Secretarial Duties

Secretarial Duties

Penny Anson, BEd, has many years' experience teaching secretarial subjects at a variety of levels. She is currently chief examiner for RSA Secretarial Duties Stage II. In addition to teaching she continues to work with companies in industry and commerce; recently this has included work in the field of desktop publishing under contract to the Economist Intelligence Unit. Formerly a Lecturer II at Halton College of Further Education, she now teach at Poynton High School in Cheshire.

Secretarial Duties

A New Approach

Penny Anson

Consultant Editor: Joyce Stananought

Chambers *Commerce Series*

© Penny Anson 1988

Published by W & R Chambers Ltd Edinburgh, 1988

British Library Cataloguing in Publication Data
Anson, Penny
  Secretarial duties.—(Chambers commerce series).
  1. Office practice
  I. Title
  651   HF5547.5

ISBN 0-550-20709-0

Typeset by Waddie & Co. Ltd, Edinburgh

Printed in Great Britain by
Richard Clay Ltd, Bungay, Suffolk

Contents

Chapter 2   The Company You Work in — Its Size, Structure and Staff

Chapter 3   Business Documentation

Chapter 4   Communication

Chapter 5 Handling the Mail

Chapter 6 Organising the Working Environment

Chapter 7 Equipment in the Office

Chapter 8 Visual Aids in the Office

Chapter 11   Safety in the Office

Chapter 12   Travel and Absence from the Office

Chapter 13   Information Sources — Where to Find Out What

Chapter 14 A Secretarial Career

Chapter 15 Secretarial Examinations — A Few Hints to Help You

Index

Acknowledgements

Thanks go to the following manufacturers who kindly supplied photographs and information without which the book would not have been complete:

Acco Europe Limited	p 128
Barclays Bank PLC	pp 186, 188, 190
British Telecommunications PLC 1985	pp 67, 73, 75, 76, 77
Fairhurst Instruments Limited	pp 149, 150
Jones and Brother	pp 141, 142, 143
NOBO Visual Aids Ltd	p 177
The Data Protection Registrar	p 20
R Weston (Printers) Ltd	p 50

Thanks are also due to the London Chamber of Commerce and Industry (LCCI); Pitman Examinations Institute (PEI) and the Royal Society of Arts (RSA) for permission to use past examination questions.

I would also like to thank the many practising secretaries and their executives who kindly returned completed survey questionnaires. These proved invaluable in obtaining a comprehensive view of the modern secretarial role in a variety of establishments. Thanks also go to those secretaries and managers who gave their valuable time in contributing to my research and in doing so helped me form a complete picture of the duties performed by, as well as expected of, today's secretary.

Finally and most importantly I would like to thank my husband Robin and my sons, Sam and Joe, without whose constant support and unfailing encouragement the book would not have been written.

Preface

Secretarial Duties should prove to be an invaluable guide to students and practising secretaries alike. The style is clear, straightforward and ideal for easy reference. For the secretarial student the text aims to cover the syllabuses of the major examining bodies in secretarial subjects, particularly those of the RSA, LCCI and Pitman. Particular account has been taken of the practical aspects of the secretary's role in the modern office. For the practising secretary wishing to develop her career the text can be used as a handy reference guide to good secretarial practice. In addition it offers an insight into the new technology which is becoming increasingly common place in today's offices.

Each chapter covers a major subject area and is divided into easy to understand sections. The *Do You Know?* sections can be used as self-assessment or class exercises and each chapter contains at least one *Secretarial Task* which aims to present a realistic secretarial problem. For students preparing for examinations there are additional questions taken from recent examination papers.

Throughout the book the term 'he' has been used to refer to the executive and 'she' to the secretary in order to make clear the distinction between the two roles. It is taken for granted that there is a sizable and growing number of female executives — even though the number of male secretaries continues to be very small.

P.A.

Chapter 1

The Secretary

Why become a Secretary?

Many established secretaries, and indeed their executives, may suggest to you that the posts they hold are among the most important in the company. Without their support, skills and organisational powers the executives would soon find themselves becoming disorganised, slowly sinking into a world of chaos! Exaggerated this picture may be but it most certainly is the case that for many companies the secretary holds the organisation together. A good secretary can provide the order and organisation within which the executive can operate efficiently and successfully.

When secretaries in a recent survey were asked the question 'Apart from the traditional skills and qualities what, in your opinion, makes a secretary special?' among their answers were:

> 'The ability to act on her own initiative.'
> 'Being able to listen to two conversations at once!'
> 'Being indispensable to her boss.'
> 'Being completely trustworthy and efficient.'
> 'Ability to use her brain and THINK!'

Managers from a variety of companies on the other hand, when asked what made their OWN secretary special, said:

> 'She makes my life as easy as possible – handles minor enquiries, organises me and so on.'
> 'She gives me that extra personal attention which enables me to do my own job more efficiently.'
> 'She anticipates my needs.'
> 'She's always smiling and is pleasant to have around.'
> 'She knows my likes and dislikes and she will stand up for herself.'

The answer then to the question 'Why become a secretary?' is that you will provide an essential administrative and supportive role within your company, one which is valued in its own right and which will also give you satisfaction and fulfilment.

1.1 Skills, Attributes, Personality

It is difficult to be clear about the type of training you should aim for—many secretaries reach positions of excellence with the minimum of formal training. It is possible for a secretary to have received only basic instruction in shorthand and typewriting many years ago and to have worked her way through to become secretary/personal assistant to the managing director of a multinational company. Or she may have transferred across to a responsible administrative position which in turn provides her with her own secretary. This is not to say that you must be satisfied with a small amount of training. Increasingly secretaries are expected to have a good all-round education, to be well qualified in secretarial skills and to have a good command of the English language. For many executives, personality is nearly as important as qualifications since with the right attitude to work and an absence of personality problems a great deal can be accomplished. Some executives would rather have a secretary who is less qualified but cheerful and willing to learn than one who is well qualified but miserable and obstructive.

(a) Skills—what must I be good at?

A secretary starting work today is generally expected to have a good basic English qualification, together with typewriting, audio-typing and word processing skills. Some executives also insist on shorthand. Many, however, accept or prefer audio typewriting as an alternative and may expect a shorthand qualification only as a measure of the applicant's overall capability. Secretaries today are increasingly highly qualified, some have degrees, and many have several 'O' levels and some 'A' levels in addition to secretarial diplomas and certificates. (For more details on training and qualifications see Chapter 14.)

(b) Attributes

You should consider the following list as the minimum requirements of a good secretary. Few secretaries will excel in all the attributes and those that do should wear a halo! But whatever their weaknesses everyone has positive aspects to their character. We can all picture someone we know, of whom we perhaps say something like: 'she never smiles much but she's so reliable' or 'she's very confident in her job, but I wish she wouldn't gossip so much!' You should build on your own strengths and strive to improve on any of your weak points. A list of all the attributes a good secretary should possess is long. She should:

- be able to organise time, documents and people
- be able to work in a team
- have a good telephone manner
- present herself well – manner, clothes, hair etc.
- be confident in daily routines
- be confident in non-routine tasks
- be flexible about type of work and times of work
- be loyal to the company and colleagues
- be discreet in terms of work and colleagues
- have the ability to be cool, calm and collected – be 'unflappable'
- be technically competent
- have the ability and confidence to work unsupervised
- be able to cope under pressure
- be quick-thinking in a crisis or other urgent situations.

(c) Personality

We can't all have the perfect personality, if indeed there is such a thing as perfection! Many would argue that 'we are what we are' or that 'a leopard cannot change its spots'. What you can do, however, is watch and take note of other people and learn from their good points and their bad points. Develop your own strengths and learn from the reactions of friends and colleagues. You may wonder why one receptionist has been promoted while another with the same qualifications is left behind. Perhaps the successful one is cheerful, helpful, organised, and dresses appropriately while the other is brusque, short-tempered, untidy and casual about arrangements and visitors. Try to identify your own strengths and weaknesses – build on the strengths and work on the weaknesses. As a guide, the following list, based on suggestions of both secretaries and executives, should give you some idea of the kinds of personality and characteristics which you should be developing. You should:

- be of a pleasant disposition
- have confidence in yourself
- be patient in circumstances beyond your control
- be a willing worker and avoid laziness
- be positive and don't procrastinate—work doesn't go away!
- keep a calm attitude to life and work—it will rub off on others
- be friendly towards colleagues and visitors—they will appreciate it and be friendly in return
- appear bright and ready to tackle problems and people cheerfully
- be enthusiastic about your job, even on bad days.

The secretary who could answer all the requirements—skills, attributes and personality—would indeed be wonder-woman. It is more important for the would-be secretary to identify the general and particular needs of her executive and to ensure that she provides the right sort of support to enable him to concentrate on his own job. In some offices where the pressure is on all the time, one of the most valuable assets a secretary may have is to 'think on her feet'. In another, where tasks may require lengthy sessions in order to get to grips with a problem, perseverance and patience will be valued. Other secretaries may find themselves in positions where they are constantly meeting important people, arranging and attending meetings and so on; in these situations self-confidence, powers of organisation and maturity will take her a long way. Some executives or employers are happy to have a secretary who may not be a perfect organiser or typist, but whose sense of humour helps them through a harrowing day.

1.2 Duties and Responsibilities

(a) Where does the secretary fit in?

What does a secretary actually do? What makes her different from a shorthand or audio typist? Is there, in fact, any difference?

There are indeed many levels at which a secretary can operate and your company may assign duties, responsibilities or job titles to staff which differ considerably from those in another company elsewhere. Many students hold misconceptions about what a secretary actually does. Colleges sometimes give their courses a bewildering array of titles and too many students are of the opinion that once they have done their one or two year stint they will walk straight into a job as top secretary/personal assistant! Students should indeed be ambitious but they must also be prepared to gain experience at the right level in accordance with their skills and qualifications. (Chapter 14 gives you more detailed information about training and qualifications, but remember that if you can convey that you have the right personality for the job you will be at an advantage in an interview and on the promotion ladder.) In other chapters you will find, in some detail, information about many roles and duties with which the typical secretary will be concerned.

Start at the bottom?
Many secretaries are promoted from junior positions—word processor operators, typists, audio/shorthand typists. If you advance your career by this route you can expect to take on many more tasks and roles as time passes; your responsibility for your own job will increase, you will have more autonomy in terms of planning your day and you will be expected to use your initiative much more.

Become qualified first?
If you take a recognised secretarial course at school or college you may begin your career at a higher level and immediately take on the responsibilities of a personal secretary.

The secretary in a paperless office?
Before you go on to read the following chapters, remember that today's secretary is not a glorified shorthand typist. Her normal working day will, indeed, include many routine tasks but she can also expect a much broader role in terms of contact with people and equipment. It is not unusual for a secretary never to use shorthand and there are high technology companies where paperwork generally is becoming a thing of the past and the secretary's contact with paper may be limited to incoming correspondence, orders and so on. One well-known business systems company, in fact, keep all their records and carry out their communications via their own computer network and the secretaries within that company are trained to be competent in several computer functions. Although such a company may as yet not be typical it is true that an increasing number are making moves towards the 'paperless office'.

Typical duties:

Daily

- deal with incoming and outgoing mail
- operate Fax and Telex
- receive, deal with and make telephone calls
- store information (on paper and on disc)
- carry out word processing and data processing (and house-keeping)
- keyboard correspondence, reports, etc.
- photocopy documents
- keep diaries
- arrange appointments
- receive visitors.

At other times

- arrange lunches/dinners
- book hotels for visitors
- make travel arrangements
- collect and present statistics/data
- arrange printing/publicity leaflets or similar
- arrange conferences, exhibition stands, etc.
- prepare reports
- organise stationery and requisitions
- arrange theatre tickets or similar
- supervise junior staff
- complete and chase expense claims
- relieve reception/switchboard.

(b) During a typical day

Many of the daily tasks are considered in detail in subsequent chapters. However, one area which is often overlooked by the up-and-coming secretary is that of the diary.

(i) Diary

It is said by many a successful executive and secretary alike that without their diaries they are lost. On the other hand there are a fortunate few who carry their diaries in their heads and have very clear and reliable memories of all arrangements made. Many executives are not good diary keepers and depend on their secretary to keep the entries up to date (this is all right so long as he doesn't lock the diary away when you need it!).

More than one diary?   In addition to their desk diary many executives will have a pocket diary. This gives you responsibility for three diaries and if you work for more than one executive then the number will increase proportionately! The pocket diary travels with them so that they can make entries while out of the office; they or you can transfer the entries to the desk diary when they return to the office. Remember also to make the entries in your own diary or diaries (one for each executive if you need it).

You must ensure that each executive keeps you up-to-date with the arrangements he makes and this may not be an easy task in some instances. Some executives are particularly elusive but you must be persistent and encourage them in good habits. This is easier if you can have a pre-arranged time when you are both in the office to up-date diaries, discuss provisional appointments and so on.

Provisional in pencil.   Always confirm appointments with your executive immediately if he is in the office and not busy. If you are unable to confirm you must make PROVISIONAL appointments and enter them IN PENCIL immediately in both diaries. Only enter them in ink when BOTH PARTIES have confirmed the arrangements. Remember also to confirm arrangements in writing whenever you can − use Fax and Telex if it is urgent and a letter if there is more time. Take care that both you and your executive get all the important details − name (correct spelling), company, place of meeting, times, and so on. Some arrangements can be quite complex and may need further attention. You can use your diary and follow-up file (see Section 6.2) for such reminders or action. Make sure you both have diaries which give you sufficient space for your needs. Some companies have their own diaries specially printed but if you are not in such a company then take care to get one which is of the right size for the number of entries you need to make.

Remember

Provisional in pencil
Confirm in writing

Allow breathing space.   One more point to make sure of is that you do not pack the schedule too tight. Remember to allow breathing space, time to eat and time to travel−and time for things to go wrong!

Some secretaries prepare daily or weekly schedules for their executive based on his diary appointments (internal and external). This gives a clear picture of the week's events and allows the secretary to make any necessary further preparations.

Check at the end and beginning of each day.   Refer to the diaries, both your own and your executive's, to check on the day's events:

At the end of the day	— ensure that any new entries are in both diaries
	— prepare documents, files, data, etc. for the next day's meetings; place them together ready for the next day in the appropriate place—your desk, your executive's desk, in new files, etc.
	Always refer to your follow-up, tickler or other reminder file (see Section 6.2) at the same time as you refer to the diaries. Make a clear note, in order of priority of the day's jobs and keep the list on your desk and tick them off when complete.
At the beginning of the day, as soon as you arrive	— check your executive's desk diary in case he made arrangements after you left the previous evening— transfer any new appointments to your own diary.
At the end of the year	— scan the old diary for any important information which should be kept; either transfer the information (annual reminders, birthdays, company celebrations) to the new diary or enter into permanent records (files, datafile, telephone book).

Remember

Don't throw old diaries away immediately. You may find that you need to refer back later for information, for instance, dates of meetings, the name of the person your executive met and so on. Some executives and secretaries keep all old diaries (they can be moved to a permanent store with other dead files; see Section 6.2).

(ii) Answerphone
Check for messages when you arrive in the morning:

      – note down and deal with urgent matters

      – record others on paper or electronic mailing system

      – pass messages to relevant people

      – deal with matters in order of priority.

(iii) Mail
Your second priority is to deal with incoming mail and procedures for this are dealt with fully in Chapter 5. Remember, however, that mail today can also arrive in your office via a computer, fax machine, telex or down a telephone line at any time of the day or night. In addition to opening mail which is delivered by the Post Office remember to check immediately on incoming Fax and Telex messages.

Some executives like to deal with all mail themselves, however straightforward, but if you are capable and have the initiative you will soon find that you are answering routine mail on behalf of your executive. Not only does this give you increased job satisfaction it also relieves your executive of routine tasks, giving him time to devote to more specialised matters. Try to establish a pattern with your executive of times convenient to you both, usually once in the morning and once in the afternoon, where you can deal with correspondence, discuss matters and arrange meetings. He may at this point merely hand you an audio tape or he may prefer to give dictation. Encourage him to let you have the original correspondence so that you can take correct spellings, names, references and so on. Always note down any special instructions such as number of copies or if it is a draft copy. Don't entrust any instructions to memory because you will invariably forget something.

Problems with dictation?   For some executives dictation does not come easily and you may find yourself waiting unduly for him to organise his thoughts before he speaks and even then he may make several frustrating changes. You must be patient in such cases and perhaps tactfully suggest that he gives dictation equipment a try, or passes some of the routine letters to you to answer. A simple 'Shall I do a letter similar to …?' is all that is necessary. At the other extreme you may be confronted by a fast thinker and fast talker but he too may not take kindly to the suggestion of a dictation machine, in which case you have no alternative but to put in some extra hours to increase your shorthand speed!

Organising yourself. However your executive likes to give you the day's correspondence you must always ensure that you are ready. He may begin dictating a letter the moment he walks in through the door, having given it careful thought on his journey to the office, or he may have prepared an urgent fax message himself which needs immediate transmission. Be prepared and make your own life easier:

- Have pencil or pen ready.
- Have notepad ready open on desk.
- Have the date written at the bottom of the page for easy reference.
- Have an elastic band around the used pages to help you to find your place easily.
- Cross out all previously transcribed material and jobs which have been completed.
- Note the initials of the person currently giving you dictation or instructions.
- Keep a clear margin on all pages: while learning shorthand you may have wondered at the purpose of such a margin in the office. Hopefully you will have used it for drills and corrections or it may have remained empty for much of the time. In the office the margin is essential—use it to make notes, alterations, insertions and so on. Like diaries, it is sensible to keep well-labelled shorthand books (date from and to) for a year or two.

(c) The rest of the day

In some offices mail and correspondence can take up the major part of the day. But of course, during the course of the day there are many other routine daily tasks to be done—sending fax and telex messages, word and data processing, photocopying and so on.

(i) Is it urgent?

Deal with urgent or priority matters immediately. No-one can predict what these might be—sending urgently needed information, tickets, samples, equipment, etc. or making last minute travel arrangements. If you don't know how to solve an urgent problem yourself then try asking for advice from a specialist within the company or an outside specialist body. For instance you may be confronted with an immediate problem if your executive has left that morning for a conference where he is giving a paper and has left his lecture notes behind on his desk. What do you do? You've forgotten all you learnt at college about urgent delivery and the post clerk is away ill. The first thing to do is to keep calm and the second thing is to contact the Post Office with an explanation of the problem and request for advice. The answer you will probably get is 'use Datapost for delivery within twelve hours or Intelpost for immediate transmission and receipt'.

Remember

Urgent problems may happen at any time of the day but whatever else you are doing you must always give them your immediate attention.

(ii) Telephone?
Telephone calls, too, will take up a chunk of your day, particularly when your executive is out of the office. You will find information about the telephone and using it effectively in Chapter 4 but do remember that the telephone is a vital link in the business world and just the nature of your voice and the manner in which you deal with a call can be an important factor in the success of your company or department. Be bright, clear and purposeful on the telephone and, as with correspondence, try to act as a filter for your executive's calls. As you gain confidence you will be able to deal with routine calls, again leaving him free to deal with other matters.

(iii) Visitors?
Like telephone callers, visitors need polite, careful and positive treatment and a bright, neat and confident approach is desirable. Again, like telephone callers, one of your tasks is to politely stall or divert unwanted and unnecessary visitors. Visitors who are expected and/or welcome should be treated in an appropriate manner. Visitors may already have been through reception, signed a visitor's book and been given an identity badge. If this is the practice in your company you will probably have been contacted and asked either if they should be brought to your office or if you will collect them (never allow a visitor to wander through your premises unaccompanied, for obvious security reasons). If you are acting as relief receptionist remember always ask someone else to accompany a visitor; again, for security reasons you should never leave reception unattended. Some large companies have porters to accompany visitors from one place to another.

When you receive a visitor always greet him or her cheerfully. Many would-be secretaries, when completing examination papers, are mistakenly of the opinion that all visitors should be offered a seat, coffee and magazines to read. Common sense will tell you what to do and when to do it. Certainly a visitor who has travelled some distance for a meeting will appreciate an opportunity to use the cloakroom and some refreshment. An expected visitor who has to wait for some time will also appreciate refreshment and something to read. In a large company your library may organise trade and other magazines and newspapers for reception. In your own office it is also a good idea to have such material available.

You must use your discretion regarding unexpected visitors and there is no substitute for experience here. As you get to know your job, you will begin to recognise visitors to whom you should give time, refreshment and so on. Sales representatives can be a nuisance although you must take care not to dismiss all of them as a waste of time. There are those salesmen whose advice and support your executive will value. For instance if your company is concerned with a technical process such as weaving fabrics from man-made fibres, the fibre salesman will also advise on technical matters such as machinery adjustments and problems encountered in processing the fibres. Salesmen such as this must be offered the usual welcome and attention.

Introductions   A small point, but one which is often overlooked, is that of introducing people to each other. Historically men have been introduced to women but today there are many businesswomen who do not care for such unnecessary niceties and are happy to be introduced on an equal basis. More importantly, it is normal to introduce juniors to seniors:

'Mrs Old, may I introduce Miss Young, our new office junior. Miss Young this is Mrs Old.'

Be confident when you make introductions and don't forget to look directly at the person you are speaking to.

When you, yourself, are being introduced, again be confident. Smile and put out your hand to shake hands. At this point in your career you may not feel confident offering your hand to someone else but you will find that with practice it will become an automatic gesture when you are introduced.

Visitors while your executive is away   As you gain confidence and experience your executive may expect you to take a more positive role with visitors. Apart from greeting routine visitors you may be expected to stand in for him if he has to leave the office urgently. This may merely mean passing on information or it may involve entertaining a visitor for lunch or even dinner. Be prepared for such eventualities and if it happens in the early stages of your career, don't panic. Keep yourself cool and calm and have confidence in yourself—your executive would not ask you to stand in for him if he didn't have confidence in you.

Record all visitors in a book   Whatever the circumstances, remember to keep a clear record of visitors—name, company, nature of business and reasons for the visit together with a note of any further discussions you may have had with them.

(iv) Storing information—on paper and on computer
Your normal day's work will produce many documents which may be on paper, disc or microfilm, and reference to Chapter 6 will tell you a great deal about the technicalities of storing information. Remember that information is no longer confined to paper and that it is more necessary than ever before that you have a routine and are systematic about handling the data with which you deal. Some rules to guide you are:

- file papers every day
- replace microfilm/fiche immediately it is finished with
- back up computer documents daily
- label discs accurately
- lock discs away at night
- keep one set of backup discs in a separate office or even a separate building

Try to set a time aside regularly each day to carry out these tasks.

(d) Weekly/monthly tasks

Making arrangements
A competent secretary will be entrusted with arranging a number of events—from travel to conferences. Of the tasks listed earlier in the chapter as weekly or monthly several are discussed in some detail in later chapters. It is true, however, that during the course of her day the secretary moves efficiently from one job to another and gives little thought to which section the particular task falls into and there is

much overlapping. A secretary organising a conference, for instance, may find herself concerned with travel, meetings, safety, publicity and so on, all of which are covered in depth in different chapters throughout the book.

(e) Departmental tasks

The remainder of your day will be spent doing tasks which may be specific to your department. For instance:

in Personnel	—applications, interviews, appointments, staff records
in Sales	—business documents, sales figures— collection and presentation
in Marketing	—promotional material, surveys, advertisements, exhibition stands
Company Secretary	—legal documents, reports
Office Services	—supervision of junior office staff, reports on proposed new systems or equipment, general administration documents, filing, forms.

Once at work you will find yourself involved in a variety of other tasks. Some of these will be mundane and others will provide the interest and sometimes the excitement that will make your job one which gives you all the enjoyment and satisfaction you hoped for when you set out on a secretarial career.

1.3 Your Working Environment

What is usually meant by 'working environment?' For some it conjures up pictures of old, cold, draughty offices and for others new, bright and spacious rooms. If you are happy with your working environment and are generally comfortable you will probably have the enthusiasm to work well. Not only are you happier but your executive, and company, will benefit. On the other hand if you and your colleagues are constantly either too hot or too cold, find that the lighting is not good enough and feel that the place is not clean, you are unlikely to give your best to the job. You will grumble and be unmotivated and probably more prone to illness and absence with predictable results.

Try to be positive about the environment. If things are not going well or you feel improvements could be made— perhaps the cleaners are cutting corners, or the maintenance people are not mending lights immediately they have been reported— make sure you report the shortcomings. Many large companies have a system for reporting faults.   '

Open plan or traditional offices?

Open plan and cellular offices have become established in today's business world although there are many who would advocate that the loss of the traditional closed-room office is a sad one.

It is unlikely that you will be expected to make a major contribution to any decisions regarding change-over from one to the other but you may be asked to suggest points in favour and against. Firstly ensure that you know the difference:

Traditional

- individual rooms/offices for management (sometimes shared)
- separate room for secretary/typist
- the larger the office the more important the executive!
- separate conference/meeting rooms
- typing/word processing pool separate
- other specialist services may or may not be centralised.

Open plan/cellular

- traditionally found in newer buildings but there are some older suitable buildings
- very few dividing walls
- sections divided by screens, plants, filing cabinets
- departments have 'areas'
- noisy equipment in separate rooms
- individual meeting or conference rooms
- canteen facilities separate.

Why has open plan become popular?

- Heating/lighting and other overheads are cheaper.
- More staff can be accommodated in less area therefore reducing rental costs.
- Studies show productivity is higher—staff are constantly under scrutiny—cannot hide behind closed doors.

- Communication is easier—less far to walk and no barrier of closed doors.
- More economical use of space.
- Easier to change space arrangements by moving dividers, etc.
- Enables flexible arrangement for moving equipment and accommodating new staff.

Why do some businesses and staff prefer traditional offices to open plan?

- Noisy, therefore concentration is difficult (glass screens, dividers and plants can help).
- Staff prefer not to be 'on show' with no privacy.
- Confidential discussions can be difficult if meeting rooms are not available.
- Security can be a problem—it is easier for 'passers-by' to read confidential papers, computer displays, overhear conversations.
- People believe that air conditioning can have unhealthy side effects, such as headaches, and can spread colds.

1.4 Your Working Hours—Flexitime or Traditional?

Flexitime gives an employee the opportunity to be flexible about working hours. Most companies who operate the system stipulate:

(a) the minimum number of hours per week each employee must work
(b) the times of the 'core' hours, i.e. the latest they may start in the morning and the earliest they may finish—e.g. 10.30am-3.00pm.

Provided that employees are in work for the core hours they may choose when to make up the remainder of the time. For instance, if you are an early bird you may like to start at 7.00am or even earlier. If, during the course of one week you work in excess of the standard week you can benefit by working fewer hours in a subsequent week. Some companies allow their employees to build up sufficient credit hours to enable them to take extra days off at a later date.

There are companies who have gone over to this system whole-heartedly while others have kept to the traditional working hours.

A company dedicated to flexitime finds that its employees are able to choose to work at times which suit both their mental state and their home circumstances. Thus people who don't warm up till late morning, or who work particularly well in the evening when the office is quieter can choose to start and finish late, while those with home commitments find it easier to arrange their work and home timetable around each other. Where cover is required after office hours, flexitime can reduce the need for overtime. For instance, if a centralised computer department needs to operate with extended working hours, flexitime could avoid expensive shift work where time and a half or even double time would have to be paid. Here flexitime is clearly an advantage to the company but not so good for the employee!

Although flexitime works well for some companies those who reject it do so on the grounds that:

- staff need to be in the office at the same time as those in other companies in order to meet, talk and negotiate during 'normal office hours'—they cannot afford to lose custom through specialist staff being unavailable
- flexitime requires organisation and administration which is costly
- flexitime can discourage long hours. It can reduce flexibility since staff can become obsessed with how many hours they have worked that week, with the result that there is an actual reduction in output and dedication to the company.

1.5 Confidentiality and the Secretary

(a) Gossip

It is often incorrectly assumed that anyone working in an office will keep information confidential. Sadly this is not the case and we all know someone, if not ourselves, who likes a good gossip. Office gossip is generally centred around people, what they have to say and what they do, either with themselves or each other and it cannot be denied that much damage can be done by such uninformed gossip. Do not let yourself become a party to this type of idle chatter and if you should have cause to know of any ill-informed and malicious gossip then take tactful and appropriate steps to put the matter right. If a junior is involved then you will probably have the authority to speak to him or her and carefully indicate that such chatter should be avoided. Point out that not only is it unfair and unkind to the victim of the gossip but it also does the junior no good since it suggests to the management that he or she is untrustworthy.

(b) Security of records

Maintaining the confidentiality and security of documents, files and computer data is a matter which is being given an increasing amount of attention by companies and government alike. The Official Secrets Act has been around for many years and you will have to sign it if you work in a government department or in a company which has connection with government matters and secrets. The Data Protection Act of 1984 is a further attempt by the government to protect individuals and companies from misuse of personal and other details stored on computer by many thousands of companies.

Fig. 1.1   *Data Protection Act 1984*

DATA PROTECTION ACT 1984

Purpose of the Act

Computers are in use throughout society — collecting, storing, processing and distributing information. Much of that information is about people — 'personal data' — and is now subject to the Data Protection Act 1984.

The Act gives new rights to individuals about whom information is recorded on computer. They may find out information about themselves, challenge it if appropriate and claim compensation in certain circumstances. The Act places obligations on those who record and use personal data (Data Users). They must be open about that use (through the Data Protection Register) and follow sound and proper practices (the Data Protection Principles).

More generally, in the office it is vital that you are aware of everyday security procedures:

- lock files away at night
- lock away money and valuables at all times
- keep personal files locked all the time
- keep confidential documents out of sight and locked away when not in use
- lock away credit card numbers, passport numbers, and similar information
- do not have confidential conversations where you can be over-heard
- always accompany visitors
- do not leave original copies around after photocopying, faxing, etc.
- lock dictation tapes away when not in use
- destroy or lock away used carbon paper and carbon ribbon
- if you issue keys keep a careful check on their whereabouts and times of return.

There are added risks involved with the increased use of computers and high technology equipment:

- avoid leaving information on screen unattended—save and remove disc or exit from program
- scroll work off screen if a visitor comes to your desk
- keep passwords locked away—don't allow them to be seen on screen
- lock away carbon ribbons
- immediately shred misprints
- lock discs away in disc boxes and in cabinets
- keep backups of important discs locked away in a separate office or building.

1.6 Electronic Office, Traditional Office or a Combination?

Where will I work?

It is becoming increasingly difficult and artificial to separate out 'the electronic office' from the other equipment and tasks performed by a secretary. For some secretaries the computer is just as essential to them as the fountain pen was to their grandparents or great-grandparents.

Communication, records, data and wordprocessing are all becoming everyday features of office life and you may well even now be saying 'So why all the fuss?'

Hopefully, within this book you will find that there is little fuss—that it all fits together like an office jigsaw—and that you can find traditional features interlinked with technological advances—exactly in the way today's offices function.

Do You Know?

1. What characteristics make a secretary special from other office workers?
2. Why a secretary might need to 'think on her feet?'
3. What routine tasks a secretary can expect to carry out?
4. What a 'typical day' for a secretary might entail?
5. What a 'non-typical day' might entail?
6. How to make sure that your diary works for you?
7. How to make sure that your executive's diary works for him?
8. How to make sure an appointment isn't overlooked?
9. How to cope with unexpected visitors?
10. How to treat expected visitors?
11. How to carry out an introduction?
12. What suggestions to make to improve an open-plan office?
13. Why many people prefer open-plan?
14. What people don't like about open-plan?
15. Why many staff prefer flexitime?
16. Why many companies don't operate flexitime?
17. How to ensure confidentiality of paper work in the office?
18. Why gossip should be discouraged?
19. How to ensure confidentiality of computer based information?
20. What the significance of the Data Protection Act 1984 is?

Secretarial Task One

Emma Jackson, a friend of yours, is opening her own travel agency office in your local town centre.

You are secretary to the Personnel Director of a large travel agency. As part of your job you are involved in the appointment of new office staff. You assist in preliminary selection for interview and you are sometimes involved in the interviews themselves. Emma knows of your experience and involvement in this area and has asked for your advice in her own staff selection.

She will need a Secretary/Receptionist and has asked particularly for some ideas on qualities and personality that the successful applicant should have. She would also like some guidance on points to raise in the interview to assess the applicants' knowledge of the secretarial role and duties to be performed during a normal day.

Set out clearly all the points that you consider important. Bear in mind that Emma Jackson mentioned in conversation that she would like to be able to make quick reference to your points and ideas both now and in future if she should need to.

Examination Questions

1. Mr Hemmings, the Managing Director, has asked you to see him this week to discuss a farewell presentation for Mr Blackstone, but you know that Mr Blackstone does not want this 'fuss'. He has said he would not attend such a function if one was planned and has asked you to let him know if this is suggested. How might you deal with this matter, bearing in mind that it is the Managing Director who has approached you and asked you to treat the matter as confidential; and what personal qualities will you need to exercise in handling the situation?

   RSA SD

2. How should the Receptionist and the Secretary to a Middle Manager work together regarding the making of appointments and the reception of people to see the Manager with and without appointments?

   LCCI SSC OP

3. Your firm is considering introducing flexible working hours. Suggest

   (a) the resulting advantages to individual staff and to the firm
   AND
   (b) the possible effects on the organisation and admin- stration of the firm.

   LCCI PSC OO&SP

Chapter 2
The Company You Work in— its Size, Structure and Staff

How much do I need to know?

As a secretary you may be working within a small company with only one or two managers. On the other hand, at the other extreme, you may find yourself working for a large multinational company with many hundreds or thousands of employees and a complicated management structure. During the time you spend with a company you will learn a great deal about its organisation and management. An induction course will probably provide you with the groundwork where you may be introduced to the company by way of a talk, video and tour of factory and offices. On this background information you will build a broad knowledge of the company, its staff and departmental structure and the way they all fit together and connect.

If you understand something of the structure of both your own and other companies with which you deal you will be in a much stronger position in terms of success in your current job and potential for future advancement. You may well say, however: 'but why do I need to know how other companies are organised—surely I only need to know about the one I work in?' Such thoughts are shortsighted. A good secretary needs a broad awareness of the overall structure and organisation of her own company, together with more specific knowledge of how the complete departmental and personnel jigsaw fits together.

2.1 What Makes Each Company Individual?

Companies come in large, medium and small sizes, although how the size is estimated can vary. Some companies are large in terms of numbers of customers but small in terms of staff employed. Others may be large in terms of factory space or turnover but small in terms of number of employees. For example, a car manufacturer who produces cars largely by automated machinery will need large factory areas and large numbers of customers, but few factory workers.

Regardless of the size of the company, however, a secretary must not only know how its management and labour force are structured but also something of how it is controlled and financed. If she is working for a small company owned by one person, or two or three partners, she will experience the problems and successes of running a small business at first hand. If, however, she is secretary to the Personnel Manager of a large limited company her interest and awareness will be concentrated on specific matters such as staffing, training and staff welfare; her job may not be directly concerned with financial problems and successes.

Be aware of all aspects

Whatever the type of company or its business, you as a secretary should be concerned with the broader aspects of company structure and organisation since your future will depend on the success and smooth-running of the organisation. An understanding and an appreciation of why a company runs as it does and why its management is structured in a particular way will help you to cope with problems, developments and restrictions which may arise during the course of your working life.

During your career you will, in all probability, have several jobs in different size companies and it will help if you have an overall picture of how the pattern fits together. What for instance makes Marks and Spencer different from your corner shop? 'A silly question', you may say, 'apart from anything else M & S is bigger!' True, of course, but it is not difficult for the average shopper to come up with other differences apart from sheer size: number of shop floor staff, number of branches, range of goods, number of administrative staff and so on. To appreciate these and other differences more fully you will find many books which give you more detail. It may help to think of a situation you could find yourself in—starting a business of your own. Such a venture may seem an unlikely event at this stage in your career, but there are many young, and older, people who have made a success of their own business, having started early on in their working lives. Secretarial agencies, and companies offering word processing and typewriting services, have all had small beginnings which led to large organisations with branches in every major town.

2.2 How a Business Grows

(a) Types of company

Stage 1　Most people start a business with a skill or service in which they are accomplished. You are good at secretarial skills, so imagine that you start up a small successful typing service working on your own from your own home, deciding your own hours, your own expenditure and your own pace of work. To begin with you use your own name and call your company *Parker Secretarial Services.* You do well and expand, renting office space above a local shop. You benefit financially from your successful business but you also bear all the costs and losses. You are, in fact, a **sole trader**.

Fig 2.1　*Parker Secretarial Services – a sole trader*

Parker Secretarial Services

23 Alderdale Grove,
Newtown NT4 7HQ

Telephone: Newtown 75261

Stage 2　The following year you do particularly well and a friend joins you in business. She is prepared to invest some of her own savings and introduces more capital so that you can buy more equipment which in turn enables you to take on more work. You become a **partnership**. You now call the business *Parker and Anderson Secretarial Services* and you share the profits between you. You also share the worries and no longer bear the brunt of any financial losses entirely on your own. In addition you have the benefits brought about by having two people contributing ideas and energy but you also run the risk of disagreements on procedure and policy decisions.

Stage 3 After some time you have become a successful local secretarial agency and need to take on more staff. As you grow profits increase, but so do the financial risks. The bank has lent you large funds but is reluctant to loan any more at this stage. You would like to open another agency in a neighbouring town but don't have enough capital. You ask two successful executives with whom you regularly do business if they would be prepared to invest in your company. Provided you become a private limited (limited liability) company the business executives are happy to invest. In return for their investment (or shares) they receive dividends (a type of interest or reward) the amount of which will usually depend on how successful the company has been that year.

Now that the company is growing the risks to your own finance are great. By becoming a **limited liability** company, however, you do not bear the entire responsibility yourself. The company is no longer owned by one person alone and becomes a legal entity in its own right. Should the company cease to be successful and become bankrupt the liability of the shareholders is limited only to the amount they invested—their own personal wealth remains intact. Some sole traders and partnerships are unwilling to form limited companies because to do so requires legal and other expenses, and much documentation. Also they may be concerned about experiencing some decrease in the amount of control they have over the business. You, however, decide to go ahead. Once limited, the company itself is recognised by law as a 'corporate entity'. There must be at least two shareholders but there is no upper limit. You may now include 'Ltd' at the end of your company name and in fact many companies choose shorter, snappier names which give a suggestion of the type of business they are in. At this stage you change your name to 'Town Secretaries Ltd'.

Now that you are a profitable limited company you have more investors and more capital which enables you to expand further. As a result your staffing requirements increase and you consider it wise to employ some specialist staff—you need a marketing manager to sell your services, purchasing staff to purchase equipment, trained word processing staff and other office support staff.

Fig 2.2   *Town Secretaries Ltd. – a limited company*

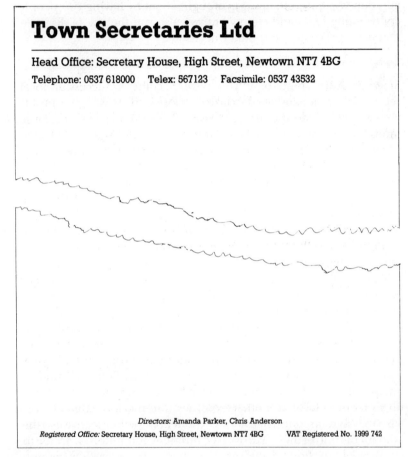

Town Secretaries Ltd

Head Office: Secretary House, High Street, Newtown NT7 4BG

Telephone: 0537 618000   Telex: 567123   Facsimile: 0537 43532

Directors: Amanda Parker, Chris Anderson

Registered Office: Secretary House, High Street, Newtown NT7 4BG   VAT Registered No. 1999 742

Stage 4   You move from success to success and finally decide that the only way open to you to increase your capital and to expand is to become a **public limited company (plc)**. Again more costs, administration and legal documents are involved, which can be a deterrent to many companies. Your company is now called *Town Secretaries plc* and your shares are now sold freely on the Stock Exchange and control of the company is in the hands of the shareholders. Public limited companies are usually large in terms of buildings and work force and may be international or multinational, although not necessarily so.

Note: a recent alternative for many growing companies has been the Unlisted Securities Market (USM)—a sort of halfway-house to full quotation on the Stock Exchange.

(b) Links with other companies

You may find yourself working in a company which does not fit any of the above categories. A large proportion of the working population works in what is referred to as the 'public sector'—local government, education, civil service, health service and so on. Your employer may, on the other hand, manufacture goods or provide a service such as banking, insurance, or tourism. It is important to note, however, that all organisations and their departments do not work in isolation. For instance, if your company makes tables and chairs and you work in the accounts department you will have connections with banking; if you work for the Company Secretary you will be in contact with insurance companies. Such associations continue right through the company and each type of business and organisation will have its own connections. Wherever you fit into the pattern it is important that you are aware of the jigsaw and your company's place in it.

2.3 Your Department

The natural progression for any growing company is to divide into specialist departments. A successful business depends on employing staff who are particularly good at their jobs—they may have had specialist training and/or experience in the area. They will also have a personality which suits the job. Your company is unlikely to have exactly the same departmental structure as a similar company on the other side of town but fundamentally it will not be too different. For instance, all trading companies need someone who takes responsibility for sales. The 'someone' may be the owner/manager or a whole department of many staff, each of whom has specific duties connected with the selling process. Some duties may even be passed over to other specialist departments such as Marketing or Public Relations. The same will be the case for handling the accounts. A sole trader will do everything himself and a small company may divide the work up between two or three people. In a public limited company, on the other hand, the Sales Department may be subdivided into countries, regions and areas and there may also be other associated specialist departments to handle market research, publicity and public relations.

Remember that whatever the size and type of company you work for, the basic formula remains the same. The figure below shows a typical example of the structure found in a large limited company—private or public.

Fig 2.3   *The structure of a limited company*

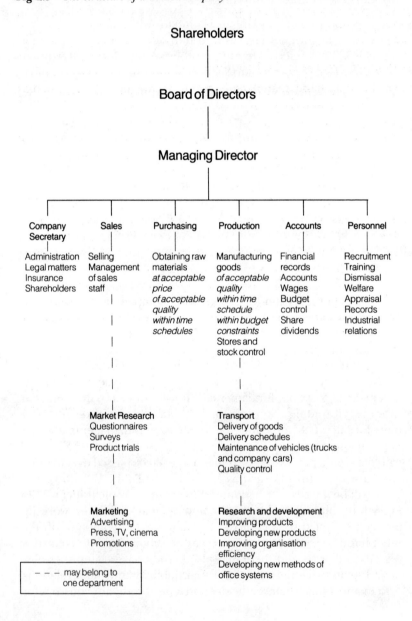

From the chart it is not difficult to see that the new secretary has much to learn about the structure and functions of the people she will be dealing with in her company. The purpose of this chapter is to give an outline of departmental structure on which you can build. For further study it is worth referring to any of the many excellent books available where more can be found about the specific aspects of company business.

Departmental tasks and routines

Most people have more than one job during their working lives—they move from company to company, department to department. There are, of course, secretaries who remain faithful to one company for their entire working life and thus become one of the most valuable assets that company may have. Wherever you go during your career as a secretary your basic function will remain the same—to carry out general secretarial tasks in order to support and assist your executive and other staff within the department. There will be specific differences some of which may be obvious to you, others you will learn more about with experience. Subsequent chapters in this book will give you helpful information about both routine and non-routine tasks which you are likely to be involved in as a secretary. Duties and tasks specific to departments are not so easy to discuss in detail since many companies operate on very individual routines. Generally though if you work in any of the above departments you can expect to be involved in a selection of the following additional tasks:

Company Secretary	– meetings procedure
	– dealing with confidential material
	– dealing with legal documentation
Sales	– processing sales documents
	– collecting and sending out information to sales staff
	– collecting and processing figures
	– organising travel, expenses, etc.
Market Research	– preparing and producing questionnaires
	– processing questionnaire results
	– mailshots

Marketing	— preparation for advertising campaigns
	— documents and letters for promotions
	— making arrangements for exhibitions
	— organising travel, expenses, etc.
Purchasing	— sending out enquiries
	— organising travel, expenses, etc.
	— purchasing documentation
	— forward planning
Production	— preparing production documents
	— preparation and up-dating of progress schedule
	— stock control
	— typing/word processing technical reports
Transport	— typing delivery schedules
Research and Development	— typing technical reports
Accounts	— completing accounting documents
	— typing financial reports
	— completing budgeting documents
Personnel	— completing and maintaining confidential records
	— organising: induction courses
	training programmes
	interview arrangements

Knowing who to contact

Once established in a department you cannot isolate yourself from the rest of the company and it is as important for you to be familiar with what goes on elsewhere as it is for you to know your own department:

- if you need information not immediately available in your own department you must know where to look for it

- if you want promotion you need broader knowledge

- you may be asked to help out while another secretary is absent or on holiday

- you will need to pass some documentation to other departments to deal with

— you may need to make enquiries about an aspect of production or sales, etc.

— you may need to collect figures from other sources for research, reports, etc.

2.4 The Management Structure

Having got to grips with the departments, their functions and your position within them as a secretary you must also be aware of how the management structure fits into the jigsaw. The triangle below may help you to picture the structure of an average company:

Fig 2.4 *The management structure*

SHAREHOLDERS

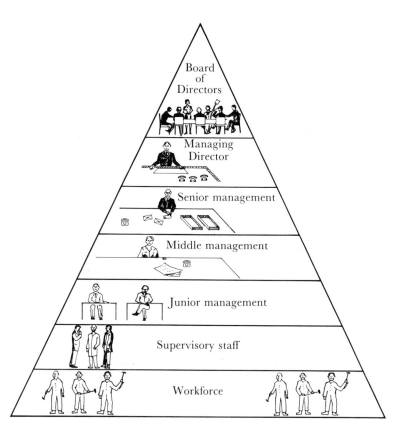

When you begin your career as a secretary you will probably move into the triangle somewhere in the middle, that is, secretary to a junior or middle-level executive. The position depends on the size and type of the company and it would be unwise to be specific about what title such a manager or executive would hold. The degree of responsibility you will have and the scope of your duties will also vary tremendously with the size, type and function of your company.

Who are the key people?

Shareholders—provide capital, buy shares and receive dividends; elect Board of Directors

Board of Directors—overall responsibility for finance, staffing and policy

Chairman of the Board of Directors—elected by the Board of Directors; may have additional business commitments in other companies

Managing Director/General Manager/Chief Executive—appointed by the Board; responsible for day to day running of the company and for appointing other executives and management

Departmental heads—may be referred to under other names: director, executive, manager; responsible for running their own departments or areas and for their staff.

2.5 Administration

(a) Where does the secretary fit in?

Looking upwards and/or across in your department there will be your executive and others above him as we have just seen. In a large organisation a busy executive may also have a Personal Assistant or you may perform that function yourself in addition to your normal secretarial duties.

Looking in other directions there may be a junior secretary or shorthand/audio typist, reception staff and clerical staff offering specific or general support to you, your own and other departments in the company. Remember that the company does not exist for the 'offices'—the offices exist for the company, although the two are dependent on each other. Without the company business the offices would not need to exist; but without the offices the company would probably cease to function efficiently and go out of business.

Fig 2.5. *Lines of responsibility*

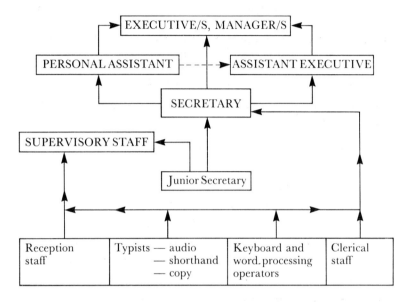

(b) What is the function of the office and what tasks does its staff carry out?

The office:

— receives, processes and transmits information—written, spoken and computerised

— sorts, analyses and classifies information

— records information on paper and computer.

Information may be received by telephone, mail or computer and may be in the form of words, figures or diagrams. In processing, information may be collected from one source, then used to prepare charts or reports, finally classified and stored in a filing or other record system. The final process may be transmission of data—as letter or memorandum, or by telephone, fax or telex.

(i) The Office Manager/Office Supervisor/Administration Officer
She or he has overall control of the clerical and secretarial function, organises and co-ordinates the work of the department and is directly concerned with:

- appointment and control of staff
- co-ordinating clerical work with and for other departments
- organising equipment and its efficient use
- establishing an acceptable working environment

(ii) A Personal Assistant/Private Secretary
She takes a more administrative role which holds increased responsibility above that of secretary. Apart from the secretarial function she may also:

- have direct responsibility for some administration
- handle confidential work
- carry out some deputisation for her executive
- have responsibility for junior staff
- be involved in interviews and in the appointment of junior staff.

(iii) A Clerical or Secretarial Supervisor
In larger companies she may be responsible for large numbers of secretarial support staff and

- co-ordinate typing, shorthand and audio services
- be responsible for sending fax and telex
- be responsible for scheduling work and ensuring that schedules are kept to
- assign work to typists and word processor operators
- make decisions or give advice about the best way to produce work, e.g. word processed or typed
- request training, as required by the company or using her judgement
- selecting the most appropriate training. in house (on-the-job), day release or block release.

(iv) Shorthand Typist/Audio Typist/Word processor and Keyboard
    Operators
They all have specialist skills which will be used according to the needs

of the company. While the means are different for each, the functions are basically the same:

Shorthand Typists—take dictation in note form and reproduce perfect copy for mailing or internal use.

Audio Typists—transcribe from pre-dictated material and produce perfect copy for mailing and internal use.

Word processor Operators—'input' (type or keyboard) material from disc, printed, shorthand, audio or handwritten notes, into a word processor or computer which may be printed immediately or stored for later use and/or amendment. Such material may be reports or standard letters for circulation, legal and other documents which need to be stored, amended, added to or changed. WP operators will also have responsibility for disc management and 'housekeeping'. Several WP operators may work together under a separate supervisor who has responsibility for assigning work and for its co-ordination.

(v) Clerical Staff
They are responsible for processing and recording information in many forms: paper, microfilm, computer. Much of the information will be specific to each department and may include collecting figures (such as sales), transferring figures from one source to another form (e.g. in the accounts department—transferring payments received from paper records to computer records) or recording information received (such as putting staff absences on to record cards or into a computer).

(vi) The Office Junior
She generally 'helps out' in whichever duties are assigned to her—messages, filing, general typing, word processing, maintaining records, etc.

(vii) The Receptionist
She receives all visitors, records the details in a reception register and communicates necessary information to departments; she takes responsibility for the reception area and may have a small switchboard; she may also do a small amount of typing and/or have a computer terminal at her desk.

(viii) The Telephonist
She may work alone or be one of a team in a large organisation; she receives all incoming calls (except any on private lines) and

- connects the caller to the person they wish to speak to
- asks for further information in order to make the correct connection
- finds an alternative person if possible
- only takes messages if it is the policy of the company to do so,
- otherwise connects the caller to the department for him to leave a message.

2.6 Qualifications, Qualities, Experience

Regardless of status and level in the hierarchy there are basic rules for qualifications and qualities necessary to do any job. All staff should:

- treat knowledge gained at work as confidential
- have a command of English sufficient for them to do their job satisfactorily
- have a level of education sufficient to enable them to carry out their job satisfactorily
- be competent at any special skills required for the job
- have passed any examinations set down by the company as a requirement for holding the position
- have followed a course which enables them to understand and carry out their duties
- be strong in aspects of personality which are particularly necessary for the job.

More than these essential points, the following should provide a brief guide to the types of qualifications and personal qualities a secretary can expect her fellow employees to have:

(i) Personal Assistant/Private Secretary

- good English and communication skills
- competence in basic skills—audio, shorthand, typewriting/ keyboarding

— success in higher level secretarial examinations and/or good experience and excellent references

— an ability to organise both herself and others.

(ii) Clerical or Secretarial Supervisor

— experience and qualifications in the skills and secretarial area
— good organisational ability—staff and work
— ability to keep to schedules
— ability to assign work appropriately to typists, operators, etc.
— consistency in ensuring that final product is of required standard
— a broad knowledge of skills and machinery in use
— an awareness of the overall management structure
— a knowledge of the requirements of each department and managers
— some responsibility for the training and careers of her staff.

(iii) Shorthand Typist/Audio Typist/Word processor and Keyboard Operators

— examination passes at levels of competency in accepted examination boards (RSA, LCCI and regional boards)
— ability to transcribe or interpret material accurately, neatly and quickly
— ability to spell and use a dictionary
— ability to punctuate and paragraph acceptably
— ability to work on own initiative
— ability to take, remember and act on instructions
— a flexible approach to work assigned and hours of work (within reason)
— ability to meet deadlines and work under pressure
— an understanding of any systems in use in the job—electronic typewriters, dictation equipment, computer hardware, word processing and other software, printers.

(iv) Clerical Staff

— basic education and competence in English skills and arithmetic skills (with calculator if required)
— ability to use office machinery and understand minor faults

      — ability to organise daily work procedures

      — ability to prioritise work

      — competence in organising the work load and environment

      — willingness, in the case of junior staff, to take instruction.

(v) Receptionist

      — a cheerful disposition

      — a smart appearance

      — ability to communicate well with visitors

      — an organised manner and an organised mind

      — ability to use her discretion when in doubt

      — ability to be discreet about company matters

      — an 'unflustered' disposition

      — some clerical or receptionist training, preferably with recognised examination passes in reception duties

      — ability to keep calm at stressful or busy times.

(vi) Telephonist

      — a clear telephone voice

      — a cheerful manner

      — ability to be precise about information

      — ability to think quickly and interpret the information she is given

      — ability to cope under stress (during busy periods)

      — ability to cope with awkward or dissatisfied callers

      — some specific switchboard training (available from British Telecom).

2.7 Office Services—Centralised or Departmental?

Throughout the book you will find reference to services which are centralised or run on a departmental basis. At work too you may find yourself in one company in which each department organises its own affairs. Or you may work in one in which all functions are run on a centralised basis. While at work you will tend to take the status quo at face value and accept the system which your company operates as being satisfactory. However, it is important that you have some background information which will throw some light on the reasons why one company has chosen one system and why another, similar company, has opted for the alternative. Remember, though, that 'the middle road' is often the one that many companies take.

Centralised services

Services and facilities which are used by all departments are often found to work better if they operate from one room or office within the company. One of the most common services is that termed 'Reprography'—printing, photocopying and associated services. Companies which produce large amounts of printed material find it more economical to have specialised staff organised in one room or area, operating more sophisticated machinery, than to have many items of smaller equipment dotted around the company and being used inefficiently. Filing, too, can operate efficiently in one area. With a capable supervisor, secretarial services can also operate more efficiently when housed together under the control of one person. Frequently audio and word processing equipment is directly linked to the secretarial services department and work is assigned by the supervisor to whichever typists or operators she thinks are suitable. Many managers prefer to have a personal secretary of their own although at middle management level such individual attention is becoming a luxury few companies can afford! A secretarial pool is favoured by many companies since it allows for more efficient use of several secretaries serving a greater number of managers.

More specifically it is useful to consider the advantages and disadvantages of the two systems, but do remember that you are likely to find a mixture of both in many companies and sometimes a bias towards one. Remember too that the system operated will depend to a great extent on the physical layout of the office area.

The size and structure of the building will have much to do with how the internal structure is organised; if the building is old with predominantly small offices, housing a centralised typing or word processing pool may prove very difficult. Equally, new buildings are generally built to house open plan (or cellular) offices and in such a building noisy machinery is more likely to be placed well away from the general clerical work force.

The advantages of a centralised system:

- noisy equipment can be isolated away from the main work area
- staff can be trained in specialist services

- better and more sophisticated equipment can be purchased since fewer machines are needed
- space can be used more economically
- heating and lighting is used more efficiently
- systems and equipment can be standardised
- quality of work can be improved through specialisation and can be standardised
- staff are freer to concentrate on their own specialist areas.

The disadvantages of a centralised system:

- may be resisted by traditional staff
- too much specialisation can lead to decreased job satisfaction
- too much bureaucracy can lead to frustrating delays which have a knock-on effect along the line
- decrease in breadth of experience for junior staff
- an urgent job may have to wait its turn in the queue
- if one central machine breaks down the whole job may be stopped; with smaller machines spread around the office one breakdown would be much less serious.

Remember

No two companies are identical in structure. This chapter can only serve to give you a basis on which you can build.

Look out for news items about well-known companies; take note of their advertising campaigns and market research studies and try to find out a little more about the departments and people in a company which you or your family or friends may have connections with.

Do You Know?

1. The difference between a sole trader and a partnership?
2. What type of business might run as a partnership?
3. Why many companies are reluctant to become limited companies?
4. The difference between a private limited company and a public limited company?
5. Who the key people in a company might be?

6. Which executive acts as a link between the Board of Directors and the remainder of the work force?
7. What the main duties of the Personnel Department might be?
8. Which department might be responsible for stock control?
9. Which other department does the Marketing Department have direct links with?
10. What particular qualities staff in the Sales Department might have?
11. Which staff are likely to come under the control of the Administration Officer?
12. What personal qualities might be expected of a secretary?
13. What training and qualifications an aspiring secretary would be expected to have?
14. What qualifications a good audio typist would be expected to have?
15. The key differences between centralised and departmental services?

Secretarial Task Two

Five years ago John Butterworth began a business which made ice-cream. During his first two years the summers were hot and his business did very well selling ice-cream to local shops and restaurants. After the first year of successful business he opened an ice-cream parlour to sell his own ice-cream.

When the business started John employed Joanne Garston to help make the ice-cream and when he opened his first parlour he took on Mike Chadwick to serve behind the counter. The summers were very hot during the next two years and the business went from strength to strength. During that time production increased and John opened three new parlours. He took on six new production staff in addition to six staff in each parlour working on a rota basis.

Because growth was fast John took on his first management staff with little thought for their specific capabilities. They now tend to work together in a haphazard way and it would seem that success has come due rather to the weather than good management. In addition to John there are four other staff, taken on to help in administration, sales and general management.

The management staff are:

Hilary Stephens who is a qualified accountant and who spends most of her time overseeing the ice-cream parlours—their organisation, stock and staff.

Alex Burton who is very outward going and confident but has no formal qualifications and is employed to manage the factory. He takes care of ordering new stock and processing the orders. He also takes some responsibility for safety in the company.

Michael Lewis has experience but no qualifications. He does voluntary work for the St John's Ambulance Brigade. He is popular with staff and he finds that they often talk to him when they have problems. Currently he helps with deliveries and organising purchasing and sales.

John has recently taken on a promising young typist Pat Robbins who attends a day-release secretarial course at the local college.

John himself organises transport of prepared ice-creams to his own parlours and local shops and restaurants. He also takes care of all customer accounts and processes payments for raw materials.

You have been John's secretary since the early days when the business started. You know the organisation inside out and John respects your opinion and has faith in your judgement. You have a reputation for being a good judge of character and aptitude and have also had experience in interviewing junior staff.

Business this year, however, has not been good and John has been unable to give his staff the wage and salary increases he would like. He blames it on a bad summer but the staff are of the opinion that it is mainly due to bad management on his part. The general complaint is that there is no clear management structure and that jobs are either done twice or not done at all. In addition blame is often wrongly apportioned when things go wrong. Standards at the ice-cream parlours are not good and there are an increasing number of customer complaints. The local restaurants which the company supplies have complained about both late and wrong delivery of ice-cream and in fact four restaurants have placed their orders elsewhere during the last six months.

John has suggested a meeting between himself and the three management staff to thrash out the problems and hopefully come up with some solutions. He wants to firstly identify where the problems are, secondly suggest an alternative management structure and thirdly produce a report assigning responsibilities to each member of the management team.

Problem
Before the meeting John has asked you to prepare some initial suggestions which he can add to his own ideas and around which he

can structure the meeting. Since he values your experience and judgement he has asked for your ideas in three areas outlined below. He has asked you to prepare a draft document which he can amend and to which he can add his own ideas before the meeting:

(a) identifying the problems
(b) suggesting a new management structure
(c) giving your suggestions for assigning specific responsibilities and job descriptions to the staff (including yourself and John).

John has suggested that the last two items could be clearly presented in the form of a chart and the whole in a draft report.

Examination Questions

1. What do you consider to be the main areas of responsibility of the Supervisor of a large typing unit and what qualities should she possess in order to do her job effectively?

   LCCI SSC OP

2. Indicate and comment on the *basic* functions of management.

   PEI SP Adv

Chapter 3

Business Documentation

3.1 —And You

'Why do I need to know about invoices and so on—I'm going to be a secretary, not a clerk'

The answer to this common cry is that as with so many aspects of secretarial work the degree of your involvement will depend to a large extent on two factors:

 — the size of the company in which you work
 — the department in which you work.

If you find yourself in a small to medium sized company you will meet some form of business documentation during the course of your working day. In a large organisation your involvement will depend on your department—Accounts, Purchasing and Sales are the departments which commonly deal with documentation as business transactions pass through the system. You may also find yourself carrying out an administrative role and be responsible for junior staff who do much of the routine paper work. Whatever your situation you should know what the normal procedures are. An understanding of these procedures also gives you a deeper and more useful knowledge of your company.

Without realising it most people handle 'business documentation' (orders, bills, receipts) as a regular part of their daily lives.

After buying a pair of shoes a **receipt** is given—a small but important piece of paper which becomes vital if the goods are unsatisfactory and have to be returned; on returning the goods, another piece of documentation, a **credit note** may be given.

Many people make purchases through mail order—clothes, household goods, etc., either directly after writing a letter to

46

enquire about the price, or through a mail order **catalogue.** In either case an **order** will probably be completed.

If you have to wait a long time for the goods you may receive an **advice** note to say that the goods are on their way.

Items may come by post or by the company's own van and the driver will ask you to sign a piece of paper to say that you have received the goods (**delivery note**).

If you pay for the goods after they have been delivered you will receive an **invoice** or **bill** and if you don't pay up quickly you'll get a **statement of account** giving you details of how much you still owe.

'This is fine,' you are saying, 'but how much more do I really need to know about all this? I'm going to be a secretary. I know most of this already and any more will be a clerk's job, not a secretary's.' In many instances this may be the case. You probably do know quite a lot about business documents from your own everyday experiences and much of the detailed work will be the job of purchasing clerks, sales staff and so on, particularly in a large organisation. But it must be remembered that a secretary needs a wide knowledge of such procedures in order to have a good understanding of her company's business. In a small company where she and maybe one other person are the only office staff, there will be no escaping documents and forms involved with buying and selling. It will probably be the secretary's responsibility to complete and follow through all business documentation.

3.2 —And the Secretary

In any manufacturing or service company, buying and selling is happening all the time. Take, for instance, a company making and selling shoes. What will they be concerned with?

Buying	Selling
Raw materials:	Finished products:
leather	shoes
plastics	boots
thread	sandals
fasteners	
dyes	
chemicals	

So while the company is buying its raw materials (which have to be of the right quality, the right price and delivered at the right time) they are also selling the finished product (which also has to be at the right price, to make a profit, in plentiful supply and of good quality).

3.3 Documents in Detail

'Cards with Hearts'—selling a new product

Imagine yourself as secretary in a small company manufacturing greetings cards. You are going to launch a new card for Valentine's day—pop up hearts and paper flowers. Let's call our company 'CARDS WITH HEARTS' and follow one aspect of the whole procedure through, from deciding on raw materials for the new card to selling it to the retail shops.

(i) Enquiry

An **enquiry** is made into purchasing raw materials. In this case adding paper flowers to our cards is a new venture and we will need to get the best deal we can. We need to know:

> price of paper flowers
> discount available
> when delivery can be made (how long it will take to make the flowers)
> quality (we will probably need some samples)
> range of colours.

The enquiry can be made by telephone or in writing (printed form or letter) or by reference to a catalogue or price list.

(ii) Price list/catalogue

A company which sells standard items in large numbers, e.g. office equipment, often publishes a **catalogue** which it updates regularly. The prices are printed either next to each item or on a separate **price list.** This enables prices to be updated easily and regularly without having to reprint the entire catalogue—which can be an expensive process.

(iii) Quotation/estimate/tender
We need to know how much it will cost to buy the paper flowers ready-made and will probably ask for some samples. Where (as in this case) the enquiry is for a non-standard item or service, then each enquiry will be given individual treatment. An estimate or tender for a building contract can take days or weeks of preparation and may include prices of materials and labour, dates for completion and so on. It can, of course, be a simpler document altogether, such as the quotation for making the paper flowers required for the greetings cards.

(iv) Order
Once our company 'Cards with Hearts' has decided on its supplier (whoever offers the quality we require at the right price and can deliver within the required time) our purchasing staff will place an **order**—sometimes by telephone but always backed up in writing. *ORDER FORMS OFTEN COME IN SETS OF SEVERAL COPIES.* The top copy goes to the supplier and other copies may go to other departments within our own company—Stores and Accounts are the two most likely.

(v) Advice note
Once our paper flowers are ready for despatch our supplier may send an **advice note** advising that they are on their way.

(vi) Delivery/consignment note
Our paper flowers will arrive with a **delivery** or **consignment** note which must be signed by the recipient on receipt of the goods.
    The goods may be sent in several ways depending on their bulk and the speed they are required. Normally they will arrive by:

    a company's own transport (e.g. Tesco, Sainsbury)
    an independent transport company (e.g. BRS)
    one of the many Post Office services available.

If the company's own transport is used then the document is a **delivery note.**
    If the company uses transport from outside (a specialist transport company) then the document is a **consignment note.**

(vii) Invoice
The **invoice** is the **bill** for the goods or service and is always numbered.

It is often printed on several copies of NCR paper and gives details of:

    date of sale
    name and address of buyer
    order number
    details of goods/service:
        description
        quantity
        catalogue/reference number
        unit price
        VAT
        discount

Fig 3.1   *A computer prepared invoice*

R. WESTON (Printers) LTD

Letterpress · Lithographic & Thermographic Printers

Dixon Street · Manmore Common · Wolverton WL2 7QT · Telephone: Wolverton 722

DELIVER TO:

INVOICE No.	DATE	ACCOUNT No.	CUSTOMER ORDER No.	DESPATCH DATE	DELIVERY NOTE No.	AREA CODE		INVOICE
080781	11/06/87	W480	TEL.	09/06/87	87129	5		

QUANTITY ORDERED	QUANTITY SUPPLIED	QUANTITY TO FOLLOW	PRODUCT CODE	UNIT	DESCRIPTION	UNIT PRICE	VALUE	VAT
50	50	0	25-1463	1 box	Paper flowers assorted colours	1.250	62.50	1

VAT	RATE	VALUE	TAXABLE	VAT			
1	15.0	62.50	51.56	7.73	The sale of these goods is made subject to our terms and conditions of business, a copy of which will be supplied on request.	TOTAL VALUE	62.50
						TOTAL VAT	7.73
					V.A.T. Registered No. 137 8894 16 DRG (UK) LTD.	INVOICE TOTAL	70.23

DISCOUNT OF   :0.94 MAY
BE DEDUCTED IF PAID WITHIN 30 DAYS

If we like the flowers we may send a **further order** or we may pay immediately.

(E & OE—errors and omissions excepted—at the bottom of an invoice indicates that the company issuing the invoice is not liable if any errors have been made in prices, etc. on the invoice.)

The 'invoice pack' (multiple copies) often forms the basis of the other documents already mentioned:

- one copy stays in purchasing
- one copy goes to sales
- one copy goes to stores
- one copy goes to accounts
- one copy goes ahead of the goods (advice note)
- one copy goes with the goods (delivery note)
- **the** *top copy* **goes to the customer (invoice).**

These 'packs' of documents are prepared either singly for use in typewriters or as continuous stationery. They may be printed on NCR paper with different coloured sheets or with one-time carbon interleaved. Some sections may also be blanked out when they are not relevant, e.g. the price is not important on the advice note or delivery note, and therefore will not appear on that document.

Is VAT important?

VAT must appear on all invoices where VAT is payable—normally a separate column is assigned for VAT.

(viii) Trade discount? Cash discount? What's the difference?
Trade discount is a deduction from the price quoted in the catalogue or price list. The wholesale or manufacturer allows a percentage discount to customers 'in the trade', typically 15% to 30% but may be higher.

Cash discount is again a reduction in the advertised price but in this case only if payment is made within an agreed period of time. The amount is usually stated on the invoice under 'Terms'. Cash discount is effectively a reward for prompt payment.

(ix) Credit note? Debit note? What's the difference?
Credit and debit notes are issued when the amount on the invoice has to be changed, either decreased (**credit note**) or increased (**debit note**).

A **credit note** indicates by how much the original invoice should be reduced—just as if you receive a credit note for returned goods in a shop. It may be issued if:

- goods are faulty, returned and not replaced
- a mistake has been made on the invoice and the customer has been charged too much.

A **debit note** adds to the original amount owed by the customer and may be issued:

- — if there is a mistake on the invoice and the total is less than the correct amount owed
- — more goods than were ordered have been delivered and the customer agrees to accept them
- — a charge for carriage has been omitted on the invoice.

'CARDS WITH HEARTS' may receive a debit note if our supplier has made a mistake with our order, perhaps sending more than were ordered, but in spite of this we decide to accept them in addition to our original order.

Remember
VAT must be shown on both credit and debit notes if applicable

---

(x) Statement of Account (often referred to as STATEMENT)
Usually in business, bills are not paid immediately on receipt of the invoice. This does not mean necessarily that the customer is un-reliable. There are two main reasons:

- — customers who make purchases regularly prefer to make payment for several invoices together—this is a more efficient use of time and money
- — some customers make a habit of not paying bills until they receive a reminder!

The **Statement of Account** is usually sent out to all customers at the end of the month and gives the customer up-to-date information regarding how much they owe, the dates of the invoices, debit notes, credit notes, etc. *Do not* confuse this Statement of Account with a bank statement which gives details of bank transactions.

A Statement of Account shows:

- — any amounts outstanding (from previous accounts)
- — details of all invoices, credit and debit notes—numbers and dates (although not details of goods)
- — details of any payment made since the last statement
- — total amount owed by the customer after each transaction.

Remember

A Statement of Account shows a 'cumulative total' i.e. the figures are added or subtracted as each item is included on the statement.

(xi) Payment

After receiving one or more statements we will pay for the goods by **cheque**. A **receipt** will probably not be issued unless it is asked for.

3.4 Know What's What

The secretary in a small company is likely to come across these documents in the normal course of her day, more so than in a large company where they will be handled by specialist staff.

It is good practice to be in the habit of checking all documentation—figures, VAT, goods and so on since oversight and omission can have disastrous repercussions. Remember that as secretary you may not only be dealing with stationery accounts or the cleaning bills. Even if you are not directly involved in the completion of these forms it is imperative that you know their purpose, source and destination. At any time you could find yourself:

- stepping in to help
- working in sales/purchasing/accounts or, in a small company, all three where some or all of the documentation will be your responsibility
- being responsible for overseeing junior staff who carry out routine form filling
- following up enquiries related to documentation.

What is a proforma invoice—is it different?

Yes it is. A proforma is sent out *before* the goods are delivered and payment must be made before the goods are delivered. A proforma may be used where the supplier is not sure of the credit worthiness of a company and wants to be sure of payment before sending out the goods.

Fig 3.2   *Movement of documents*

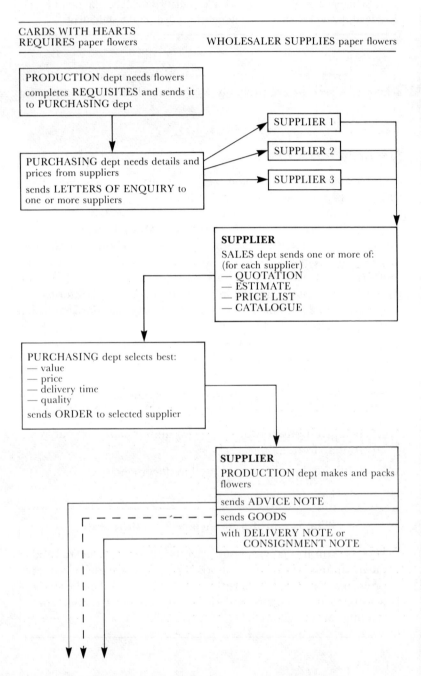

CARDS WITH HEARTS
REQUIRES paper flowers   WHOLESALER SUPPLIES paper flowers

PRODUCTION dept needs flowers
completes REQUISITES and sends it
to PURCHASING dept

SUPPLIER 1

SUPPLIER 2

SUPPLIER 3

PURCHASING dept needs details and
prices from suppliers

sends LETTERS OF ENQUIRY to
one or more suppliers

SUPPLIER
SALES dept sends one or more of:
(for each supplier)
— QUOTATION
— ESTIMATE
— PRICE LIST
— CATALOGUE

PURCHASING dept selects best:
— value
— price
— delivery time
— quality
sends ORDER to selected supplier

SUPPLIER
PRODUCTION dept makes and packs
flowers

sends ADVICE NOTE

sends GOODS

with DELIVERY NOTE or
        CONSIGNMENT NOTE

Movement of documents continued from page 54

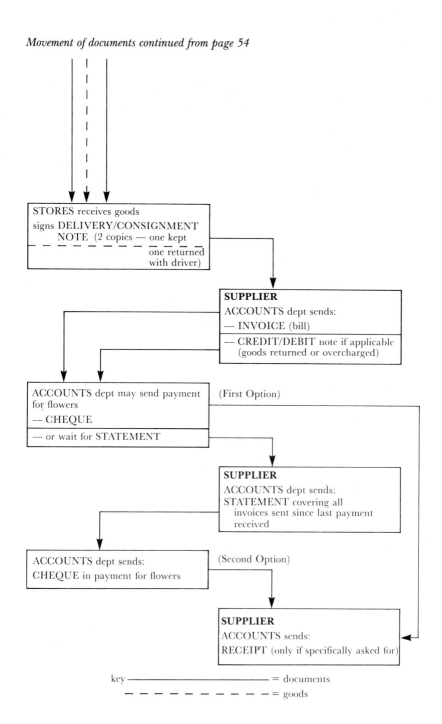

STORES receives goods
signs DELIVERY/CONSIGNMENT
NOTE (2 copies — one kept
one returned
with driver)

SUPPLIER
ACCOUNTS dept sends:
— INVOICE (bill)
— CREDIT/DEBIT note if applicable
(goods returned or overcharged)

ACCOUNTS dept may send payment
for flowers
— CHEQUE
— or wait for STATEMENT

(First Option)

SUPPLIER
ACCOUNTS dept sends:
STATEMENT covering all
invoices sent since last payment
received

ACCOUNTS dept sends:
CHEQUE in payment for flowers

(Second Option)

SUPPLIER
ACCOUNTS sends:
RECEIPT (only if specifically asked for)

key ——————————————— = documents
— — — — — — — — — — = goods

Do You Know?

You are secretary to the Managing Director of a small company—he wants a new chair. Do you know:

1. How to find what's available?
2. How to find out the price?
3. How to make out an order?
4. What to do with the delivery note when it arrives?
5. What information to expect on the invoice?
6. What document will tell you details of any other purchases you have made during the past month?
7. When you might expect trade or cash discount or both?
8. What document to expect if you return the chair before payment is made and a replacement is not required?
9. What document you will receive if the invoice contains a mistake—it states the price of the chair as £50 instead of £150?
10. If the statement states 'TERMS: 10% 7 days 5% 28 days, otherwise net', do you know what this means?

Secretarial Task Three

Your executive, the Managing Director of 'Cards with Hearts', is thinking of installing a drinks machine within the factory and has asked you to find out some prices for purchase/rent, etc. Write a reminder note to yourself outlining what you must do to get the information he requires.

You are also responsible for the purchase of all items of stationery used in the company. Sometimes a junior deals with documents as they come in and they frequently get mislaid. Prepare a check list for yourself and the junior which will ensure that all documentation is dealt with in the correct manner, both outgoing and incoming.

Examination Questions

1. Taking each of the following departments in turn, name two forms or documents that would normally be handled by a clerk in that department and explain the nature of the information that each form would be likely to carry:

    (i) The Costing Department
    (ii) The Accounts Department
    (iii) The Main Stores
    (iv) The Personnel Department
    (v) The Production Department

    LCCI SSC OP

2. The following documents are all used when processing a purchase. You are required to place them in the order in which they would be likely to be used and to describe the purpose of each document.

    (i) Statement of Account
    (ii) Advice note
    (iii) Purchase requisition
    (iv) Quotation
    (v) Cheque
    (vi) Order
    (vii) Enquiry
    (viii) Goods received note
    (ix) Credit note
    (x) Invoice

    LCCI SSC OP

3. Explain the circumstances under which a firm would send out the following documents:

    (i) A Statement of Account
    (ii) A debit note
    (iii) A delivery note
    (iv) An enquiry
    (v) A proforma invoice

    LCCI SSC OP

Chapter 4

Communication

Success depends on good communication

'But I didn't know about it'.

'I'm not a mind-reader'.

'I wrote it down but I can't find the paper I wrote it on'.

Familiar? Of course! These are words which even the most efficient of us have uttered at some time in our lives. Unfortunately for many of us they are uttered far too often and the question we should be asking ourselves is 'Why?'

The answers, too, are equally familiar:

'It was on the noticeboard for a week'.

'You never concentrate'.

'You should use your diary for its proper purpose'.

Of course, in the atmosphere of the home, school or college classroom most problems of this sort can easily be put right by asking a fellow student who hopefully was listening at the right time. In business, however, the solution is not always so easy and many a problem finds its roots in 'poor communication'.

Good communication is vitally important to the success of any organisation. It may take one of several forms—from a casual conversation, in passing, to a formal letter or contract of acceptance. The secretary is fundamental to effective communication in a company since she is frequently the mainstay on whom several people depend. Not only does she take responsibility for physically typing letters, memos, etc., she also acts as an intermediary in conversations, both face-to-face and through the medium of the telephone.

4.1 Communication is Instinctive

From birth communication is instinctive—babies cry when they are hungry and gurgle when they are happy. With only a small vocabulary a toddler in need of a biscuit will communicate this very effectively to her parents with such 'words' as 'bitbit' or 'biddit'. In no time at all, and with no effort, the toddler becomes a child with a full vocabulary for whom verbal communication is a sixth sense. When you were at junior school you rarely stopped to think about what you were going to say to your friends in the playground—for the most part you just said what you had to say—whether friendly or not, depending on your mood for the day. Generally life goes on in a similar pattern, except that with growing maturity we take greater care not to offend, and learn to take the rough with the smooth and on a bad day not to 'take it out' on our fellow workers. However, our basic instincts do not change: we want to speak—it happens without conscious thought—like eating and sleeping. All too often however, we think after we have spoken: 'I opened my big mouth and put my foot right in it'.

So if communication is so natural why all the fuss? Why write a whole chapter about something which we have been doing very well thank you since the day of our birth? Let's look at the essential factors which, as secretaries, we should bear in mind when communicating with our colleagues at work. Where do we go wrong, if we go wrong?

Firstly, successful communication only happens when the communicator and the recipient are 'on the same wavelength'.

Fig 4.1 *Successful communication*

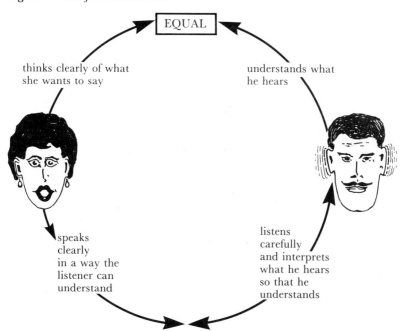

'But what has this to do with the secretary in the office?' Perhaps you have already been on work experience and been given a job to do by someone who has been doing it for years and has given you the sort of explanation which leaves you feeling that you knew more about the job before you arrived! Perhaps you have begun a course in information technology or word-processing taught by a 'computer teacher' who has baffled you with RAMs, ROMs, bytes, Ks in your first lesson—all important material, but perhaps you weren't quite ready for it then; again, you came away feeling more confused than enthusiastic. Why does this happen? The answer, of course, is that communication has not taken place at the right level for the particular situation.

(a) Think before you speak

Again, back to our picture—to communicate well, you must communicate in a way which the listener will be able to hear, interpret if necessary, understand and remember.

To communicate in speech effectively, i.e. so that you are understood, there are a number of key points which you should remember.

- Try to organise in your mind what you want to say before you say it. If necessary make brief notes before you speak, particularly for an important telephone call.
- Speak clearly and logically, i.e. don't start at the end and work backwards.
- Speak at a level suitable to your listener—speaking 'above someone's head' is a sure way to poor communication.
- Take note of your listener—is she still concentrating and understanding or does she look as though she is thinking about what she's having for tea. Perhaps you are not being clear; perhaps you are being too longwinded and she's hungry!
- Speak and write simply. Don't use long words or sentences where short ones will do. They may sound grand but all too often they lead to misunderstanding and lack of attention on the part of the listener.

(b) Keep it simple

Instances of unnecessarily long or complex sentences, or even sentences couched in jargon, are easy enough to find. Take for example the following:

— Amendments to a local authority District Plan:

> 'Line 5. Delete 'bottlenecks'. Insert 'localised capacity deficiencies'.'

What was wrong with 'bottlenecks'? A simple term which everyone understands.

— An otherwise straightforward letter asking for payment of an overdue account:

> Dear Madam
> With reference to my recent letter I note that your account is still £70.05 overdue. In view of the time which has elapsed I shall be most grateful if you will regularise this out of order situation.

What is wrong with saying 'I shall be most grateful if you will send a cheque in payment without delay'?

— Can we even begin to understand what the architect who wrote this had in mind?

> It is necessary to state that urban forms are a product of the modulated interaction between static determinants and the builders of urban formation subject to spatial mediation by the composite network of dynamic or functional conceptual forces.

(c) Listening is just as important

However straightforward a sentence may be, success in communication is only achieved if the listener plays her part:

- Listen carefully to what is actually being said—don't just switch
  off when you think you have heard enough—the important
  points often come at the end as an afterthought!

- If you don't understand, ask the speaker to explain or clarify
  what they have said, perhaps even to draw a diagram or put the
  important points together in a list.

- Don't try to do two things at once while listening to important
  instructions or explanations. You cannot catch up on the filing
  while having an important conversation. Apart from annoying
  the speaker you will probably miss some of the instructions and
  lose important papers.

- Make a point of remembering the important points in a
  conversation. It is a good idea to make a note immediately of
  any points to be followed up, reported on, etc. either in your
  diary or your follow-up system.

But, you are saying, communicating isn't all done by speech. We've
all heard about 'body language'. And what about all that paper that
accumulates in an office? What about the computers we are expected
to be able to use? What about the visual aids we need to understand?
Where does this fit in? The answer is, of course, that it fits in in exactly
the same way—all the same rules apply, except that for 'speak' and
'listen' we can substitute 'write', 'read', 'draw' and 'indicate'.

4.2 Choosing the Appropriate Form of Communication

In the majority of cases the secretary has no choice: the telephone
rings, she answers it; the executive dictates a letter, she types it. But
there are many times nevertheless when a choice has to be made and
the higher up the ladder a secretary rises, the more it will be her
responsibility to make that choice.

What are the areas of communication the secretary will be
concerned with? Broadly speaking they fall into the categories of
Internal and External, Written and Spoken; indeed many of these
areas are common to all categories.

Fig 4.2 *Choosing the appropriate form of communication*

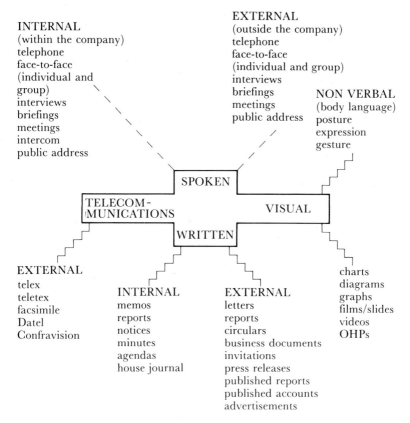

INTERNAL
(within the company)
telephone
face-to-face
(individual and
group)
interviews
briefings
meetings
intercom
public address

EXTERNAL
(outside the company)
telephone
face-to-face
(individual and group)
interviews
briefings
meetings
public address

NON VERBAL
(body language)
posture
expression
gesture

SPOKEN

TELECOM-
MUNICATIONS

VISUAL

WRITTEN

EXTERNAL
telex
teletex
facsimile
Datel
Confravision

INTERNAL
memos
reports
notices
minutes
agendas
house journal

EXTERNAL
letters
reports
circulars
business documents
invitations
press releases
published reports
published accounts
advertisements

charts
diagrams
graphs
films/slides
videos
OHPs

Of course in practice—in the daily hustle and bustle of office life—the secretary will find herself moving from one task to another, smoothly and without fuss, and will not have time to stop to consider which box this message or that call falls into.

Consider the secretary's day—what will it entail?

– Opening and reading incoming mail.
– Preparing replies to standard and non-standard mail.
– Preparing routine and non-routine memos.
– Preparing meeting documents.
– Preparing reports.
– Making and receiving routine telephone calls.
– Coping with 'difficult' telephone calls.

— Receiving visitors.

— Conversing with visitors while they wait.

— Dealing with 'difficult' visitors.

— Everyday conversations with colleagues.

— Issuing instructions to junior staff.

— Receiving instructions from superior staff.

— Passing on information, written and spoken.

— Dealing with correspondence by telephone or written reply.

— Taking dictation/audio typing.

— Taking minutes of meetings.

Selecting the appropriate method

Amongst all these tasks, and more, how is the secretary to choose the best method of communication? What factors are going to influence her choice?

A serious accident in a factory offers no choice—an emergency call would be made immediately. But in the normal course of events the choice is not always so obvious and this is where many problems in a business lie. The secretary should ask herself some or all of these questions:

— Is it urgent?

— How far must the message go?

— Is the time of day an important factor?

— Must the message be transmitted word for word?

— Must cost be taken into account?

— Is the method chosen reliable?

— Must the message be in writing?

— How many people need to receive the message?

— Must the message be delivered personally?

— Is the message long and complicated or short and simple?

— Is the message confidential?

999 calls, thankfully, do not happen every day. But even so, in many instances, the secretary will have no choice in the matter. 'Write to Mrs Bradbury will you Joan and say . . .' or 'phone Mike Jones and ask him for lunch next Tuesday' is the usual way. However, it is also

important for the secretary to be able to select the most appropriate form of communication in any given situation. Sometimes she has time to consider the many options open to her, as in the case of despatching important documents abroad, when safety rather than urgency may be of paramount importance. However, more often than not, time will be the ruling factor and a decision has to be made quickly. It is vital, therefore, that the secretary should have the relevant information at her fingertips or, if it is not available to her, that she should know where to find out whatever she needs to know to help her make a quick decision.

The first important decision to be made is between oral and written communication, so let us look at the pros and cons of these two methods, together with the various options available within the two categories.

4.3 Oral Communication

The advantages of communicating by speech are fairly obvious:

- It is quick—there is no waiting for mail, etc.
- Feedback is immediate—the speaker gets an immediate verbal reply, either face-to-face, or on the telephone.
- Non-verbal responses can be observed—these may indicate feelings which the participants may be reluctant to actually say.
- More people may participate—for example in meetings.
- Valuable spontaneous ideas and decisions may result from face-to-face conversations.

Because of the important advantages of oral communication and because it is second nature to us, many people in business rely heavily on discussion and conversation. Unfortunately many problems arise because they have not given sufficient thought to the equally important disadvantages which may arise:

- The **spoken word is all too easily forgotten**—a written record is often vital.
- **Some material needs more careful planning** than spontaneity allows for and is therefore more suitable to the written word.
- **Oral communication can easily get out of hand** and become uncontrolled.

- Legally **a written record is often required.**
- There may be some **time delay** if the relevant **people are not immediately available.**
- If more than one person is involved there may be **practical problems in getting everyone** together at the right time.

In spite of the disadvantages of spoken communication, the secretary will be required to communicate in this way for a good part of her working day. She will communicate on a variety of different levels and in several different directions—up to higher management, across to staff on the same level as herself and down to staff for whom she is responsible.

The means of communication will be based mainly on 'face-to-face' (one-to-one or in a group) and by telephone (external and internal).

(a) 'Face-to-face'

Communication takes place between herself and her superior/ superiors in routine discussions, in interviews, in meetings, in business discussions where she may be asked to make enquiries or to take an active part, and generally around the office with colleagues during the course of a working day.

Face-to-face discussions are valuable in that they can be planned or spontaneous. They also offer instant visual feedback which is so important. However, there are times when face-to-face is not possible or is inconvenient or when an individual would prefer not to have eye contact, perhaps in a delicate situation or when he wants to keep discussion to a minimum.

(b) Telephone

This is probably the second most widely used means of communication between individuals. In addition to many of the advantages of face-to-face discussion the telephone also offers the obvious advantage of immediate conversation with someone at a distance:

- immediate feedback
- it is not subject to the vagaries of the postal system
- it is often more convenient to pick up a telephone receiver than to write a letter, telex, or arrange a meeting.

However, using the telephone has two major disadvantages and some minor ones:

- the cost of calls can be immense if used indiscriminately, e.g. for long calls at peak rate times

– in the main it is not suitable for group discussions, unless the appropriate equipment is installed, which can be expensive

– the recipient of the call may not be immediately available when telephoned

– tone of voice can be deceptive and can convey a misleading attitude if facial expressions cannot be seen

– 'cold' calls, e.g. for the purpose of selling a product, can be too abrupt a way of making an introduction and can make people defensive.

(i) Using the telephone
As a secretary you may find yourself using the telephone in one of three ways:

– **in a small company** as secretary/receptionist/switchboard operator

– **in a small/medium company** as relief switchboard operator in addition to your own telephone in your own office

– **in a medium/large company** you will be concerned with your own telephone (or telephones), dealing with internal and external calls.

Fig. 4.3 *A small switchboard*

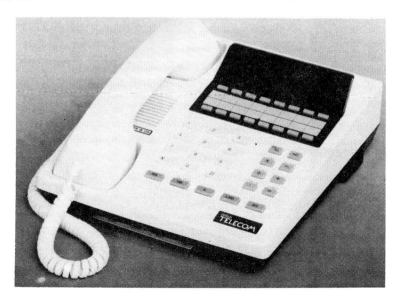

In all cases the procedures are the same:

- Always have a message pad to hand.
- Answer promptly—don't linger while you finish a previous task.
- Speak slowly and clearly.
- If on a switchboard give name of company.
- If the call has come to your telephone via the switchboard give:
  your name and/or position;
  a greeting (Good morning/afternoon or perhaps 'hello' if the call is internal and the caller is working at the same level and is well-known to you).
- Deal with the call in an appropriate manner—there will be several options:

  the call may be regarding information with which you normally deal, e.g., arrangement of meetings, receiving statistical information, recording progress, etc. In these cases the call would be dealt with in a routine manner and will normally cause no problems. Ensure that you record information accurately. It is wise to repeat essential information back to the caller to ensure that you have made no mistakes.

  The the caller may wish to speak to your superior who is unavailable, in which case you must:

  1. apologise for his absence (there is no need to say where he is—just say that he is unavailable)
  2. ask if you may (a) take a message (b) ask your superior to call back or (c) put the caller through to someone else who you think may be able to help (it is helpful to check first since there is the danger of annoying the caller if he has to speak to too many people without receiving any concrete help).

Remember

Dealing with callers in your executive's absence needs careful consideration since important contracts worth many thousands of pounds can be lost by mishandling of telephone calls.

(ii) Taking a message
The essential ingredients of a message are:

- Name, company and address, if appropriate, of external caller.

– Name and department of internal caller.

– Caller's telephone number and extension.

– Date and time of message.

– The message itself—you may have to sift the essential information from the non-essential—but always check back with the caller that you have recorded the important points, including accuracy of name, company and telephone number.

– Any further action, e.g. whether to telephone the caller back, or whether the caller will phone again, etc.

– Your own name, clearly written, so that any problems which arise can subsequently be taken up with you.

Remember

Always take the caller's name, company and telephone number even if he has not asked to be called back. This information is vital if any queries arise.

(iii) Telephone calls to the secretary

Many calls will be for you as the secretary, perhaps arranging appointments, interviews, meetings, giving apologies, asking for literature, etc. In these cases it is important to deal with the calls efficiently.

– Have your diary handy, to refer to for appointments, etc.

– Have note-pad and pen ready for important details—*never use odd scraps of paper,* they get lost.

– Double check details with caller.

– Have information ready if you know beforehand that someone will be requiring up-to-date sales figures or meeting details, for instance. It doesn't create a good impression and wastes time and money if you have to say 'could you wait while I look it up?'

– Keep the caller informed of what you are doing if you do have to leave the telephone to find information. Sometimes it is easier and more convenient to offer to call back rather than leave the caller waiting while you spend some time routing through files or finding someone else who can give you the information.

Helpful hints

Be polite, friendly, concise, organised and calm.

Answer your telephone promptly and do not ignore a neighbouring phone if there is no one there to answer it. You can at least take a message and, by doing so, may avoid losing an important contract.

Always record at least the name and telephone number. Make sure a longer message is precise, concise and accurate.

(iv) Making telephone calls
There are certain basic rules to follow when making telephone calls.

- Have the telephone number you are calling written down in front of you. You may have to call several times before you get through. Looking the number up wastes time and money.
- Plan what you want to say before making the call—make brief notes which you can understand easily.
- Wherever possible know who you want to speak to—the name of the person or department. If unsure you may be able to refer to the reference on any correspondence which you have.
- Ensure that you are speaking to the right person before beginning whatever you have to say—it is very frustrating to repeat a message several times to the wrong people.
- Have any papers to which you may need to refer during the call ready by the telephone.
- When your call is answered say who you are and ask for the extension number, department, or name of person you wish to speak to. If you are unsure, briefly state the nature of your business to the operator who should then advise you.
- Be prepared to:

    leave a message—even with an answering machine

    speak to someone else who may be available

    phone back later

    'hold', i.e. wait for the person you wish to contact to become available. This may take some minutes and you must remember that time costs money. However, sometimes this may be the only way to get to speak to a busy person.

(v) Create a good impression

All calls, both internal and external, require the same approach and treatment, fundamental to creating and maintaining a good impression of your company

- identify yourself, your department, your company
- speak clearly
- speak slowly
- speak politely
- be friendly
- be prepared
- be concise
- be organised
- take details of—name
  company
  date
  time
  message.

Remember

Time costs money. Whenever possible, make calls in the afternoon and particularly try to avoid long distance calls in the morning unless they are absolutely necessary.

Make no personal calls unless they are urgent. Many companies have private call boxes for the use of staff.

Don't 'hold' when you can make a call later unless you know that the person you want is particularly difficult to get hold of.

Don't confine yourself to your own telephone. Be prepared to answer someone else's phone, particularly in an open-plan office. You may avoid the loss of an important contract—you may know the whereabouts of the person being called or you may otherwise be able to help. Remember that the telephone is a vital factor in the success of any company and each unanswered call adds to the possible frustration and annoyance of the caller.

(vi) Coping with difficult calls

Telephone calls unfortunately don't always follow the 'text-book' pattern. There will always be the difficult calls, the callers who are awkward, cross, rude, long-winded or difficult to understand. Sometimes they have reason to be so. At other times, perhaps they got out of bed the wrong side' or maybe just lost an important contract and it is your misfortune that you are the next person they speak to! As secretary you must be able to deal with these in a calm and efficient manner. Sometimes a caller will be annoyed for a very good reason— perhaps he has already explained his problem to four different people before getting through to you. This may have happened because your switchboard operator was at fault in not ascertaining the exact manner of the caller's business before putting him through. One well-known store requires its switchboard operators always to ask a caller's business even if the caller seems to be sure of who he wishes to speak to. On the other hand the caller himself may be at fault for not organising his call before he started, i.e. he did not ascertain who he needed to speak to from your switchboard.

Examples of difficult telephone calls:

Long-winded callers   need careful handling. They may be valued customers and naturally must not be offended. A careful inter-ruption at an appropriate pause and 'I'm very sorry Mr Torrent, would you excuse me, I have to be at a meeting in a few minutes. I'll look into the matter immediately I return and call you back then' will avoid offending and gives a promise of immediate attention.

Cross or rude customers need a calm, unruffled, organised approach. Never get cross or rude yourself—you will only make matters worse. Tactfully keep the caller to the point and make sure that the facts are clear and correct. If the problem becomes too great for you to deal with, offer to pass the matter on to an alterna-tive, appropriate person. Always make a clear, accurate, unbiased record of the call. If the matter becomes serious, it is essential that you remember all that was said.

When customers or clients are difficult to understand—perhaps you are on a bad line, or English is not their first language—it is important that you help them. Ask simple, straightforward questions which can be answered clearly. Perhaps the caller is making a complaint about some goods. You should phrase your questions clearly and simply:

> On what date did you buy the goods?
> What is the name of the shop you bought them from?
> What town is the shop in?
> What price did you pay for the goods?
> What is wrong with the article?

In this way you are more likely to get clear answers than if you merely asked 'what is the problem?'

(vii) Internal communication

Intercom is a means of communicating by means of an internal telephone system within an organisation. The calls may be made through either a separate telephone system or through the same system as for external calls. Each department, head of department, secretary, desk, etc. will have its own internal telephone number and it is important that as secretary you ensure that both you and your superior have an up-to-date list of such numbers. In some companies these internal telephone directories will run to pages while in others, a small firm of architects for instance, there may only be two or three telephones, one for the partners and one for the secretary.

(viii) Mobile communications

British Telecom have made great advances in mobile telephone facilities over recent years which have provided increased mobility for telephone users. Portable handsets are readily available as are telephones with loudspeakers, both of which enable the user to move away from his desk while making calls. Calls can be made as easily from the other side of the room as from, for example, a moving car or while visiting a new factory site. Such services are equally available for internal and external calls.

Fig 4.4 *Mobile telephone*

Mobile radio payphones
British Telecom are introducing the **Trainphone** which enables calls to be made from trains on main line routes and some intercity coach services. They are also currently developing a **Ferryphone** which can be used on ferries travelling from Britain.

Radio paging
Sometimes referred to as one-way or two-way radio, **radio paging** is an extension of the traditional 'loudspeaker', 'tannoy', or 'paging' system and operates by means of a pocket radio receiver. When called the receiver emits a signal. The person, on hearing the signal, can then listen to a message—with a two-way system the person receiving the message can also give a reply. The common name 'walkie-talkie' is an apt one. Although used mainly by police, firemen and those in similar jobs, their use in spreading to other areas and 'cellular radio' is becoming an important part of the telephone network.

Bleeper systems
Bleeper systems are a recent development from the traditional 'loud-speaker' or tannoy and represent an extension of radio paging. They are now as well used as telephones in some jobs. Any individual may carry with him a pocket-size receiver which, when called, emits a high pitched 'bleep'. The person carrying the 'bleeper' knows, on hearing the signal, to go to the nearest telephone and call a pre-arranged place—usually the switchboard—who will pass on whatever message they wish to convey. Some systems are able to emit several different tones, each of which identifies the person who is calling the bleeper. For example, an architect visiting several sites may be called mainly by his secretary, in which case he will need no more than one tone. On the other hand, a doctor in a busy hospital may be required urgently in any one of many places. He would be able to identify which ward, department or location had called and could immediately telephone or go there. These devices are valuable to people on the move in that they are no trouble to carry around, are unobtrusive in their tone and there is no problem with confidentiality since conversations only take place at a telephone.

(c) Conferences at a distance with the help of British Telecom

The cost of calling several people together from several parts of the country, sometimes for a meeting which may last only a short time, can be immense: hotel bills and travel expenses for more than one or two people can soon total several hundreds of pounds, apart from the loss of valuable time in travelling and the inconvenience of being absent from the office. British Telecom offer a number of services which enable busy executives and their staff to have oral or face-to-face discussions and conferences with other personnel throughout the country.

(i) Confravision
Groups of people can be linked by sound and vision throughout the country at specified times from studios in several major cities. Perhaps your superior asks you to arrange for the sales staff from your office in Birmingham to have urgent discussions with the staff from the Glasgow office about seriously declining sales. Normally this would involve either several long telephone calls with information being passed through several people, or several people travelling and staying overnight at considerable expense. Through British Telecom you can book studios in Birmingham and Glasgow for example by giving as little as two hours notice. Once in the studios all participants are able to see each other on video screens and can hear what is being said by means of microphones which can be switched off if confidential discussions are necessary. It is also possible to arrange for the entire conference to be recorded on tape. Mobile studios are also available for companies who are situated too far away from a studio.

Fig 4.5 *Confravision – close up of screens*

Fig. 4.6 *Confravision studio*

(ii) Videostream

A videoconferencing service which offers instant transmission of moving pictures between the conference rooms in two different organisations. No special studios are required as a range of free-standing terminals are available which contain both camera and monitor.

(iii) Confertel

An audio conference system which allows a meeting to take place between several telephone users, in or between any countries, and using the ordinary telephone lines. Once connected, callers can take part in discussions between several people.

(d) Helpful equipment

(i) Telephone answering machines

A major problem for small businesses with limited office staff is that of answering telephone calls when the office if empty.

Professional people such as architects, doctors, surveyors and many others carry out much of their business away from the office and many have part-time office staff. For these people telephone answering machines solve many of their problems. These machines can be left on for 24 hours—when a call comes through, a pre-recorded tape is activated which plays an appropriate message. It usually gives the name of the business and gives details of when the office is open, for instance, or where the caller should phone (in the case of doctors), or any other appropriate message. Some machines will automatically switch off after this message has been relayed to the caller, others will ask the caller to leave a message after they hear a 'tone', usually a high pitched bleep. Many callers are reluctant to speak to an answering machine but for many businesses it is a valuable way of ensuring that important business is not lost through enforced absence from the office. The machines are purchased and connected to an existing telephone system. With the latest machines (Voice Bank is operated by British Telecom), it is even possible for the would-be receiver of the message to call up his own answering machine from any telephone and instruct it to relay any messages already recorded—without him having to return to his office or home.

Fig. 4.7   *Voicebank*

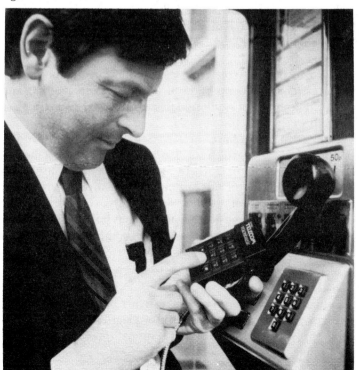

Don't be shy with an answering machine!

Say who you are, your telephone number and your reason for calling.

Ask to be called back or say when you will call again.

Remember

If you have an answering machine in your own office to
    switch on when you go out
    check for incoming calls when you return
    follow up incoming calls—relay messages, call back, etc.

(ii) Memory telephones

Many standard telephones, which can be purchased from British Telecom or other companies, are able to 'store' any number of telephone numbers. The simpler phones are limited to 10 numbers while the more complicated and expensive ones can store as many as 400 or more. These numbers can then be called merely by pressing one or two buttons which cause the full number to be dialled automatically. This facility is extremely useful where many long numbers, particularly international, are dialled frequently. An individual directory will be necessary to record the codes for each number. With the greater telephone memory, it is important to use the coding carefully and systematically otherwise it is questionable whether there is anything to be gained from such telephones.

These telephones also have the facility for automatic redial of a number previously tried which was perhaps engaged and some will ring out when a line is free, where all lines have previously been engaged. Other facilities include last number redial, digital display of dialled number and cost of call, diversion of calls to other extensions or numbers, background music while the caller is holding (sometimes worse than silence!), the list is endless and becoming longer with each new telephone introduced to the market.

(iii) Callmakers

Commonly used numbers (up to 400) can be called without dialling. Numbers are recorded on plastic cards or magnetic tape, or can be dialled by pressing only one key. They save time and are more convenient for long telephone numbers.

Remember

Try to make distance calls after 1.00 pm. Even only a few morning calls can be very costly.

Keep the length of calls to the minimum—some companies issue departmental telephone bills, to encourage economy.

Only make urgent personal telephone calls. Many companies have public telephones installed. Not only are private calls costly, but they take up important telephone time with the result that callers may not be able to get through.

4.4 Written Communication

Communication via the written word is probably the second most common method of transmitting ideas and messages and covers a wider variety of media from letters and memoranda to reports and minutes. In this changing world of telecommunications and computer technology why does the written word survive? Its advantages are obvious:

- ideas can be explained fully
- there is a written record for reference
- identical copies can be distributed simultaneously to relevant people
- oral discussion can be endorsed in writing
- a record exists for legal purposes
- it allows time for accurate translation of foreign languages.

In spite of these advantages there is no doubt that the written word is being superseded by new means of communication and indeed some would argue that we write fewer letters, both business and social, because we are lazy and prefer the convenience of the telephone. It is also true that there are many times when alternative methods of communicating are more appropriate in terms of speed, accuracy and spontaneity. Why is this?

Let us look at the disadvantages of written communications:

- it costs time to send internal memos, or letters by means of the postal system. It is not unusual for a letter posted first class in London to take two days to reach its destination on the other side of the city while an identical first class letter, also posted in

London, takes only 24 hours to reach Manchester, 200 miles away!

- it costs money to guarantee delivery of written correspondence within 24 hours. Datapost, for instance, the only Post Office service which guarantees next day delivery costs over £10
- it takes time to prepare lengthy and accurate written communications
- confidential papers may go astray if not treated appropriately
- feedback takes time—letters can remain unanswered on the recipient's desk for days
- poorly written letters can lead to misinterpretation

The terms letters, memos, reports and minutes are, to a certain extent, household words but within the context of the office it is vital that the secretary knows:

(a) which method is appropriate to each situation
(b) the correct form each should take.

Many times the secretary will be asked to 'write to Mr Beardsall and say . . .' or to 'send a memo to John Stone in Marketing telling him . . . .' The secretary will, it is hoped, know what 'writing a letter' means and what 'sending a memo' entails. Other times it may be said to her 'Let Mike Arndale know that I can't manage lunch next month'. In such instances the secretary will consider several factors before communicating with Mike Arndale:

- the time available before the lunch date
- how easy Mike Arndale is to contact
- whether this information should be passed on in writing
- whether a telephone call is sufficient.

The secretary may also be expected to arrange meetings either on a regular basis or *ad hoc*. Again she must decide what method to use after considering all the facts at her disposal. For example an informal meeting of all sales staff may require a simple phone call followed by a memo to each person, whereas a meeting of Directors would require her to send an official Notice of Meeting and Agenda.

When at work the secretary will be concerned with written communication of two main types: that which is for an internal destination and that which is for an external destination. Referring back to Figure 4.2 it can be seen that internal communication is concerned mainly with memos, reports, and notices. It is important that the secretary recognises when to use each since it will often be her responsibility to make the decision.

To the experienced secretary, choosing the form of communication should be no problem. The new, inexperienced or potential secretary needs more guidance.

(a) Memorandums

More usually referred to as memos, these pieces of paper can vary from a short, informal note between two managers to a long complex document from a manager to perhaps the Managing Director setting out details of a proposed contract with another company. A memo is essentially a written communication sent within a company (it may go from one site to another, even in another part of the country). It differs from a letter in that it has no address, no salutation (Dear. . .) nor any complimentary close (Yours . . .). The wording may be formal or informal depending on the nature of the material and the personnel involved. The importance of the memo lies in the fact that it provides a written record for reference which can be used by the sender and the recipient. It should be filed in the usual way along with other related documentation. The memo in Figure 4.8 shows clearly a typical layout, although the order may vary from company to company. Although not essential, most companies require a heading since this makes it easier to identify the content of the memo and it is also useful to refer to for filing purposes. Sometimes a memo is sent covering more than one topic; it must be remembered that this can make filing slightly more difficult although an easy solution is to photocopy the memo and file one copy in each relevant file.

Filling in a Memo Form

- Titles—Mrs, Mr, Ms, Miss—may be omitted from the sender's name, although they are normally included in the recipient's name.
- First names and surnames may be used.
- Include the name of the destination department or the position of the recipient in order to avoid confusion.
- Include the sender's position and/or department for the same reason.
- Begin with a subject heading.
- Do not begin Dear. . .
- Do not finish Yours . . . (sometimes a signature is included at the end of the memo).
- Include an indication of any extra copies which may be sent to other personnel for clarification, e.g. 'cc Accounts'.

Fig 4.8   *A memo*

TOWN SECRETARIAL SERVICES

Internal Memorandum

To   All Heads of Departments   **Date**   16 January 19....
From   Amanda Parker   **Ref**   AP/lw
           Managing Director

Subject   USE OF NEW COMPANY STATIONERY

The new company stationery is now available from stores and is to be
used for all correspondence from the 1st of next month.   Please
ensure that staff in your department are aware of the change.

(b) Reports

The secretary's involvement with report writing will vary from
company to company and from report to report. She may be asked to
put together regular routine reports on current sales progress, the
material for which she receives from sales staff based around the
company who report back to her at regular intervals, or she may be
given the draft for a more detailed report which she has to put
together more formally. On the other hand she may merely be
required to present a report, perhaps a lengthy document regarding a
new contract, which has already been written in a formal manner. For
each of these instances it is important that she knows the correct
format—whether the report is short or long, formal or informal.

A short report will normally consist of three major sections:

- the introduction (giving background details, stating the current
  situation and outlining the reason for the report)
- the findings (information gathered on the subject)
- the conclusions (details of recommended action).

This information may be presented formally or informally, even as a
memo outlining the situation and recommended action.

A longer, formal report will follow a more detailed pattern although not all sections will necessarily be included:

- title page (with author's name, date of presentation and name of company or organisation commissioning the report)
- contents page
- terms of reference (and outline of the reasons for the report)
- the procedure or method of approaching the research carried out (modus operandi)
- findings or results (often in several sections)
- conclusions
- recommendations or suggestions for action
- appendices (supplementary information, often including research figures, which may be useful to the reader)
- bibliography (list of books, articles, journals, etc. which have been referred to during the course of investigation or research).

Fig 4.9 *Report on the canteen facilities at Middlemore College*

REPORT ON THE CANTEEN FACILITIES AT MIDDLEMORE COLLEGE

TERMS OF REFERENCE

On 10 March 19.. Mr P Stephens, Principal of Middlemore College, set up a committee to investigate complaints of inadequate canteen facilities for Middlemore students and to make any necessary recommendations.

The members appointed to the Committee were Mr D French, Vice-Principal, Mrs P White, Lecturer in Domestic Economics, Mr T Lisseman, Lecturer in Business Studies and Miss B Wasley, Secretary of the Students Union.

EVIDENCE

The Committee interviewed Mrs S Fox, the canteen manageress, on 11 March 19.. . Mrs Fox said that she was two full-time staff short on the approved establishments, that one of the part-time assistants, Mrs L Taylor, was ill and would not return to work for at least two weeks and that none of the staff had been replaced; furthermore there were now over a thousand students in the college while the canteen was designed to cater for 400 only. Mrs Fox pointed out that there were long queues, particularly mid-morning and mid-afternoon and many students did not get served until after the time they should have returned to lectures. To obviate queuing and crowding, it was Mrs Fox's opinion that her staff should be brought up to its full establishment as soon as possible. Mrs Fox also thought that if the present system of staggered break-times was further extended the queues would be less.

The Committee then interviewed, in the course of the week ending Friday 14 March 19.. some 20 students, representing a cross-section of the student body. (See Appendix I for list of names and departments). The interviews were carried out using a questionnaire (see Appendix II).

The views of the students (recorded in detail in Appendix III), supported by Mrs Fox's comments, were that the canteen was understaffed and over-crowded at break-times. The present system of staggered breaks was hampered by some lecturers' practice of not keeping to the allotted times, by either finishing their classes too early or too late, so that groups of students arrived in the canteen at the times allocated to other groups.

CONCLUSIONS

1   The canteen is understaffed.
2   The canteen is inadequate in size to cater for the numbers of students using the facilities.
3   The problems are aggravated by the non-observance of the time-table by some members of staff.
4   The break timetable is probably not satisfactory even when it runs to schedule.
5   Alternative forms of providing refreshments should be investigated.

RECOMMENDATIONS

1   The Middlemore Chief Education Officer should be asked to take steps to bring the canteen staff up to the allotted numbers.
2   The teaching staff should be firmly requested to keep strictly to the existing break timetable.
3   The break timetable should be re-examined with a view to extending the total period in which the canteen is used during both morning and afternoon.
4   A committee should be set up to examine the possibilities, problems and economics of installing drink and snack vending-machines on each floor in the college in order to lessen the pressures on the canteen facilities.

SIGNED

Mr D French
Vice-Principal   ....

Mrs P White
Lecturer in Domestic Economics   ....

Mr T Lisseman
Lecturer in Business Studies   ....

Miss B Wasley
Secretary to the Students' Union ....

Date: 20 March 19..

APPENDIX I   List of students interviewed
APPENDIX II   Questionnaire
APPENDIX III   Full details of comments resulting from
               questionnaire and interviews

(i) Writing reports

It can be quite a daunting task for the new secretary to be asked to write a report. The first thing to do is to obtain a previous report which has been prepared on a similar subject and follow the same style. It is important that reports are presented in an impersonal unbiased way and that they are not emotive. To this end they are always written in the third person—this means that phrases such as 'It was found to be', 'It can be concluded that' are used in preference to 'I think' or 'We found'.

(ii) Presentation
The presentation of a report must be clear, concise and free from ambiguity. A good typist's reference book will give a clear outline of the presentation but it is important to remember that the report must be easy to read. Very often the reader will be short of time and will want to read only the important points and may concentrate on the conclusions and recommendations. It is vital, therefore, that each section is clear and easy to read. Various systems of numbering are available to use and many companies have their own house-style which must be followed. Always think of the logic of the numbering system you choose and remember that too many combinations of numbers and letters can lead to more confusion. A safe and clear method is the one used in this book which follows logically through chapters and sections. An alternative is to begin with numbers and add in capital and lower case letters for subsections. Numbers only may be used, as in Example 4. Any of the examples below, consistently used, are acceptable:

Example 1	Example 2	Example 3	Example 4
1 (a)	A1	A (i)	1
1 (b)	A1 (a)	A (ii)	1.1
1 (c)	B1	A (iii) a	1.2
	B2	b	1.2.1
	B2 (a)	c	1.2.2
	B2 (b)		1.2.3

Report writing—helpful hints

Understand and keep to the terms of reference

Consider the tone of your report—is it appropriate to the type of report you are writing and for the people who will read it?

Keep within the time allocated to produce the report—stick to deadlines

Consider the length—has it been stipulated? If so allocate research effort and writing time accordingly

Consider the degree of formality required—this will affect the style, length and tone

---

(c) Letters

(i) Considerations

Letters are arguably one of the most common types of written communication in use in the office. They cover as many topics and take as many forms as there are types of business. The secretary's involvement will vary from straightforward transcription from tape or shorthand to complete responsibility for obtaining information, and writing the letter.

Most correspondence falls into one of four categories:

General	letters of thanks, enquiry, apology, etc.
Specific	letters of confirmation, appointment, outlining problems, estimates, etc.
Circular	promotion material (advertising and selling goods and services).
Standard	form letters giving standard information, e.g. asking for outstanding payments, holiday information (specific names, addresses and appropriate information can be inserted on each letter).

Most normal daily correspondence will be produced on a typewriter—manual, electric or electronic—but there is an increasing trend for secretaries to use word processors for their daily workload. Circular and standard letters are particularly suited to word processors and have eliminated the drudgery of retyping many 'top' copies of important documents and speeded up the 'fiddly' and sometimes slow process of filling standard letters with variable information.

(ii) Putting the letter together in the correct way

This should be second nature to a secretary. Unfortunately it is not always so. Many companies will have a 'house style' which is followed throughout the company. If this is the case there will usually be a booklet or folder that you should keep in your desk setting out the patterns and practices for all company correspondence and documents.

Typing a letter requires a few initial considerations.

- What size of paper? A4 is generally more suitable and increasingly popular—there is nothing to be gained from squashing too much on to A5.
- Is it to be posted by any service other than normal delivery (first or second class)? If so this should be indicated on the letter (e.g. Special Delivery).

- Is it Private or Confidential? This should be indicated on the letter.
- Should any date other than the day of typing be indicated? (Sometimes a letter which is to be posted tomorrow will require tomorrow's date.)
- Who is the letter to be addressed to: the company, a person, or marked 'For the attention of'? (Some companies request that all correspondence be addressed in this way.)
- How many carbon copies are required?

On completion of the letter always:

- Check accuracy very carefully (an incorrect number could cost the company thousands of pounds through a lost contract).
- Check that all enclosures are attached.
- Type an envelope of the correct size—don't cram too much paper into a small envelope.

Don't leave any of these until later—they are more likely to get forgotten. Do them immediately.

Remember
check accuracy   check enclosures   check envelope

(iii) Composing letters for yourself
This is by far one of the more difficult tasks for an inexperienced secretary and yet it is one at which she must be competent. Writing a successful letter requires some thought and planning:

1. Have all the information you need at hand before you start:
   - name and address of addressee
   - previous relevant correspondence
   - any material to which you need to refer or from which you need information for your letter
2. Plan an outline of what you need to say, including reference to previous correspondence or telephone calls
3. Structure the letter in paragraphs and include reference to:
   - reason for letter (telephone call, letter, enquiry) with date
   - substance of letter (date of interview, details of estimate, etc.); this may run to several paragraphs
   - further action required by sender or recipient.

The tone of the letter is important and with experience you will gain confidence in writing in an appropriate style. To begin with, where you are unsure it is always preferable to be more formal than necessary. People are rarely offended by formalities but they may not be impressed with a letter which is too friendly. It is important to remember too that a letter is a written record and as such must be worded carefully and be free from ambiguities.

Remember

Be concise, but not so brief as to omit important information.
Keep the wording simple and clear.
Keep to the point.
Use a polite, friendly, but not over-familiar tone.
Check thoroughly on completion that you have said everything you want to say.
Check carefully for mistakes and ALWAYS correct them or retype if necessary.

(d) Copies

— Always take a copy of anything you type—carbon copy or photocopy.

— Always correct mistakes on carbon copies as well as on top copies.

— If more than one copy is required use different coloured paper to distinguish one from the other.

— Mark copies immediately with the name or department where they are to be sent and remember one must always go in the file.

It is very common these days for companies to use photocopies in preference to carbon copies on the grounds that they are a more accurate record and may be cheaper in the long run; it is quicker to produce one or more accurate photocopies than to work through the process of collating and lining up the paper required for carbon copies—top copy, carbon paper, and at least one flimsy. In addition, correcting carbon copies takes time. It is argued in terms of operator time that photocopies are more economical. On the other hand it should be remembered that photocopies are usually produced on ordinary paper which takes up more space than 'flimsy' in the filing system. This too is inefficient.

Correspondence–helpful hints

When taking shorthand, always make notes for yourself very clearly, preferably in your margin or down one side of your notebook if you use a page divided into two.

Before beginning to type, check your notes for special instructions regarding urgency, enclosures, number of copies, etc.

If working from audio tape it may be necessary to check the end of each piece of work for special instructions before beginning to type. There will always be those dictators who add at the end of the dictation 'Take an extra copy on pink flimsy please' or 'Put in the heading . . .!' If you don't check first you will have typed the whole letter (which may be long) before you find these extra instructions! You will usually get to know the culprits and you may find it very difficult to change their habits–but don't give up!

(e) Notices and bulletins

A **bulletin** giving internal information to all or only a few employees, may be issued on a regular basis, perhaps weekly, or when there is something specific to be communicated. It can be issued to individuals, in which case several copies will have to be made, or it can be put on one or more noticeboards. It can vary in length, from a few lines to a document of several pages, and usually covers several topics.

A **notice** will generally be displayed on one or more notice boards and must be clearly set out so that it can be read easily. Each notice should cover one topic only. Notice boards themselves need careful organisation since they can very soon become cluttered and unmanageable. Clearly marked areas for specific topics, departments, etc. not only look neater but make identification and reading easier.

In terms of preparation the secretary may be involved only to the extent of typing or word processing the bulletin or notice, or it may be her responsibility to collect information from several sources and to put it together in the appropriate way. For bulletins in particular she must have a specific routine whereby all material has to be submitted by a specified date and she has a strict timetable for typing, printing or photocopying, and distribution.

As with all written communications it is important that the material for the bulletin is put together in an organised and logical manner and the wording should be clear and unambiguous. It is not necessary to impress other employees with your loquaciousness and verbosity! Keep the style clear and easy to read otherwise employees will not read carefully, or at worst will not read at all.

(f) Invitations

The number of invitations to which you, as secretary, have to reply will vary enormously according to the type of work or business you are involved in. Formal replies to formal invitations are no longer essential although it is still considered good manners to reply in the third person if the invitation is to a particularly formal occasion. In the majority of cases it will be up to the secretary to both reply and decide the manner in which she will do so. Always try to match the tone of the invitation and bear in mind the degree of formality of the occasion. Conference invitations are often formally presented but in the majority of cases require a letter of confirmation of attendance or even merely a form to be filled in. On the other hand, an invitation to an important reception or banquet would require a more formal reply.

(g) Advertisements

If the secretary has responsibility for junior office staff she may be involved in their appointment. It may also be her responsibility to advertise for other staff, such as cleaners and canteen staff, particularly if she works in Personnel. The first stage in such appointments is generally to advertise and as such it may be the secretary's job to put together an appropriate advertisement. For standard appointments, such as cooks and cleaners, the advertisement may already be prepared and may only need minor changes. On the other hand, for a new or different post the wording will need careful consideration. Remember, again, to be concise, specific and to include all the important information. Use a previous advertisement as a guide and remember to give priority to the important information. Perhaps the name of the company is a big attraction—many people would like to work for television or radio. Or perhaps the job itself is interesting. Maybe the job is not so attractive but the salary will be good. The advertisement must convey the right information to the right people so the place and timing of the advertisement is of equal importance. A large company will often advertise in a national paper, some of which have special days for specific categories.

It is usually the case that the highly paid jobs are advertised more widely, since companies want to attract the best person for these jobs which are likely to carry greater responsibility. Other jobs will be advertised in the local press, job centres and staff agencies. Always bear in mind the people at whom you are aiming your advertisement.

(h) Telex and Teletex

Telex is a service provided by British Telecom and is available 24 hours a day provided the receiving machine is switched on. The message to be sent is prepared in advance on the Telex keyboard and a copy of the message is printed at both ends on continuous stationery, which may also have one or more carbon copies. It can be recorded on perforated tape which can be played back and printed before transmission in order to check the accuracy of the prepared message. Once the Telex is ready to send, the operator dials the number of the recipient (a Telex directory is published regularly) and the message is transmitted automatically at speeds far in excess of those which a keyboard operator could manage. Since calls are charged on a similar basis to those of the telephone, i.e. according to distance and the time taken to transmit, it is important that messages are transmitted as quickly as possible.

The advantages of Telex are its speed and accuracy—the message transmitted is received almost immediately and provided there is someone available to deal with it at the other end a reply can be made with little delay. Telex messages are particularly suited to overcoming two inevitable problems associated with international business:

- time differences, for example between America and Britain (office hours overlap for only half the day)
- language problems, for example between Portugal and Britain—a message can be translated before sending or after receipt.

In addition, many business people find that Telex enables them to transmit messages quickly without becoming involved in lengthy discussions or arguments.

Most Telex machines being installed today have video screens and messages are prepared using a word processor, with transmission much faster than punched tape.

Teletex is an extension of Telex and uses the existing Telex network together with PSTN (Public switched telephone network), and PSS (packet switched data network). It is hoped that it will eventually replace Telex and provide an integrated electronic mail service where messages may be stored, edited and retrieved in a similar manner to word processed and other computerised information.

(i) 'Fax'—Facsimile transmission

Fax, like Telex a few years ago, is making its mark on the business world in a big way. Companies who possess Fax machines are finding them to be a fast, efficient and reliable means of transmitting copies of documents, letters, photographs across the country and even between countries.

Fax machines are essentially copying machines which by means of the telephone system can electronically scan material of any kind—printed, handwritten, photographed, etc., and send an exact copy to another machine simultaneously. It is perhaps the ultimate in fast, accurate transmission. The only limitation today is that there must be a compatible machine at the other end. As with all new developments the equipment is initially expensive and unattainable for many small companies. However, the cost of the machine is soon offset by the costs saved from alternative means of sending documents, particularly where urgency is a factor. Many companies will now use Fax in preference to Special Delivery, which is not always reliable, or Datapost which can be costly and inconvenient—not only are there the costs of sending the documents, etc., but photocopies must also be taken since originals should never be mailed without ensuring that there are further copies remaining in the office. Fax is also replacing Telex in many businesses.

The use of Fax is not confined to companies that possess machines. Major Post Offices have Fax machines available for public use, Intelpost, for transmission and reception. The major inconvenience here is that someone needs to travel to the Post Office and at the other end another person will have to collect it. This may be time-consuming but could still be quicker than relying on Datapost, Red Star or Special Delivery. Telex, of course, is as quick, but does not enable exact copies of plans, photographs, manuscripts, etc. to be sent; it also involves time in retyping documents or letters. All these factors should be considered by the secretary when making a decision regarding how to send a message or documents.

Companies are now finding that it is cheaper to send messages by Fax. It is also quicker in operator time and for the busy executive it avoids the need to get involved in telephone calls when time is short.

In spite of growing popularity there are some disadvantages to Fax: (i) confidentiality—documents are seen by the sender and recipient; (ii) legibility—quality is not always good; (iii) receipt—to establish that the document has been received a telephone call may have to be made; (iv) the person to whom the Fax is sent may not always be available if an immediate reply is needed.

(j) Datel

Datel operates via the British Telecom network. It is a system whereby data can be sent from one terminal to a central computer where it is processed and stored and is available for retrieval when required. It can be thought of generally as an internal service whereby a large company with several branches can receive data, statistics and other information via a modem. The whole process is fast and can operate over any distance. It is particularly suitable for up-to-date sales figures, accounts, stock records, etc.

4.5 Transmission of Information via the Post Office

The Post Office is an institution which we would find it difficult to live without were it to cease functioning overnight. From the simple stamp to the urgency of Datapost, the Post Office has become an essential part of our business and personal lives. While many of the traditional mail services are being rivalled by alternative methods of getting information from point A to point B, some of their methods are prohibitively expensive for smaller companies. Companies in city centres find couriers or motorbikes unsurpassable in terms of speed and security for physically moving documents and papers around within an hour or less for only a few pounds. Nevertheless in spite of these and other developments the Post Office remains the backbone of the written communication system.

For the most part using Post Office services is second nature and plenty has been said on the merits and demerits of the first and second class postal system. Remember though that the Post Office offers other services, many of which are given publicity in clear leaflets available from Post Offices. For comprehensive details of all services refer to the POST OFFICE GUIDE which is published annually and available from Post Offices. Your company will probably use many of the Post Office services and if it has specialist mail staff they will be aware of a whole range of available facilities. If you are in a small company you must ensure that you have some idea of what is available and it may help to consider the essential services you are likely to come across in four categories: SPEED, SECURITY, POST WITHOUT PAYING and PERSONAL SERVICE. It must be remembered, however, that this *is* only a brief list; there will be other services which you will need to use, whose details you will be able to find out about from other sources.

(a) Speed

(i) Datapost

The only Post Office service which guarantees next day delivery. It is an overnight service and there is a basic, relatively high, fee plus an additional charge for packets over a given weight.

(ii) *Special delivery*

Mail is almost certain to be delivered next day but this is not guaranteed. The package must be handed over the Post Office counter and postage plus a fee paid. A Certificate of Posting is issued and limited compensation is paid if the mail goes astray. If the mail does not reach its destination the next day, the sender is entitled to a refund although it must be remembered that this will not rectify the situation if the material was needed urgently.

(iii) *Other services*

Fax, Telex, Electronic Mailing (see other chapters) and British Rail's Red Star (station to station plus delivery if required).

(b) Security

(i) *Registered Post*

For first class mail only. The packet is kept separate from the remainder of the mail and is signed for when accepted at the Post Office, and on delivery by the recipient. Registered Post mail is recognisable by special envelopes crossed with black or blue lines. Lines may be drawn on an ordinary envelope. A blue numbered stamp is stuck on the packet. A fee is charged and compensation is paid if mail is lost. Registered Post is suitable for valuables and money.

(ii) *Recorded Delivery*

Gives proof of posting and proof of delivery but compensation is not as great as with registered post. Normal postage plus a fee is payable and the recipient signs on delivery to say it has been received. Recorded Delivery is suitable for valuable documents and items (money and jewellery *may not be sent* via Recorded Delivery). The package is recognisable by a yellow, numbered label. The sender receives a certificate as proof of posting which has the same number as that on the label.

(iii) *Compensation Fee*

Available for parcels only, it provides for compensation in case of loss or damage. The sender completes a certificate of posting stating how much compensation is required and receives a stamped certificate from the clerk. Compensation Fee is suitable for larger valuable items.

(iv) Other security services

Private motorbike service (usually operates in major cities).
Private courier.
Private security companies such as Securicor.
Personal delivery—company car or by hand.

(c) Post without paying

(i) Business Reply Service
First or second class. Envelopes are easily recognisable—pre-printed
with the company's name and address and their licence number, and a
large '1' or '2' enclosed in vertical black lines. A customer may use these
envelopes or cards to reply to advertisements or for sending payment
without paying any postage. The company using the service obtains a
licence, pays an initial fee and the postage for every envelope posted.

(ii) Freepost
No special stationery needed, but a licence is necessary and a fee is
payable. Anyone writing to the company must include 'Freepost' in
the address and no postage is required. The licensed company will pay
the postage.

(d) Personal service

(i) Private bags
All mail to and from a company is placed in a lockable private bag and
either taken to the Post Office or collected and delivered by the Post
Office. A fee is charged for the service.

(ii) Private boxes
A private box is rented at the Post Office and mail can be collected
at any time. The box number must appear in the address (e.g. PO
Box 42).

(iii) Redirection
If a company or individual changes its postal address, the Post Office
will automatically redirect the mail for an agreed period. A fee is
charged.

(iv) Post Restante
Mail may be sent to any main post office to await collection for a given
period. Mainly useful to anyone travelling for long periods and who is
staying in different places for unknown lengths of time.

4.6 Communicating Visually

In many instances effective communication depends on visual interpretation of information, statistics, etc. This can take many forms from computerised 3D pictures to traditional graphs and pie charts. In many instances it is one of the secretary's duties to prepare information for visual representation, perhaps for meetings, circulation, conferences, etc. It is important that the appropriate type of chart is chosen since wrongly shown information can be misleading and worse than no chart at all. Briefly the most common forms of visual representation are:

> Line graphs, pie charts, bar charts.
> Visual control boards.
> Diagrams and charts.
> Slides, films, OHP transparencies.
> Models.
> Maps.
> Computer generated pictures.

For more detail on these see Chapter 9.

Do You Know?

1. How you would communicate the following information:

   Weekly sales figures to the Managing Director?
   Asking six candidates to attend for interview in two weeks' time?
   A change of interview date at the last minute to the same candidates?
   Copies of photographs required urgently in your office in Germany?
   Routine acknowledgement of receipt of an order?
   Results of an investigation into canteen facilities?
   Arrangements for an annual dinner dance to all employees?
2. The main areas of communication a secretary must be competent in?
3. How to be prepared for making and receiving telephone calls?
4. The essential ingredients of an accurate telephone message?
5. How to handle difficult calls?
6. The different services available to enable calls to be made without payment by the caller at the time of telephoning?
7. The advantages of communication by writing?
8. The different methods available of producing written communications?
9. How to enumerate a report?

10. How to reply to an invitation?
11. The advantages of using Telex?
12. Why Fax is growing in popularity in business?
13. What Datel offers businesses?
14. Do you know the difference between:
    (a) a letter and a memo?
    (b) a notice and a bulletin?
    (c) Telex and Fax?

Secretarial Task Four

Problem 1

You have just been given a new electronic typewriter to work on to replace your old manual machine. You are very impressed with the improvement in the speed at which you can work and at the neatness of the documents you produce. The rest of the office staff in the company are still working on manual or old electric typewriters and you feel that the office would benefit if there was an overall change-over to electronic machines throughout the offices. You have talked to your executive about this and, while he sympathises with what you say, he thinks that you should write a more formal report which he can submit to the Managing Director who is more traditional in his ideas, particularly since such a complete change-over would be very costly. He has also asked you to take into account the fact that there would be extra costs in terms of ribbons.

Collect sufficient leaflets and catalogues from local suppliers and write the report asked for by your employer. You will also find additional help in Chapter 7.

Problem 2

You consider the company for which you work to be very traditional in its means of communication. Its business is expanding rapidly, particularly internationally and growing numbers of sales staff are required to contact the office on a regular basis. They frequently grumble to you that it is not always easy or convenient to use public call boxes, particularly from long distances, and they do not feel it is very appropriate to use customers' telephones for lengthy and costly calls. In addition they do not always have the correct change for a call. You feel that you have some responsibility to at least report on the position to your chief and to make some recommendations. Prepare an account of what you would do and what you would say.

Problem 3
An important contract has just been lost to a rival company. Your offices are open plan and you are aware that telephones are frequently left unanswered. You also know that much of the negotiation with the prospective company has been by telephone. Your employer has asked you to put some notes together suggesting ways in which office staff can help in the avoidance of such a loss in future. How would you ensure that all staff were made aware of the problems and recommendations you have made?

Examination Questions

1. Suggest five methods of internal communication which you might use during the course of a normal working day. For each method named you should suggest an appropriate use related to the work of the Production Department.

    LCCI SSC OP

2. Your office needs to send information frequently to other branches for action today. Describe briefly four means of communication explaining in what context each could be used.

    LCCI PSC OO&SP

3. Mr Landers, Office Manager, is interested in using video-conferencing for regular meetings of Comlon International plc. Write a memo to Mr Landers describing video-conferencing and listing the advantages and disadvantages of using such a system.

    LCCI PES SA

Chapter 5

Handling the Mail

How much will I be involved?

The extent to which the secretary handles the mail will vary according to the size and policy of the company for which she works. A large organisation will normally have an established system and specialist staff for dealing with the bulk of incoming and outgoing mail, and in such a case the secretary's involvement will be confined to correspondence and documents within her own office only. In a small office, however, with only limited secretarial and office staff, the secretary must be prepared to take an active part at all stages, from the time the post arrives to the time it leaves the office or reaches the Post Office.

Be efficient and be prompt—in large and small organisations it is up to the secretary to establish, and keep to, a routine which enables correspondence to be dealt with efficiently and without delay.

5.1 Incoming Mail

(a) Routine

First of all let us consider the routine to be followed.

   (i) *Deal with mail first and without delay.* It should be ready for the recipients to deal with as soon as possible, preferably as soon as they arrive in the morning. This may mean the secretary making a point of arriving earlier as a matter of course, but if this is not possible (you may work for someone who prefers to make a 7.30 start to avoid the traffic) then deal with the mail as soon as it, or you, arrives.

  (ii) *Sort* mail into departments or personnel.

 (iii) *Open* mail if it is the policy of the company to do so. **Never open** Private and Confidential mail unless authorised to do so.

(iv) *Date and time stamp* mail as received:
   stamp envelope if mail is unopened
   stamp each document if mail is opened
   don't obliterate printed or typed information.
   Both date and time are important in case of further enquiries regarding receipt of mail.

(v) *Check* that enclosures are as stated in the letter. If enclosures do not correspond with those stated then take follow-up action:
   make a note on the letter of omissions
   telephone and/or write to sender, pointing out omission.

(vi) *Record* any cheques, cash or other payment in a remittance book.

(vii) *Sort* mail into order of priority—
   urgent (usually special delivery or first-class)
   non-urgent (possibly, though not necessarily, second-class)
   journals
   advertising and promotional material.

(viii) *Ensure* that the right person gets the right mail. If a letter is not addressed to a specific person or department then use your initiative to deduce where it must go. If in doubt look at the:

references	your original reference may be quoted if the letter is a reply to one of yours
subject heading	you may know who is dealing with the project, account, enquiry, etc.
content	scanning the letter will give you an idea of who to pass it to
sender's name	you may have some knowledge of who is dealing with this client, enquiry, etc.

(ix) *Don't throw envelopes away* until an agreed time has elapsed (usually three to four days)—there may be further enquiries regarding date of receipt, correct address, contents, etc.

(x) *Photocopy correspondence and documents* which need to be seen by several people.

(xi) *Circulate magazines,* journals, etc., which are not suitable for photocopying (see Section 5.2).

(b) The secretary's role

Assuming that the secretary in a small office (perhaps an architect's office with three partners and one secretary) is involved from the time the post arrives, then she must be aware of the routine to follow throughout. In a medium to large organisation, such as an international chemical company or local government offices, her involvement will be much more specific and confined to the mail within her own department.

Be organised
It may be that the mail is delivered by the post staff to your desk. It may come opened or unopened, sorted or unsorted. Whatever the case you must pick up the routine as outlined above at an appropriate stage. Once you are dealing with the correspondence itself, establish a pattern which ensures that nothing gets overlooked or forgotten. Far too many misunderstandings and frustrations occur in business because mail has not been answered or acknowledged, more often than not merely because of inefficiency and an untidy desk (although those guilty of such disorganisation would argue that at least they know the paper they want is there somewhere!)

Establish a routine

Follow a set pattern:
- *Sort* correspondence into order of priority (as outlined above).
- *Ensure* that the mail is available to your executive early in the day, preferably when he arrives (if this is practical – he may be an early bird!).
- *Prepare* any files or documents which he may need to refer to in connection with the day's mail.
- *Extract* routine correspondence which you are able and authorised to deal with, for example travel or conference arrangements, interview arrangements or supplying data. (Your executive may like to see all correspondence before you extract any.)
- *Check* for enclosures and deal with omissions (as outlined above).
- *Record* any remittances (cheques, etc.) in a remittance book and follow the procedure of your company. The entries may have to be endorsed by someone in authority, perhaps the chief cashier.
- *Photocopy* or circulate any correspondence which needs to be seen by more than one person – as outlined below in 5.2(b).

5.2 Internal Circulation

(a) Photocopying

There are several instances when documents need to be seen by more than one person and are suitable for photocopying.

1. **One letter, several topics:** correspondence which covers more than one topic may need to be seen by executives in different departments. Passing the letter round causes unnecessary delays and there is always the danger that it will go astray or sit in the middle of one of the inevitable piles of paper which accrue on some executives' desks. Always photocopy such documents and put the initials of the executive concerned at the top of his copy. It is a good idea to indicate on the original who has received copies.
2. **For reference:** correspondence which needs to be seen by other executives for reference purposes only should be dealt with in the same way.
3. **Articles:** extracts from journals which are of relevance and interest to particular executives and which are suitable for photocopying.
4. **Urgency:** lengthy documents, reports and so on which are of urgent interest to several people should be photocopied and circulated.

(b) Circulation

Complete journals and magazines are mostly unsuitable for photocopying since the cost of such a task would be prohibitive. There is, too, the additional problem of copyright and you should take care that you do not breach copyright laws when photocopying articles from publications. One approach might be to send round a brief digest of the articles of interest or relevance to a department with a note that the original is available from the library or other department and may be borrowed if required. These, along with any other documents or journals which need circulating and have not been photocopied, should be sent through the internal mail system with a **circulation, routing** or **action slip** attached.

Circulation or routing slips should indicate:

— who has sent the document
— what the document is
— a list, in order (alphabetical or priority) of who is to see it
— space for their initials when they have seen it
— space for the date it was passed on
— who the document is to be returned to
— the date by which it is to be returned.

All the above information is vital in order that the path of the document can be easily followed and chased should it get lost. The secretary, too, should keep an identical record of the slip for reference purposes.

Fig. 5.1   *A circulation slip*

CIRCULATION		
FROM		
DATE		
NAME	DEPT.	PASSED ON
RETURN TO		
BY		

Action slips are slightly different in that while they indicate similar information to a circulation slip, they also show the action that each person is expected to take, such as collecting further technical information, preparing a report, obtaining information on prices, etc.

Fig. 5.2   *An action slip*

TO:	DATE
FROM:	

☐ NOTE AND RETURN TO ME   ☐ FOR YOUR INFORMATION
☐ SEE ME ABOUT THIS   ☐ FOR YOUR COMMENTS
☐ PLEASE ANSWER   ☐ PER OUR CONVERSATION
☐ TAKE APPROPRIATE ACTION ☐ NOTE AND FILE
☐ FOR YOUR APPROVAL   ☐
☐ INVESTIGATE AND REPORT   ☐

COMMENTS

J.T.

(c) Delivery

Mail for circulation will usually be delivered by hand. A large company may employ a post clerk especially for this purpose and several deliveries and collections may be made within the space of one day. In a small company it may be your own responsibility as secretary to deliver any internal mail.

ENVELOPES—Often special envelopes are used for internal mail. In many cases these envelopes are constructed to be long-lasting since they are reused and may contain several documents to be sent from one department to another. Some envelopes are constructed with several punched holes to make it easy to see if they contain mail or are empty. They are printed with ruled lines on which names can be written, crossed off and reused many times.

(d) Procedure

Internal mail may arrive on your desk or be collected at any time during the day. Have baskets or trays clearly labelled to accomodate incoming and outgoing internal mail. This will make your post clerk's job easier and ensure that nothing gets lost or overlooked.

5.3 Preparation of Outgoing Mail

(a) For signature

Outgoing mail will have been prepared at various stages during the day and will consist of letters and documents prepared by the secretary herself, material dictated by her executive, reports, internal memoranda and other documents. In many cases the executive will pass on the original letter for the secretary to refer to for names, addresses, references, dates and subject heading. The original letter should be kept with the reply until after signature and mailing, when they should both be filed without delay.

Once again it is vital that the secretary keeps to a strict routine in order that nothing gets lost or mislaid:

- *Copies* Always ensure you take one or more carbon copies or photocopies of letters, documents, etc. (some companies internally circulate copies of all letters sent out). Different coloured copies may be used for different purposes and it is important to keep to such coding. Such a system might use white for central filing and pink for internal circulation.

— *Carbon copy or photocopy?* Taking more than one carbon copy can be a messy, time-consuming and unhappy job for the inefficient typist. However carbon copies do enable use to be made of coloured, cheaper bank paper for reference purposes. Bank paper is also less space consuming than bond. However companies are making increased use of photocopiers which can save time and thus, contrary to some opinion, also save costs when more than one copy is required.

— *Envelopes* Always type the correct size envelope to accomodate any enclosures at the time of typing the letter. Remember to include any special mailing instructions, e.g. Recorded delivery, Special delivery or Confidential.

— *Enclosures* Collect enclosures together as soon as possible— either at the time of typing the letter or as soon as they are available.

— *Signature book* Keep letter, enclosures, copies and envelope together in a folder or signature book until they have been signed. Signature books are specially designed for this purpose and are particularly useful in that they keep letters separated from each other, thus avoiding the danger of enclosures from one letter becoming mixed up with another. In addition holes may be pre-cut out of each leaf of the book so that it is easy to see through from one division to the next and thus when the last letter has been reached.

— *Signing: by the executive* Plan your day so that morning and afternoon mail is signed well in advance of the time designated for final delivery or collection by mail room staff. In a large organisation this may be as early as 3.30 pm to enable the post to be cleared in time for Post Office collection. The middle of the afternoon is a time when your executive will most likely be out or engaged with visitors or meetings so it is helpful if you both can agree a time when he will normally be available to sign mail.

— *Signing: by the secretary* Sometimes your executive will not be available to sign mail and in such cases you must be prepared, by agreement with him, to sign on his behalf. This is traditionally referred to as a 'per pro' or 'on behalf of' signature.

Complete the letter in the normal way but with the addition of 'pp', 'for' or 'on behalf of' in front of his name.

For example: Yours faithfully

for John James
Sales Director

Alternatively you may add at the bottom 'dictated by John James and signed in his absence'.
    The secretary must then write her OWN SIGNATURE—it is a common mistake to insert the name of the person writing the letter.

(b) —And for posting

Yet again the secretary's involvement depends on the size of the company. Nevertheless it is vital that she is conversant with the procedures involved since, even in a large organisation with specialist mail room staff, there will invariably be times when the secretary has to deal with late, urgent mail.

The normal procedure is as follows:

- *Ensure mail is ready* for the time designated by mail staff. In a small organisation have mail ready well before you leave in order to avoid last minute panics.

- *Check that envelopes and enclosures are correct*, folded in an appropriate manner to fit the envelope. (Too many papers in an envelope which is too small can lead to damaged envelopes and the risk of lost documents. There is also a security risk.)

- *Indicate* on the letter and envelope any special posting instructions—Recorded, Registered, Special Delivery.

- *Indicate* whether mail is to be sent first or second class. Companies have different policies—some send all mail second class unless indicated otherwise and vice versa.

- *Seal carefully*—reinforce with tape if necessary.

- *Take to mail room* or place in marked tray ready for collection.

If you deal with all mail yourself:

- *Weigh, stamp or frank* all mail.

— *Place in a large envelope or pocket* specially designed for such a purpose. Don't carry mail unsecured in your hand or handbag. Ensure that it is bundled together, facing the same way and carried in an appropriate container to the post office.

— *Keep special mail separate*—Registered, Recorded, Special Delivery, etc. and make sure that you leave the office in plenty of time to reach the post office well before it closes. Failure to post a Special Delivery letter on the day of writing could have serious consequences! You may have to reach an arrangement with your executive in such circumstances, but don't just leave without informing him or someone else of your whereabouts.

— *Keep a supply of stamps* together with a stamp record (stamps bought and used) for regular mail in a small organisation if there is no franking machine or last minute mail which has missed the post room deadline.

— *Update the franking machine regularly*—units and date.

Remember

On the franking machine
Check the date—Check the rate

5.4 Dealing with Mail in the Executive's Absence

Establish a routine with your executive regarding who is to deal with urgent and non-urgent mail when he is away from the office. It may be that all mail or only selected mail, such as urgent or priority, is passed to his deputy. The rest you must deal with in an appropriate manner:

— Urgent mail: mail requiring an urgent reply which cannot be passed on must be answered explaining that your executive is away and will deal with the matter immediately on his return. Wherever possible find someone else who CAN deal with an urgent matter.

— Routine mail: reply in an appropriate manner, either giving any information required (provided you have the authority to do so) or, if your executive is away for any length of time, explain the situation and say that he will reply on his return.

— Pass on letters which need special consideration to another executive where possible and where relevant.

— Keep a record of all letters received and sent in a separate file for your executive's reference on his return and together with any information he may need to reply.

Fig 5.3 *How mail usually flows through an organisation*

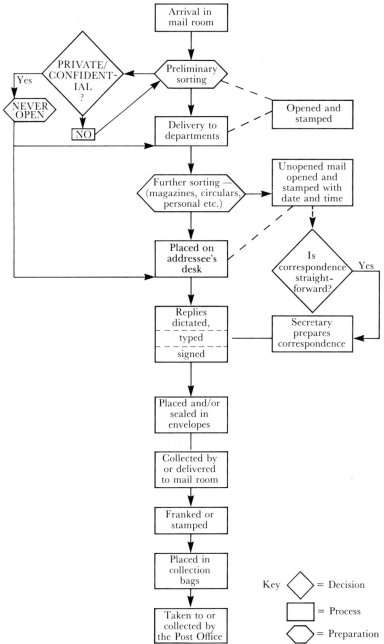

5.5 Mail Shots (or Personalised Mail)

Circularising standard mail to many hundreds of companies is now common practice and one which the secretary may find herself involved in. One of the reasons is that mail shots can be done quickly and cheaply using microcomputers. Once the secretary has the equipment (computer and software), and has mastered the technique and has spent time inputting the names and addresses, the process is relatively easy and can be repeated time and time again with minimum effort. Again in a large company such a task would be in the hands of specialist staff. In a medium or small company the secretary may be involved or may supervise junior staff. It is a wise precaution to inform the mail room of any forthcoming mail shots to enable them to plan accordingly—arriving at the post room at 4.30 pm on a Friday afternoon with 2000 letters for mailing that day may lose you the valued co-operation of the mail clerk!

There are few of us in the 1980s who are not the recipients of some kind of mail shot—the kind that says:

'Mrs Gardner, you have been chosen from all the people in Hampstead to enter our competition to win a world cruise'

or even more precisely:

'Mrs Gardner, you are one of the lucky ones in Acacia Avenue, Hampstead to enter our competition, etc.'

Many of us may consign these to the rubbish bin but the fact remains that most companies find mail shots are very profitable and are an important part of a company's contacts with its actual and potential customers. For example mail shots can be used for:

- Telling your most valued customers about a new product or service which your company is offering.
- Reaching new customers to tell them about existing or new products or services.
- Informing existing customers of a price change.
- Sending out questionnaires as part of market research.

Once a mail shot has been sent out the secretary will probably be involved in any follow-up correspondence, which may or may not be part of the original mail shot. Such a follow-up may consist of letters chasing unreturned questionnaires or a further letter regarding a new product if no interest has been shown by the recipient of the first letter.

Mail shots can vary in size from 100 letters to thousands. A government health campaign can involve mailing the entire population of the British Isles. It goes without saying that such numbers require automation and possibly the services of a specialist mailing house and the secretary will not be expected to 'lick and stick' such quantities of letters!

Easymailing:
With the Post Office, companies who do not normally use a franking machine but who issue periodic mail shots (over 150) can take advantage of this Post Office service whereby mail shots can be prepaid and franked by the Post Office.

5.6 Mail Room Equipment

The minimum equipment a secretary in a small office would need is:

    scales
    postage stamps/franking machine
    date stamp
    photocopier
    stapler
    string
    sellotape
    parcel tape
    wrapping paper

As the size of the mail room increases so does the need for more sophisticated and useful equipment. While a franking machine becomes a necessity the usefulness of other machinery depends on the volume and type of mail. Where a company's mail is large enough to warrant the use of a mail room with specialised equipment, the secretary's involvement will be minimal. She should, however, be aware of the equipment available and its uses, and reference to any specialist textbook or office supplier will give her further information. Many of the machines are extremely sophisticated and, like combine harvesters, provide many functions in one machine.

Used for booklets, leaflets, etc.

Collator	automatically, and at speed, gathers papers together in the correct order.
Binding machine	binds collated papers together.
Stapling machine	electrically operated, can staple pamphlets and booklets together at speed.

Used for mail shots, invoices, etc.

Folding machine	automatically folds to the desired size.
Inserting machine	puts folded papers into envelopes.
Sealing machine	automatically seals envelopes.
Addressing machine	prints pre-prepared addresses on envelopes or labels (can be used repeatedly but are being replaced by computer mail shot packages.

Used for destroying unwanted and confidential material

Shredder	cuts paper to small strips which cannot be read and can be reused as packing material.

Used for opening mail

Letter opening machine	slices a sliver of paper from the edge of an envelope—a fast process if envelopes are stacked carefully.

Used for posting

Franking machine	stamps envelope or parcel label with required postage and prints time and date of franking. Units of postage are purchased at the Post Office and registered on the machine. The units are automatically deducted from the register as each letter is franked. An advertising slogan can be incorporated in the printed impression.

Do You Know?

Why have ...
1. Circulation slips?
2. Coloured carbon copies?
3. Photocopies?
4. Franking machine *and* stamps?
5. Strong internal mail envelopes?
6. Separate filing trays?
7. Strict postal times?
8. Date and time stamps?

Are you confident ...
1. When to answer routine mail?
2. When not to answer routine mail?

3. How to answer routine mail?
4. When to use circulation slips?
5. When to use photocopiers?
6. What to do with the mail when your executive is away?
7. What to do if an envelope arrives without enclosures?

Secretarial Task Five

As part of your job as secretary to John Butterworth, who makes ice cream (see Secretarial Task Three) it is your responsibility to deal with all incoming mail. Mr Butterworth has been away for five days during which time you have dealt with a large amount of correspondence. The majority of the mail you have placed in a file ready for him to deal with on his return and some of it you have been able to deal with.

Prepare a list for Mr Butterworth detailing what action you have taken concerning the following correspondence:

(a) A first-class letter addressed to Mr Butterworth and marked CONFIDENTIAL.
(b) A notice of a conference to which replies are required in three days' time and in which other staff may be interested.
(c) Two letters addressed to a member of staff who left the company some weeks ago—one marked URGENT and one marked PRIVATE.
(d) An invitation to contribute to a new trade journal.
(e) A five page report of interest to all partners.
(f) A letter asking if there are any clerical vacancies.
(g) A letter addressed to Mr Butterworth and dated a week ago, refusing to settle an account and asking for an urgent meeting.
(h) A circular from the local council regarding new parking restrictions outside your offices.

Examination Question

1. Write notes for your new junior on how to handle the opening and sorting of incoming mail.
   List the items of equipment which would improve the efficiency of this task.

LCCI PSC OO&SP

Chapter 6
Organising the Working Environment

Storing documents and records

Although, arguably, one of the most unpopular tasks within an office, the storage of documents is one of the most important. It is vital that documentation is kept in a secure and organised manner since without reference to such documents a business will soon find itself in trouble. Letters, memos, reports, accounting documentation and other records form the backbone of business transactions. Without them negotiations become difficult. Also, without documents, there is no proof that a transaction has taken place and thus the whole accepted way of operating a business will collapse. Just imagine what would happen if a contract to supply a large retail chain with a new range of Christmas goods had been agreed by telephone. The supplying company will be involved in spending many thousands of pounds in order to produce the goods and will not receive payment from the chain store until after the goods have been delivered. If, on receipt of the invoice, the chain store queries the amount they are being charged and there is no written record of the original agreed price then the supplier is in a very awkward position. How does he prove that a price was agreed? He risks losing many thousands of pounds through his inefficiency. It could of course be that there has been documentation— a letter may have been written and filed incorrectly or not even filed at all. Such inefficient record keeping could be repeated many times a year by a poorly organised company with very unhappy consequences—law suits, bad debts and, finally, bankruptcy.

It is clear then that accurate record keeping is of vital importance in all organisations, large or small. But to be more specific what in the last two decades of the twentieth century do we mean by 'record keeping'— not just paper, surely? Who today has not been told that 'the paperless office is just around the corner'?

But whether or not this is true is questionable. Perhaps you have been on work experience and after a big build up at school or college

114

expected to be working on a computer for most of the day—electronic filing, computerised diary, wordprocessing and so on. Maybe it wasn't like that at all, maybe you spent most of the day at a traditional typewriter with occasional unexciting relief at the filing cabinet. 'Where is this electronic filing system they told us about?' you ask yourself.

Let us look at what really happens in the majority of offices.

Traditional filing methods—storing paper in cabinets

Such methods are not to be discounted merely because they seem out of fashion and out of favour. The majority of companies still prefer such systems for several reasons which will become evident later in the chapter. What are the traditional systems? Ask yourself or your family what happens to the important papers within the household such as birth, marriage and death certificates; employment papers; examination certificates and bank statements. Maybe the answer is 'they're in the kitchen drawer' or 'some are in my handbag and I'll have to look for the rest'. If you are more efficient in dealing with household papers you may have a small filing box with labelled divisions so that you can find papers easily.

Businesses use an extension of the filing box—cabinets, drawers, cupboards—each of which will be suited to its own needs, just as your family has a system which suits it best. Similarly, in a company, 'filing system' may mean:

The way the files are arranged within the cabinets.
The type of equipment used.
Where the files are kept—centrally or departmentally.

In the majority of jobs held by a secretary the filing system will already be in existence and it is up to her to maintain it efficiently and improve it as necessary. Because of this she must know how to use the existing system and if she does need to expand or reorganise she needs some knowledge of the alternative methods available. So let us look at the three major areas mentioned above in more detail.

6.1 Storing Documents—How to Arrange the Files

Before a decision can be made about how to store the documents it is necessary to have some knowledge of the accepted systems in current use. In the main the usual modes of classification are:

Alphabetical
Chronological
Geographical
Numerical
Subject

It must be remembered, however, that in the majority of cases there will be a combination of two or more systems, with alphabetical classification being the key to many of them.

(a) Alphabetical

While relatively straightforward it is amazing how many documents are lost within this system through lack of understanding of the basic rules. These are:

(i) *Select the name by which documents will be filed.*

It will appear on the outside of the file. This will usually be the surname or the most important word in a company's name, e.g. J R Adams will be filed under Adams J R and The Anvil Company will be filed under Anvil Company The. If there is any doubt then a cross-index must be made (see Section 6.2).

(ii) *File alphabetically by surname or word selected.*

Refer to first letter and if there is more than one file classified by this letter or name then refer to the second letter or initial and so on until a new letter is reached:

Order and Name of Files	Name of Company
ABA	ABA
Abacus	Abacus
Adam E F	Adam and Son
Adams J R	J R Adams
Adams Apple Co Ltd	Adams Apple Co Ltd
Adamson B T	B T Adamson
Adamson Stephen	Stephen Adamson
Agricultural Supplies plc	Agricultural Supplies plc
Anvil Company The	The Anvil Company

(iii) *Treat 'Mc' 'Mac' and 'M^c' as if they were spelt 'Mac':*

Order and Name of Files	Name of Company
Macclesfield Trading Co	Macclesfield Trading Co
McClory Alastair F	Alastair F McClory
MacDonalds Ltd	McDonalds Ltd
McGregor Food Services	McGregor Food Services
McWilliam George	George McWilliam
Manchester Catering Supplies	Manchester Catering Supplies

(iv) *St and Saint are filed under Saint:*

St Ambrose College
Saint Brian & Co
St Christopher Hotel The
St James' School

(v) *All other prefixes are treated as part of the name:*

Order and Name of Files	Name of Company
de Havilland Olivia	Olivia de Havilland
d'Henin Sauce Company	d'Henin Sauce Company
Dhobi Fashion Wear	Dhobi Fashion Wear
de la Mere Francis	Francis de la Mere
de Sousa Martin	Martin de Sousa
Van-Es Jan	Jan Van-Es
van Morrison Ian	Ian van Morrison

(vi) *Ignore:*

The in company titles: file by first important word and either omit *the* altogether or move it to the end.

Order and Name of Files	Name of Company
Sewing Box	The Sewing Box
St Christopher Hotel The	The St Christopher Hotel
Strong Box Company The	The Strong Box Company

Hyphens:

File hyphenated words as one word:

Reed Company
Rees-Jones G
Rees-Mogg Industry Group
Rees-Williams & Company
Reid Estates

Titles:

Place title after first word of file reference name:

Waltham Sir Richard	Sir Richard Waltham
Forrester Dr Elizabeth	Dr Elizabeth Forrester
Botham Rev Henry	Rev Henry Botham

(vii) *Numbers* are filed as though written in full:

18+ Fashions (filed under Eighteen)
100 Club (filed under One hundred)
2 Brewers Hotel (filed underTwo)

(viii) *Abbreviated Names may be filed under full name.*

If so a cross reference should be made (see Section 6.2):

BBC or British Broadcasting Corporation
ICI or Imperial Chemical Industries
TUC orTrades Union Congress

If a company name begins with a group of initials, then filing is done by the initial first:

IBM United Kingdom Ltd
ICA Computer Systems
IMA Fashions
International Fashions

(ix) *Government Departments* should be filed under the key-word:

Education and Science Department of (DES)
Defence Ministry of

with cross referencing under initials.

(b) Chronological

While chronological filing (or filing in date order) is possibly little used on its own as a filing method, it is to be found in common use within most other methods. Within any file, most documents will be stored in date order, usually with the oldest at the back of the file and the newest at the front. This is a widely recommended system and one which should be accurately adhered to since any papers which get out of sequence can cause unnecessary delays and annoyance.

Chronological filing is more commonly used in a 'tickler' or 'follow-up' file (see Section 6.2) where the date is the point of reference for each document to be dealt with.

(c) Geographical

Files are classified in areas, either nationally or internationally, for instance:

Scotland
Wales
North West England
North East England
Midlands
South West England
South East England

Within these areas there may be further subdivisions into counties, towns, regions, etc.

The final subdivisions, however, will probably be categorised in conjunction with another system which is more specific, such as alphabetic or numerical filing.

Geographical filing is particularly suited to companies who deal with many companies or individuals in different areas. Often the company will have one central office with sales staff or technical staff based in corresponding areas. A major common problem with this system is that it requires comprehensive geographical knowledge on the part of the person operating the system, otherwise delays caused by misfiling can be the result. Where this system is considered to be the most suitable for a particular company then a solution to the problem is to have some means of cross indexing (see Section 6.2).

(d) Numerical

Numerical filing is possibly the second most popular means of classification after alphabetical, but even this system cannot operate on its own and works in conjunction with alphabetical.

Each file is given a number and all files are stored in the filing cabinet in numerical order. In a large company there is the danger that the size of the numbers may grow to enormous proportions. In such cases some means of grouping files, or making numbers more easily manageable may be found. For instance all files in Personnel may be prefixed with the number 12, thus giving personnel record files as follows:

12-456	Peter Jones
12-457	Alex Thornton
12-458	Mary Butterworth
12-459	Peter T Johnson

The next file to be added, regardless of its position in the alphabet will be placed after Peter Johnson with the number 12-460.

In some cases the numbers may be reversed with the common digit appearing at the end. For example:

45612
45712
45812
45912

This is known as **terminal digit filing**.

An extension of this system is a more sophisticated decimal system which also makes classification and location easier. Such a system uses an initial number to indicate a major category and subsidiary numbers to indicate subdivisions. For example:

20–England
30–France

The next number might indicate North, South, East or West

20.1   England–Northern
20.2   England–Southern
20.3   England–Eastern
20.4   England–Western

If any further division was necessary then an additional number would be used, perhaps to indicate a particular type of industry or specific area, for example Textile Companies. All these companies would be given the number 3, Shoe Manufacturers number 4 and Wool Merchants number 5. For example the files for Textile Companies in England and France would be numbered as follows:

20.1.3   England–Northern–Textile Companies
20.2.3   England–Southern–Textile Companies
20.3.3   England–Eastern –Textile Companies
20.4.3   England–Western –Textile Companies

Similarly:

30.1.3   France–Northern–Textile Companies
30.2.3   France–Southern–Textile Companies
30.3.3   France–Eastern –Textile Companies
30.4.3   France–Western –Textile Companies

The boundaries of such geographical divisions would be predetermined and would need to be available for reference to anyone using the filing system, since one danger of such a system is that individuals have different ideas as to where a geographical dividing line might be and for some people geography of even their own country is not their strongest point!

(e) Subject

Again, working in conjunction with an alphabetic system, files are arranged according to the subject matter, for instance, conferences, exhibitions, etc. Subject filing is often the most suitable for personal or home filing where the documents may be large in number, yet small in variety e.g., tax, medical, certificates and so on.

6.2 Managing the Files

(a) Cross index and cross reference—know the difference

Cross indexing

The operator will find it difficult to find files in a numerical system without the addition of some sort of cross indexing. This means that in addition to files being stored in numerical order, relevant details from each file must be recorded on some kind of alphabetical system. This usually takes the form of index cards, strip indexes, microfilm or microfiche or computer records. Such an additional system enables a very small amount of important information to be kept in a way which is easily accessible. On the other hand it can make accessing records a more time-consuming process. The big advantage of numerical filing is that it enables an infinite number of files to be added to a system without the need to reorganise it each time a drawer or cabinet becomes overfull; in numerical filing files are given the next number and placed at the back of the existing system after the previous number. Another advantage is that it is particularly suitable for filing documents which already operate on a numerical system, e.g. project or contract numbers, account numbers, etc.

Cross referencing

Often it is difficult to decide under which letter, area or subject to place a file. For instance where would you file 'Department of Education and Science'—under E for Education or S for Science? Such organisations as the BBC pose similar problems. Should it be filed under BBC itself or British Broadcasting Corporation? In such cases some indication is necessary to show where the file is to be found. This is known as cross referencing. A small card or paper is inserted in the alternative section. The card should state in which category the file can be found,

e.g. For BBC see British Broadcasting Corporation.

Remember

Cross referencing is not confined to alphabetical filing—it is used with all systems where there may be some doubt as to the placement of files.

Don't be lazy about cross referencing

Don't assume that either you or other people will guess where the file is to be found—you will lose a lot of friends that way. Although you may, and indeed should, know your own system thoroughly, there will always be doubt and there will also be occasions when someone else will need to refer to your filing system—your chief, your junior or a relief secretary while you are ill or on holiday. For this reason it is vital that the system is easy to follow since much time and money can be lost through 'mislaid' files and papers.

(b) Absent cards

Another common cry of despair may be heard around the office when important files cannot be found and no-one admits to having them or indeed having borrowed them. Again it is vital to have a foolproof system whereby the files can be traced. The usual method is to insert an 'absent card' (sometimes referred to as an 'out card') or 'absent folder' to indicate:

> The name of the borrowed file.
> Who has borrowed the file.
> When it was borrowed.
> When it should be returned (the exact date).

The advantage of an absent folder or wallet is that it replaces the file and acts as a receptacle for documents and papers until the file is returned when they can be inserted appropriately.

(c) Borrowing and lending files—don't be casual

Make sure you know their whereabouts. Busy executives often need files when they are in a hurry. They will frequently say they have no time to fill in forms and are very convincing when they say they will return the files immediately they have finished with them. Unfortunately they are often so busy they forget to return them, and after a frantic search, the secretary may find the missing file at the bottom of a pile of papers on her executive's desk (assuming that it has not been passed on to another department, in which case the job of retrieving it becomes even harder). In such instances it is one of the secretary's duties to 'educate' her executive, and others she works for and with, and wherever possible establish a routine so that she knows the whereabouts of missing files and papers.

Wherever possible it is wise to limit the number of people who have access to filing systems in order to limit the likelihood of misplacement and loss. It is also vital to consider the security aspect. The fewer people who have access the less chance there is of files being seen by those who should not see them. Much documentation is of a highly confidential nature—contracts, legal documents, proposals for mergers, personal staff details, appointments, etc.—and it is vital that the secretary considers this at all times when dealing with documentation.

(d) Dead files

Old material should be removed periodically and placed elsewhere; some companies have rooms or the basement set aside for the purpose while smaller companies may need only a single cupboard. Dead files are kept in long term storage boxes and clearly labelled with the names and dates (from and to) and may be destroyed (usually shredded) after an agreed period of time, perhaps two or three years.

Encourage good habits

The fewer people who have access to files, and the more accurate the records of where files are at any one time, the less chance there is of any breach of security.

(e) Follow-up systems

A follow-up system is a means of reminding yourself what is to be dealt with either this week or this day. In its most simple form it exists as a diary with reminders to 'chase RM' or 'restore petty cash'. Like diaries, follow-up systems are kept to ensure that nothing is overlooked at the appointed or appropriate time.

You or your executive may have made plans two months ago for a conference which is to take place in two weeks time. Now reminders or letters of confirmation may need to be sent. Each week you may have similar arrangements to make and confirm, and it goes without saying that there are few people who are able to remember what they have to do each day without needing some form of reminder. A follow-up or tickler system is just such a reminder. Other typical uses for a follow-up system might be:

Arranging meetings.
A request for the return of a borrowed file.
Collection of sales figures.
Chasing unanswered correspondence.

A more efficient follow-up system consists of a drawer or filing box divided into twelve sections labelled with the months of the year. The front section is subdivided again into 31 consecutively numbered sections (1-31) to correspond with the days of the month. Files and papers to be dealt with later will be filed under the appropriate month or day. Every day the secretary must refer to the follow-up file to find out what has to be dealt with. As each day or month passes the now empty cards are moved back to the next month ready to receive further papers.

Checklist

Quick access—quick retrieval

Find the correct cabinet: are the cabinets clearly labelled?
Find the correct drawer or shelf: can you see several files at once?
Find the correct group of files: has colour coding been sensibly used?
Find the correct file: do the files follow the correct system?
Are the index tabs:

> – clearly visible;
> – easily read;
> – uncluttered by protruding papers;
> – secure?

(f) Colour coding can make life easier!

The use of colour can make a world of difference to the ease of use of a filing system. A glance is all that is necessary to locate a group of related files after which more careful scanning of the files can take place. A very simple use might be in the Personnel Department where red guide cards might indicate men and green may be used for women. A more extensive use of colour might be made for departments or geographical areas. Take care to keep to a simple and consistent system.

Colours need not be confined to guide cards—folders, strips, covers to files and labels all help to make the use of files so much easier. Once a system has been established, however, it is important not to be lazy or lax about continuing its use. Such aids are only effective if consistently used. It is important to keep to a simple and easily managed system. Anything too complicated can cause more problems and location of files may become even more difficult than if the colours had never been used in the first place.

Remember

Colour should be used so that:

Its presence has a meaning.
Its absence is noticed.
It conveys a message which is quickly understood.

6.3 Central or Departmental?

It is very rare for a secretary to have to make such a decision—it is more usual that a system will already be established and it will then be her major concern to use it efficiently. It may be, however, that there is some question within the company of changing from one system to another and in such a case the secretary could be asked to make enquiries and prepare a report on which any decision or recommendations will be based.

What differentiates departmental filing from central?

Central filing

- All (or most) of the company files are kept together in one room or area.
- Only trained and specialist staff will operate the system.
- Supervision and security is easier—fewer people have access to files.
- Equipment and space is fully and efficiently used.
- Equipment and systems can be standardised thus making access to files easier and quicker.
- There is less need for files and papers to be duplicated in several departments, again reducing both the security risk and the paper load.
- An efficient system should allow for quick and easy follow-up, so reducing the risk of lost papers and files.

Departmental filing

- Files relating to one department in particular are easily available to that department.
- Specialist files are less likely to become lost if they are kept within one department.

- A system can be used which is particularly suitable to each department—e.g. Sales—Geographical
  Personnel—Alphabetical or Numerical
  Stores—Numerical or Subject.
- There is less of a security risk, files can more easily be kept confidential.
- Specialist knowledge of departmental staff is greater, therefore accurate filing is easier.
- A smaller system is easier to handle.
- Junior staff have the opportunity to gain experience in filing and to learn more about the whole company.
- Files can generally be found with very little delay.

In practice it is not so easy to decide which of the two systems is more appropriate and many companies run a combination of both. While many companies operate on a departmental basis it is rare to find any one which uses only central filing and most executives and departments will keep at least a personal filing cabinet, particularly for confidential material to which only they and/or their secretary have access.

6.4 Choosing the Equipment

If as secretary you should find yourself in the position of preparing a report or proposals for a new filing system it is vital that you are aware of the equipment which would be needed to operate your recommended system efficiently. Perhaps you have only been asked to give some thought to the equipment you are already using, or maybe you realise that your system needs updating.

Investigate the facts and the facilities

Whatever the situation it is most important to support any recommendations with firm ideas, facts and information. Make a full investigation and collect plenty of leaflets, catalogues and so on—don't depend on one supplier whose range may well be limited. If your company has a favourite supplier you will probably want to be loyal, but it does no harm to make further enquiries since a good supplier will make every effort to provide you with the equipment you need. Open any office supplier's catalogue at the appropriate pages and you will be met by a bewildering array of filing cabinets, drawers and the like. Do not be downhearted although in many cases you may find that because of financial restraints you must resign yourself to using inappropriate or old equipment. On the other hand it may be that you are given a degree of freedom and capital to re-equip your office with the most suitable equipment for storing documents. Whatever the particular situation it is the secretary's responsibility to ensure that filing drawers, cabinets and so on are used efficiently and that time and space are not wasted.

Look at the catalogues and take advice

Reference to any office supplier's catalogue will show the immense array of equipment from which the secretary can make her selection. Assuming there will be some financial constraint a possible checklist of equipment to consider will look as follows:

Storage	Supplementary Equipment	Computer Filing
Cabinets:	Dividers	Binders
Vertical	Labels	Suspension kits
Lateral	Guide cards and tabs	Disk storage
Horizontal	Individual files:	
Rotary/Carousel	Lever arch	
Mobile cabinets	Ring binders	
Chest plan	Wallets	
Strip index	Clip boards	
Card index	Transparent pockets	
Expanding files		

Faced with the task of setting up, or improving, a filing system, where does the secretary begin? The first thing to do is to consider the particular characteristics and recommended application of all the different systems. Generally there is no better advice than to take time to approach a selection of office suppliers and to listen to their advice (always remembering that they are interested in selling and will only give you the good news about a product, omitting the bad!). Talk to other experts and approach other colleagues or even companies for advice based on experience. Build up for yourself a picture of what is available, on which you can make an informed decision. You will find that most equipment falls into the categories outlined in the check list above, each of which has its own particular application and function within an office.

Cabinets come in several shapes and sizes, the most common being **vertical** and **lateral**, with **rotary** or **carousel** playing an important part in centralised filing and **horizontal** being an invaluable means of storing plans and other large documents.

(a) Vertical cabinets

Vertical filing is the oldest organised method of storing papers in offices. Up until a century ago paper in offices was generally stored on a 'spike', in chronological order with the most recent paper on the top. The only problem was that the paper you needed to refer to could be some 200 papers down. It takes little imagination to picture the problems of removing 200 papers and replacing them in the right order. Pictures of chaotic Dickensian offices spring to mind! Storing papers in drawers was a natural progression and, while today vertical filing is being superseded in many offices by lateral filing, it is still very popular and the most suitable to many needs.

Vertical cabinets vary from single drawer to four-drawer, with each drawer housing a rail on each side from which are suspended the carriers.

Figs. 6.1 and 6.2   *Different forms of storage*

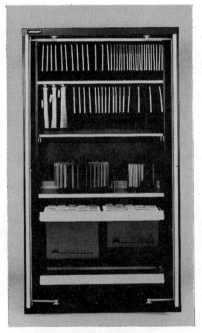 

(b) Lateral cabinets

Lateral filing is housed in wall cabinets so that the files lie side by side horizontally with the label at the end of each file visible. The cabinets take up less floor space overall than vertical cabinets and have the added advantage that no extra space is needed to open drawers. In addition records can be stored from floor to ceiling, thus saving even more valuable office space. The files are normally stored on their spines in individual or linked folders usually hung from rails or they may be supported on shelves with a plastic holder which holds the guide card indicating the name or other details of the file. These tabs may be flat or protruding or may be angled to make reading easier, since reading the guide cards is perhaps one of the major disadvantages of this system. In some cases the plastic may magnify in order to overcome this difficulty. In addition, provided the doors or fronts of the cabinets are open all of the files are visible at a time. This means that several people can access the files together thus making their use of time much more efficient. One major manufacturer of filing equipment suggests that by using lateral filing a company could increase the number of files on view seven or eight fold. This is a major advantage over vertical filing where only one person can use one cabinet at a time.

(c) Horizontal cabinets

Horizontal cabinets have been a traditional method of storing plans, drawings and other large sheets of paper. They have two major disadvantages in that:

(i) they take up a disproportionate amount of floor space
(ii) papers become easily damaged since several papers may be stored in one drawer and to find any one paper will entail sorting through many others. (Particularly since the one wanted is almost always at the bottom!)

Chest plan files are increasingly replacing horizontal cabinets. They are similar in design to vertical files except that they are individual cabinets, large enough to take plan-size sheets of paper standing vertically. They are free standing, tall, thin and often mobile. The plans are housed in suspended dividers with guide cards as in suspended vertical filing. Papers stay flat and do not get damaged through unnecessary handling and the cabinets themselves take up much less space than the more traditional horizontal cabinets.

(d) Mobile cabinets

In any office there is always a problem of moving a group of files around to several people or departments. Mobile cabinets can take the form of a single suspension drawer or an unenclosed frame on wheels.

Mobile files are particularly useful in open plan offices where staff at different desks or in different departments may need to refer to a group of files on related subjects or areas.

(e) Rotary files

Files (usually the lever arch type) stand on carousel units which rotate. They are considered to be particularly space saving since the person using the files needs only to stand in one place at any one carousel and rotate the carousel to find the file. The only movement involved is to move to the next carousel. Rotary files can halve the space needed by a lateral system.

(f) Powered filing

Here again the filing clerk needs to move very little in order to access the files. Vast numbers of files are housed in long rows in a conveyor belt type system which automatically rotates the files forwards and backwards as required by the operator. This system is particularly suitable for large centralised systems of filing.

(g) Supplementary filing equipment

Manilla folders   With or without clips to secure papers. Usually used to keep papers relating to one category or company together within the divider.

Lever arch files   Hardback files with large capacity for punched papers. Papers are held securely by a sprung bar. Suitable for large quantities of paper related to one or more subject. Files are particularly suitable for rotary systems where they stand upright with labelled spines facing outwards.

Box files   Rigid boxes with a sprung clip inside to keep papers secure. Particularly suitable for loose papers of various sizes. Normally stored upright on shelves with label facing outwards.

Expanding files   Expanding boxes predivided alphabetically into fixed pockets. Particularly suitable for 'Follow-up' or 'tickler' files and for personal filing in the home since the capacity is not great. They are obtainable in various qualities from card to rigid lockable PVC.

Wallets   Made from card. Suitable for loose papers or papers clipped together. Can stand on shelves stored laterally but are more suitable for carrying loose papers for short periods of time.

Multipart files Manilla folders consisting of up to nine subdivisions forming one file. Suitable for temporary divisions, for example for letters awaiting signature or pre-sorting before filing or other un-punched papers. The contents are held by elastic lace and the cover is printed for labelling or cross referencing.

Collapsible and rigid storage cases Suitable for long-term storage of 'dead' files.

Transparent punched pockets For use in conjunction with ring binders to store and/or display photographs, well-used documents, price lists, brochures, etc. Available in several colours for easy reference.

Plastic files Transparent or coloured front, clear pockets, compressor bar. Particularly useful for reports, projects, sales literature, etc.

(h) Indexing equipment

Many filing systems depend upon an index of one sort or another. Equipment available is much and various. The traditional index cards still very much have their place and are able to house a large amount of important information in a relatively small space. A cross index of suppliers, for instance, might give the company name, telephone number, address, Sales Manager's name and a list of goods normally purchased from that supplier. In the Personnel Department the name of the employee, his current department and employee reference number may be all that is necessary. Such information frequently needs to be readily accessible and it is sensible to use the cross indexing system to provide such information.

Cross indexing is most popularly used with numerical filing. To find a file all that is necessary is to find the name of the company or project on the card in the cross index system. The cross index card will indicate the number of the actual file in the filing cabinet.

Cards The traditional cards are small—some postcard size, some smaller and some larger—stored in small desk top boxes or rotary wheels. Guide cards with protruding tabs divide the cards up according to the system of classification used to match with alphabetic dividers.

Visible cards May be pre-printed ready for information to be inserted and stored in overlapping pockets in shallow drawers or folders. The name of the file is typed or written on the bottom edge of the card which remains visible all the time. The bottom edges of the pockets are protected by transparent plastic strips into which the cards are tucked.

Visible strip index   Ideal for listing and retrieving information which constantly changes, but which must always be updated and maintained in perfect sequence. It works rather like a directory with each 'strip' having room for one line of information only. For filing purposes the name of the file would appear on one side and the file number on the other. The strips are housed in drawers, files or on rotary panels and can be moved up or down as strips are removed or inserted.

6.5 Filing Efficiently

The efficiency of a filing system depends not only upon using the most suitable equipment and method but on the ability and reliability of the filing clerk. Complete accuracy and easy access is vital so always remember the following guidelines.

- File daily—files must always be up to date and papers readily available.
- Pre-sort papers before placing in files—don't waste time and effort in repeatedly removing and replacing files from cabinets.
- File accurately—if unsure scan the letter or document for clues. Look at the subject heading, reference, signature or company name or the contents.
- File neatly, keeping edges of papers square—lazy and casual filing leads to lost and damaged papers.
- Place most recent papers at the front (top).
- Avoid large, bulky files—remove material no longer required or out of date to 'dead' files.
- Store 'dead' material in box files or other specially designed 'archive boxes', label with name of file, dates of oldest and most recent documents and keep in separate place.
- Insert a reference to the 'dead' file number on the current file.
- Avoid removing individual papers from a file. Take a photocopy of single papers. If absolutely necessary insert a note where the paper was removed from stating date, details of paper and name of person who has removed the paper.
- Insert an absent marker or wallet if a file is removed.
- Replace files as soon as they are no longer needed.
- Use cross-references to avoid confusion and lost papers.

6.6 Microfilm

It is easy to be misled into believing that **microfilm** has all but replaced traditional filing methods. This is by no means the case, but it is true that it is becoming more and more a part of normal office equipment and systems. Its major role is saving space and microfilm is of particular value when storing dead and archive material which is not referred to on a regular basis.

(a) What it is

Microfilm is a means of storing exact copies of documents in photographic form. Documents are photographed and reduced by 24 to 72 times to the size of a postage stamp or less. They are stored either on rolls of film, sheets of transparencies or on individual cards, each of which takes up considerably less space than traditional paper documents.

Whenever a document is needed for reference the film, in any form, is viewed on a scanner, reader or VDU linked to a computer which enlarges the negative and projects it on to a screen.

You may have come across microfilm in your own public library where the catalogues of books are held either on microfiche or microfilm instead of the traditional index cards.

(b) What form it takes

Microfilm
This may be contained in cassettes or spools of 16 mm or 35 mm film (suitable for drawings, plans, etc.). Spools of film provide the larger capacity but need individual threading while cassettes are convenient to handle and less prone to damage. Archive or dead material is particularly suited to 16 mm microfilm where the order of the documents does not need changing.

Cassettes are particularly suitable for viewing several documents in any order, since it is easy to scan forwards and backwards and the cassette does not need rewinding. It can be removed from the viewer and reinserted with the same document in view.

Microfiche
'Fiche' (from the French meaning 'file index card') is a card with several film images put together in rows and columns, forming a 'grid' pattern.

The card is normally A6 (or postcard) size and may have space for information to be inserted which can be read with the naked eye (file references, department, etc.). Microfiche is available in several 'standard' formats—consequently the number of records accommodated on one A6 card will vary according to manufacturer and degree of reduction and can be any number from 100 to as many as 3000. Microfiche is convenient to handle, store and transport and is often preferred to roll film.

Aperture cards
Eighty-column punch cards with an individual microfilm frame mounted provide a means of combining key-punch data which can be used to sort cards and speed access of the microfilm image from a stack of aperture cards. They are particularly suitable for drawings and plans and can be used for reproduction of the document.

Plastic jackets
Plastic jackets hold individual strips of 16 mm or 35 mm film and provide an easy means of referring to film and make updating an easier process. Images can be copied or read via a viewer directly from the jacket without removing the individual strips of film and, like aperture cards, each jacket has space for a title which can be read without magnification. Jackets are particularly useful for material which needs periodic or regular updating such as sales figures, reports, etc.

(c) Which to choose and why

If a company is considering moving to microfilm it may be up to the secretary to do some groundwork and prepare information or a report on the proposed system. Apart from considering the systems themselves as outlined above it is important to ask some questions regarding the reasons for the changeover.

- How often will the documents be referred to?
- How many people need access to the documents?
- Will the documents be stored centrally or departmentally?
- To what extent will the documents need to be produced in print?
- What are the financial constraints?
- How many readers are needed?
- Where will the readers be situated?
- How will documents be retrieved?

These are clearly questions which the secretary cannot answer in isolation but consultation with users, suppliers and decision makers will be necessary to provide a full and useful report.

(d) Retrieval of documents

Film, cassettes and cards must, as with all record keeping, be clearly labelled and indexed. Codes or indexing can take the form of traditional numbering or may be combined with bar code readers or be linked to a computer-based retrieval system, which will be expensive but fast.

Microfilm viewers require some practice and skill for quick retrieval since the 'pages' have to be scrolled through and viewed to reach the desired point. However, speed is essential if the system is to be used effectively and efficiently. Cassettes are easier to handle since it is easier to move backwards and forwards through the film. Fiche viewers are in fact the easiest to handle provided the cards are clearly indexed and can be easily found in the first place.

(e) Why change to microfilm?

- Considerably less space is needed for filing cabinets.
- Important originals only need be kept and these may be stored securely in safes, banks and so on.
- Security is greater.
- Film is fireproof.
- Copies on film and fiche can be easier to mail.

(f) Why stick with traditional filing?

- Purchasing the equipment for microfilm can be costly if there is not sufficient material to warrant a changeover.
- Experienced staff who are efficient in traditional filing systems may be resistant to change.
- Referring to documents can be inconvenient if there is no reader easily available.
- Finding the exact frame can take time and care.
- Updating microfilm must be efficiently and regularly done to be effective.

(g) Filing by computer

By using COM (computer output on microfilm/fiche) documents can be viewed on screen at greatly increased speed. This removes much of the frustrations of viewing on microfiche readers since the speed at which the documents are translated can be as great as 120 characters per second. Documents can be turned into hard copy (printed) at will by selecting the frame, viewing it on screen and asking the computer to print.

Checklist

Setting up or changing filing systems

Is a central system available?

Is it company policy to use the central system?

Are the majority of documents confidential?

How many people need to and have authority to see the documents?

How often are the documents referred to?

What size documents need to be stored?

To what extent is space a consideration?

Is there a financial constraint or is microfilm an appropriate option?

Is time an important factor and are computers available?

Is COM a viable extension to microfilm?

Remember the personal files

Your executive is likely to have an amount of personal and confidential filing which you will probably be responsible for:

- keep the files locked at all times
- mark all papers and files confidential
- do not lend files to unauthorised personnel.

Do You Know?

The difference between:

1. card index	and	visible strip index?
2. box files	and	lever arch files?
3. microfilm	and	microfiche?
4. vertical suspension	and	lateral suspension?
5. alphabetic filing	and	alpha-numeric filing?
6. follow-up	and	cross-reference?
7. COM	and	power filing?
8. chronological	and	geographical filing?
9. microfilm reader	and	computer screen?
10. departmental filing	and	centralised filing?

Secretarial Task Six

You work for Mrs Mills, the Sales Director, who left for a business trip in Italy last night. When you listen to your tape this morning you hear this message:

> Alison, my personal filing drawer is too full. Can you organise something better please while I'm away. I don't really need some of those old files, I rarely refer to them, but I haven't any room for another filing cabinet.
>
> Can you also set out some guidelines for the junior who is taking your job while you are on holiday. I really need her to be able to cope with filing the paper work as efficiently as you do. I imagine she has some idea regarding straightforward filing but she may have problems with personal and confidential documents.

Problem 1

Write a note to Mrs Mills making suggestions for her approval on:
- (a) Which files should be removed.
- (b) Which might be disposed of and how this should be done.
- (c) How the remainder should be stored.
- (d) An alternative method of keeping the documents which might not give rise to these problems.

Problem 2

Prepare a check list for the junior giving her the guidelines Mrs Mills has asked for.

Problem 3

The absent cards you currently use are little more than slips of paper and include only the name of the file. You consider that your department needs new cards. Design such a card and write a brief memo to your departmental staff explaining its purpose and how it should be used.

Examination Question

1. The company you work for is considering changing from conventional filing equipment to microfilmed records.
   - (a) What equipment is needed to set up and operate a microfilming system? (You should BRIEFLY state USE of equipment.)
   - (b) Describe the most suitable uses of microfiche, microfilm roll and aperture cards.

(LCCI SSC OP)

Chapter 7

Equipment in the Office

How much do I need to know?

How much does the secretary need to know about equipment and machinery found in today's offices? Some people may think that modern equipment is either so straightforward and easy to use that little explanation is necessary, or so sophisticated that only a specialist can be expected to handle it. In many instances this is certainly the case but as secretary it is important that you keep up to date with the fast moving technological world of office equipment. Only in this way will you be able to make the right recommendations and decisions about the kind of equipment you need. It is also important that you are able to cope with other equipment in your offices. It is not necessary to know all the technical details, that is the job of a specialist, but you must be able to make decisions about which machine to use and when—which is most appropriate and which is unsuitable for the job you have in mind.

You need to know what you can use in your office to do general jobs, and jobs specific to your own requirements—from files to fax, date stamps to dictaphones. You must be aware of specialist equipment available to you in the company which may be centrally situated and run by specialists. Centralised machinery will offer you facilities and service which cannot economically be operated on an individual basis.

Much of the equipment and associated services to be found in an office is also discussed in other chapters—facsimile, telex, and so on—where it forms part and parcel of the services and function of that department. In fact, most machinery and equipment does not fall easily into a single slot and cannot be thought about under specific headings. Office equipment crosses over many departments, functions and jobs—office copiers, an obvious example, are used by all departments for a multitude of jobs, the same applies to typewriters, word processors, dictaphones and so on.

138

The changing face of the office

The development of equipment is moving faster than many offices can keep up with. No sooner has a 'new' model of typewriter or photocopier been acquired than more leaflets arrive announcing yet further improvements—faster, with more memory, more colours.

7.1 The Secretary's Office—What Does She Have, What Does She Need?

(a) Typewriters

Are you one of the unlucky ones, still pounding away on a traditional manual typewriter? (Perhaps you don't consider yourself to be unlucky—perhaps you wouldn't have it any other way!) More and more **manual** and **electric** typewriters are being replaced by **electronic** typewriters or **word processors**. It is not unusual for a company to exchange its entire fleet of manual typewriters overnight for word processors.

In an ideal world all secretaries and office staff would be given some choice in the equipment they are expected to use. Unfortunately all too often the choice of new equipment is made by administrators, with little or no consultation with the people most affected by the choice— the users.

What do the new typewriters offer that the manual ones didn't? Remember first that electronic is not the same as electric. Electric typewriters operate in the same way as manual machines except that the energy comes from electricity instead of your fingers and hands. Electronic typewriters, on the other hand, offer an entirely new concept.

- They are easy to operate and therefore cause less strain and tension—the keyboard can sometimes even be tilted to suit the typist.
- They have few moving parts which means less to go wrong.
- The type basket is replaced by a daisy-wheel or similar device: literally a wheel which looks like a daisy with stems each of which has a letter or character on the end; whenever a key is depressed the wheel spins until the correct letter is in the printing position.
- Some can be linked (interfaced) to a computer to double up as printers.
- Some can be used as terminals to transmit data by 'phone.

- The potential print speed is faster than any typist can achieve— 10 characters per second is about average.
- Ribbon changing is an easy no-mess operation since all ribbons are housed in cassettes.
- Corrector ribbons are available for all machines and mean cleaner, neater, easier corrections.
- Choice of daisy-wheel means choice of size and style of type— 10, 12, 15, scientific, italic, Greek, etc.

Features on these machines are as variable as the price but generally it is the case that 'you get what you pay for'. To give a fully comprehensive list of these features is an almost impossible task. As each day passes a further feature is added. Briefly, however, and starting with the most basic, they provide the following features.

- Automatic relocation and correction if a mistake is made (this can vary from within a few characters to any number of lines).
- Choice of typing pitch—usually 10, 12 or 15 characters to the inch.
- Repeat keys—selected keys or all keys repeat until the special repeat key is released.
- Automatic centring and underlining.
- Express backspace.
- Right justification—extra spaces are inserted between words so that all lines finish at the same point on the right.
- Bold typing—characters strike more than once to make the print appear darker and hence stand out.
- Type-ahead: the typewriter has a memory which enables the typist to continue typing while the typewriter catches up after a carriage return.
- Automatic carrier return (wrap-around) at the end of a line.
- Automatic line or paragraph indent.
- Line or phrase memory (useful for standard letters).
- Backup memory—stores what you have typed for a set period (on some machines this is only temporary—until the machine is switched off—on others it can be up to a number of days or weeks).
- Decimal tabulation—a tab which enables automatic aligning of the decimal point.

- Automatic superscript and subscript.
- Combined calculator functions.
- Word search—finds every occurrence of a word in the document.
- Search/skip and replace—replaces one word with another through the document.
- Page/line format—remembers margins, tabs and indents.
- Automatic paper setting (programmable).
- Automatic page end indicator (programmable).
- LCD correction screen (large or small).

Prices of typewriters have undergone radical changes over the last few years and today the company that purchases anything other than electronic typewriters is rare. While the initial outlay for the typewriter, ribbons and correction ribbon may be great, in terms of speed and quality of output, comfort, convenience and efficiency of the typist, electronic typewriters have no equal.

Fig. 7.1 *An electronic typewriter with memory*

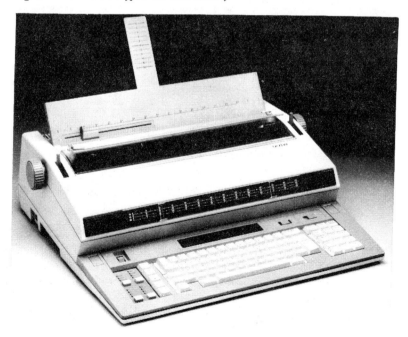

Ribbons

FABRIC	initially more expensive than film but longer lasting
	print fades as ribbon becomes well-used
use with:	
Cover-up tape:	on disposable spool
FILM: Correctable One-time Multi-strike }	initially less expensive than fabric but NOT so long lasting consistently dark print
use with:	
Lift-off tape:	on disposable spool

Coloured
normally Black/Blue/Red/Brown/Green

Fig. 7.2   *Ribbon cassettes*

Fig. 7.3   *Daisy wheel*

(b) Word processors

It is difficult to remain ignorant of the existence, use and value of word
processors thanks to widespread television, newspaper and magazine
advertising. Word processing is no longer a specialist task done by
highly trained operators. It has reached our homes and our offices in a
big way—authors, secretaries, typists, managers, students, teachers,
once they begin to use a word processor, wonder how they managed
without it and quickly consign the manual typewriter to the attic or
jumble sale. Many individuals and companies have entirely bypassed
the electronic typewriter and moved straight to word processing. A
word processor can now cost as little as a sophisticated electronic
typewriter, with the added bonus of a computer able to run additional
software such as databases, spreadsheets, diaries and electronic mail.

(i) Dedicated word processors
Up until a few years ago *dedicated* word processors were the popular
choice. As suggested by the word, 'dedicated' means that they operate
only as word processors, and can run a very limited amount of other
software. They can be very expensive and are usually operated by
specialist staff.

(ii) Computer with word processing software
The computer with word processing software (as against a dedicated
word processor) is becoming an increasingly popular choice. There
are several reasons for this move towards WP software.

   – After the initial outlay, many other software packages can be
     run on the same computer (see above).

— Minimum cost computers are easily attainable—one popularly advertised computer costs little more than a sophisticated electronic typewriter and offers greater facilities; by the same token a computer with software can cost less than a dedicated word processor and again offer more facilities (see above).

— A word processor is more powerful in terms of memory than an electronic typewriter and can store documents permanently.

— Some electronic typewriters can be more difficult and complicated to learn than a basic word processing package.

— The simpler word processing packages need little or no specialist training once the basic concepts have been learnt.

(iii) What does a word processor do?

There is no substitute for actually sitting in front of a word processor and 'having a go'. Briefly, however, a word processor can give:

— fast input (typing)　　　　wrap around (automatic return)

— on screen correction　　　proofread before printing so giving
　　delete ⎫ line　　　　　　perfect copy with no messy
　　insert ⎪ character　　　　corrections
　　overtype ⎬ paragraph
　　copy ⎪ page
　　　　 ⎭ document

— automatic:　　　　　　　　page numbering
　　　　　　　　　　　　　　indentation
　　　　　　　　　　　　　　reformatting (arranging the page
　　　　　　　　　　　　　　layout)
　　　　　　　　　　　　　　spell-checking (dictionary)

— 'merge'　　　　　　　　　create personalised letters—
　　　　　　　　　　　　　　standard letters
　　　　　　　　　　　　　　printed at speed with individual
　　　　　　　　　　　　　　names and addresses
　　　　　　　　　　　　　　automatically inserted

— standard letters　　　　　created by joining selected standard
　　　　　　　　　　　　　　paragraphs which are held on disc.

And so the list goes on. If you are unable to get to a word processor to see its full powers, or if you operate a word processor with limited facilities try to get hold of leaflets, brochures which will tell you more.

Hardware	Software
keyboard or other input device (mouse, light pen)	the computer programme: word processing
VDU (Visual Display Unit— Screen)	database
CPU (Central Processing Unit)	spreadsheet
printer	payroll
disc drive	graphics
discs (floppy, hard, compact)	electronic mail
	electronic diary

(iv) Whatever happened to the typing pool?

A centralised typing service is still a common feature of many large companies but this too is giving way to a centralised word processing service. Wordprocessors may be 'stand alone', i.e. they are self contained with their own memory store (usually floppy disc drive), or linked together with a central memory, usually referred to as 'shared logic'. Many companies prefer shared logic systems because:

- they can be cheaper to install throughout a company
- several operators can work on different parts of the same document at the same time
- equipment can be standardised
- standard or shared data can be accessed by many different people in the company.

On the other hand, shared logic systems have two major disadvantages:

- there can be delays if several terminals are accessing the same document at the same time
- if there is a central fault, the whole system may go down at once.

The problem of a central breakdown can be solved by using **distributed logic** where the terminals have a degree of 'intelligence' (sometimes referred to as being 'smart') and are not totally reliant on one Central Processing Unit.

A further alternative is to use **shared resource** where a stand-alone computer might have the facility to use a central hard disc storage, printer or other output device.

(v) Where do electronic typewriters end and word processors begin?

Some electronic typewriters are becoming so sophisticated that the dividing line between them and word processors is growing very thin.

The facilities offered on an electronic typewriter can be as various and as sophisticated as on a basic word processor. However, the major difference which can easily be identified is that even the most sophisticated typewriter still has its keyboard and 'printer' within one unit. Another important difference is in the amount of memory available. Memory is measured in numbers of characters or 'K' (1000 characters) and the amount of memory is generally considered to be an indication of its classification—typewriter or word processor. The memory of an electronic typewriter may be as little as 10 characters or as large as 7K (7000 characters) and grows with each new model introduced. It is normally accepted that the average electronic type-writer has only a small strip display screen or no screen at all, while a word processor is expected to have a full size VDU (portable WP's operate with reduced size screens) and to have a great deal more memory; nowadays 128K is considered small while 512K enables a dictionary and other software such as a spreadsheet or database to run concurrently with the word processor (multi-tasking). While it is easy for the secretary not to concern herself with such 'technicalities' and to dismiss them as unnecessary, some understanding of terminology is vital if she is to make sensible and useful choices over the equipment she is to use. Increasingly the secretary is expected to use other software such as spreadsheets and databases as part of her normal routine.

(vi) Typewriter or word processor—which should I use?
Many people are so hooked on their word processor that for them there is only one answer to the question. However, in the office you may not be in the same situation and the answer can depend on several factors with the first two perhaps being the most important.

Questions to ask yourself

Which is available?	
Which do I prefer?	
Is the document long?	wp is less tiring
Is the document complicated?	wp copes well with complicated material
Are there going to be alterations?	wp allows corrections and amendments to be made without the need for complete retypes
Is the final quality important?	wp print out gives perfect copy

Can I print it out quickly?	printers for wp may not always be immediately available if shared resources or shared logic is used
Is it to be printed on special paper (e.g. printed forms)?	may be quicker on a typewriter
Will I need to print or type the document again at a later date with or without changed data, names, details, etc?	wp stores documents and avoids the need to retype long documents
Does the same information need to be sent to more than one person?	wp offers the facility of 'mail shots' (personalised letters) up to any number
Do I type a lot of one-off letters and single page reports?	quicker on a typewriter envelopes, too, are quicker

(c) Printers

Printers too are becoming faster almost week by week. Amongst those you will come across are four major types:

Daisy wheel	impact
Dot matrix	impact
Laser	non-impact
Ink jet	non-impact

Impact

characters are printed by means of the print mechanism touching the paper

Non-impact

only ink touches the paper, there is no other contact

You may also hear them referred to as *letter quality* or *draft quality*.

Draft quality

the speed is fast but the quality of the print is not what would be expected for correspondence or other important documents

Letter quality or **Near letter quality (nlq)**

the printing speed is slower but the quality is much higher

(i) Impact printers

Daisy wheel printers reliably produce good quality print (letter quality) although their speed is slower than dot matrix or laser printers. Also daisy wheel printers cannot cope with graphics— diagrams, charts, etc. (For description of wheel see Chapter 7.1(a)).

In **dot matrix printers** the printed characters are made up of a series of close dots; the quality of the print depends on the density of the dots; nlq is produced by either printing the dots closer together or printing over a line more than once; the quality of the letter being printed is affected by the speed at which the printer operates. Dot matrix printers are particularly useful for internal work (draft reports, internal correspondence) and for business documents (orders, invoices, statements and so on). Unlike daisy wheel printers, dot matrix are not confined to pre-set letter types. Those with nlq can be used for external documentation provided they are printed on good quality paper. The type of print can be governed by the software and in many cases can be changed in the middle of the document merely by an instruction within the file or document. Dot matrix printers can also be used to print out graphics—bar charts, graphs, logos, designs and so on. The 'smarter' the printer the more it can offer.

(ii) Non-impact printers

Laser and ink jet printers offer the best of all worlds except in terms of price. Currently they are very expensive but the price is dropping as technology advances and as more are sold. They surpass even the fastest dot matrix printers *and* produce copy which is of excellent quality. These printers which are quite compact (see Fig. 7.4(a)) have played a major part in the fast growing popularity of 'desktop publishing'.

(iii) 'Desktop publishing'

Desktop publishing is a fast growing area—an extension of word processing and computer graphics. Currently the major disad- vantages of desktop publishing is the cost of the laser printing, but in some companies, the cost is well justified when comparisons are made with the costs of using specialist printers. Today's secretary cannot ignore the existence of desktop publishing which has now reached the stage (in terms of cost and frequency of use) that word processing was at a few years ago.

Fig. 7.4(a) *Desktop publishing and its application*

Looking more business-like has a way of attracting more business.

They say looks aren't everything. But it's hard to look professional when your documents don't.

On the other hand, a document that looks good makes you look good.

And that goes for everything you produce on the Apple™ Desktop Publishing system.

Reports, memos, newsletters, training material, technical manuals, forms, you name it. In different type styles, sizes and weights. Printed out on plain paper, your own letterheads, even transparencies. With illustrations, reversed-out panels, graphs and photos dropped into the text wherever you want.

Transform in-house printing.

If you now send your print work out to be done professionally, you'll have the quality — and the bills to prove it. If you do it in-house, you probably have neither.

Apple Desktop Publishing is inexpensive, fast, and simple to learn. It lets you plan better and present more convincingly.

As for the results, we think they speak for themselves.

The quality of our printing is so good, in fact, that we're actually selling the system to printers themselves. (If they don't know, who knows?)

We'll prove it, free.

We're so confident of that quality that we want you to put it to the test. Just bring us a page (the busier, the better) from one of your presentation documents and we'll redo it on the Apple Desktop Publishing system and send it back.

We call this the Apple Challenge.

 Apple
The power to succeed.

Apple and the Apple Logo are trademarks of Apple Computer Inc.

For more information or a closer look at the Apple Desktop Publishing system, contact:

Authorised Dealer

Fig. 7.4(b)

APPLICATIONS FOR
DESKTOP PUBLISHING

Accounts	Legal documents
Advertisements	Magazines
Annual reports	Manuals
Application forms	Menus
Brochures	Minutes
Business cards	Newsletters
Catalogues	Notices
Certificates	Order forms
Change of address	Overhead trans.
Charts	Plans
Christmas cards	Press releases
Circular letters	Price lists
Contact reports	Product specs.
Credit control	Recruitment ads.
Direct mailshots	Reports
Engineering drawings	Sales charts
Exhibition graphics	Spreadsheets
Flow charts	Statements
Graphs	Stationery
Holiday rotas	T'phone messages
Internal t'phone dirs.	Tech. drawings
Invitation cards	Tender docs.
Invoices	Training notes

FAIRHURST

(iv) Printer stationery

Stationery falls into two main categories: single sheet and continuous. Some printers accommodate either type, others only one.

Single sheet   With single sheet operation papers have to be loaded individually but are then automatically fed into the printer at the touch of a button. There are normally two selections—line feed and form feed. Line feed takes the paper in line by line at each press of the touch sensitive switch and form feed automatically takes the paper into the printer by a predetermined amount. Many electronic type-writers also have this facility. Particularly suited to this method are letterheads, reports and any other documents which require good quality print.

Many printers have the facility to take a **cut sheet feeder.** This saves sheets having to be loaded individually by hand. Sheets of paper are held in a **hopper,** fed in automatically when a new sheet is required and then ejected into another part of the feeder when the printing of that page is complete. Cut sheet feeders are particularly useful for long reports or when printing out mail shots.

Continuous stationery Perforated stationery is fed through continu-ously. The paper has perforated sprocket holes down each side which can be removed after printing if required.

The sprocket holes serve to secure the paper on the sprockets which feed the paper through the printer. Continuous stationery can have interleaved one-time carbon or be made of NCR paper, although this type of stationery does not work well with laser and ink jet printers where there is insufficient or no pressure (these printers work so fast that to print multiple copies quickly would be no problem).

Factors to consider when choosing a printer

Do I want quality?
Do I want speed?
Do I want multiple copies?
Is printing to be done on pre-printed stationery?
What are the cost limitations?
Will noise be a problem?
How many people need to use it?

(d) Other computer software

The secretary with stand-alone computer or terminal must be aware of other software available to her. In a large company the choice of software will be made by other people and appropriate training given where necessary.

A full coverage of the 'electronic office' could take up a whole book, and indeed there are many such books under the umbrella title of 'information technology' available to the secretary.

Briefly the areas today's secretary needs to be familiar with are:

stock control
database
spreadsheet
graphics
electronic mail
viewdata
networks
OCR (optical character recognition)
computer conferencing
electronic filing.

Computer conferencing is also discussed in Chapter 4.

(i) Electronic stock control

This is becoming a familiar feature of today's major retail outlets and one of which the public is becoming increasingly aware. Supermarkets and department stores now use a system where data which is printed on the goods, in the form of the now familiar bar code, and is scanned by means of a light pen or small flat-bed screen. Alternatively, data in the form of a code number, is punched into a keyboard. The keyboard or bar code reader is one of many terminals. The central computer immediately scans the stock record, registers the price on the terminal (cash point); at the same time it registers the sale on the stock record and immediately updates the stock figures. These systems are known collectively as **Electronic Point of Sale (EPOS)**. Supermarkets and banks are now exploring the possibilities of debiting shoppers' bank accounts directly at the supermarket tills (**Electronic Funds Transfer at Point of Sale** or **EFTPOS**). Electronic stock control using keyboards, bar codes and punched tickets is also in use in many manufacturing industries. From purchase of raw materials to sale of finished article, all figures are entered on a computer terminal. As goods are received and issued the figures are registered on the electronic 'stock card' which is automatically updated. This information can be linked and transferred to sales and purchasing documents with no manual calculations or paperwork taking place.

(ii) Electronic filing

Electronic filing can be considered in two ways:

1. The storage of documents and files which are produced as a result of any of the many software packages available:

     word processing
     spreadsheet

database
electronic mail
and so on (an ever expanding list). All of these programs
create their own documents which are stored on disc. Some of
the documents will be printed for reference purposes, others
can be kept on disc, with backups, until required. The creation
of this type of electronic filing involves no extra costs or labour
over and above that already involved in operating the existing
systems.

2. A much greater task is that of converting existing paper files to
   an electronic system. At the simplest level microfile, linked to a
   computer (CIM—computer input from microfilm, and COM—
   computer output from microfilm, see Chapter 6), is a form of
   electronic filing. Apart from using microfilm, such a task is
   gargantuan. The more common application of computer
   storage is that of **database**.

(iii) Database

Database is a valuable asset to any department dealing with change-
able or permanent facts and figures which are constantly referred to or
which need to be kept for long periods. Information which normally
would spread over large numbers of papers, files and filing cabinets
can be held in one program. Departments such as Personnel can
record details of staff—name, address, telephone, qualifications,
experience, salary, absences and so on—and refer to the information
as and when they need to within seconds. The advantages of such
programs are clear: they are space saving and easily updated, and they
are good for long term storage, easy reference and easy print out. A
database will re-sort data into any order required. For example,
records which have been stored alphabetically may be required in
numerical or age order; the database will re-sort in seconds. A
database will group records as required; perhaps all staff over the age
of 25 or all staff who can drive. Yet again the possibilities are endless,
although as a general rule more memory and powerful programs will
give a more sophisticated database with correspondingly broad
facilities.

(iv) Spreadsheet

Like databases, spreadsheets require large amounts of memory to
operate. Spreadsheets replace large sheets of paper, pencil and ruler
for doing tedious and repetitive calculations. Spreadsheets can

calculate and recalculate in seconds what it may take an individual hours to do, even with the aid of a pocket or desk top calculator. Once the outline has been established and the formulae for the calculations which need to be done have been set up, a spreadsheet will keep and update, for example, all a company's accounts. 'What if?' calculations can be repeated on the screen over and over again, avoiding the need for rubbing out on paper and recalculating by hand. Spreadsheets are no longer the province of accountants but are available to anyone who has the need for them. Many students and school pupils, with the aid of a simple and cheap program such as 'Mini Office' find a spreadsheet of use in their personal budgeting.

(v) Graphics

The sophistication offered by graphics packages is immense and a book such as this can in no way do them justice. In very simple terms, software is available which will convert statistics into visual representation, i.e. graphs, pie charts, three-dimensional drawings which can be rotated and viewed from every angle, decorative drawings, coloured pictures, notices and so on. Dot matrix printers will print basic material but for more sophisticated and complicated material 'plotters' are necessary. 'Plotters' will produce multicoloured work which can do the work of a draughtsman in seconds. A whole new world has been opened up for designers who can now ask, via the computer, 'what if?' and the computer will present the answer in a visual form. What previously would have taken hours can now be carried out in minutes. Cartoon animation is produced with computer graphics, in conjunction with light pens, colour pads and the 'mouse' (a box which when moved around next to the computer controls a pointer which selects such operations as 'drawing', 'painting', 'patterns', 'colours' and so on). Not only are graphics packages fun, they have also opened up new fields for designers of bridges, cars, textile prints, clothes, machinery, and much more.

(vi) Electronic mail

Electronic mail in fact covers a host of computer facilities—Telecom Gold, Viewdata, and a multitude of computer software which enables one compuuter to talk to another. Telex can now be transmitted directly via a computer terminal eliminating the need to print a copy of the message. There are, however, dedicated computerised mailing systems which enable one computer to 'talk to' another computer. In effect this means that a message, memo or letter sent from a computer terminal in one office to a computer terminal in another may appear immediately on the receiving screen (usually as a message at the bottom of the screen) or will be stored until the recipient refers to the system, as he would refer to traditional incoming mail. The success of electronic mailing depends on the compatability of the systems. At the moment there are limitations in this area and many systems allow only internal communication.

However British Telecom's 'Telecom Gold' is one of the most successful electronic mailing systems. To date it has 30 000 'mailboxes' and provides fast, easy, cost-effective business communications. Apart from providing facilities to send messages from one terminal to another in seconds it also gives access to telex, Radiopaging and information databases. By using Packet SwitchStream or International PSS, Telecom Gold provides a cheaper means of communicating abroad (cheaper than international telephone).

Note: Packet SwitchStream ('Public packet switched data network') is widely used for computer communications—computer data is transmitted in electronic 'boxes' and finds the quickest 'route' electronically from its source to its destination.

(vii) Viewdata
Prestel, Oracle and Ceefax are all public information services.

Prestel, operated by British Telecom, links adapted television screens to computers through ordinary telephone lines so that information and two-way services can be delivered directly to offices and homes. Information on Prestel can be updated by the minute and is available 24 hours a day. By using 'Gateways', private computers can be linked to Prestel sets via Prestel computers. The introduction of 'Gateways' has led to the introduction of home and office banking, home shopping and other services. It is hoped that these services will expand in the future. The system is two-way and customers can send messages, make bookings or request information at the touch of a button.

Both **Ceefax** (operated by the BBC) and **Oracle** (operated by Independent Television) work on similar principles to **Prestel** with the difference that they are only one-way, are broadcast like television (instead of passing down telephone lines) and are operated by means of a keypad directed at the television set.

Information offered by all three services include pages, or frames, of news, travel information, recipes, timetables, weather, sports results and much more.

Optical character recognition

Optical character readers scan printed or typed characters and convert them into signals which can be input into a database or word processing system. Banks and building societies already use OCRs to read codes (such as an account number) when sorting cheques. More recent developments are moving towards machines which can read handwriting, including those which can recognise signatures.

(viii) Computer conferencing
As with video conferencing (Confravision—see Chapter 4) computer conferencing offers the facility for simultaneous discussion, negotiation and transmission of information between several people spread around the country via a computer network. Contact can be made between departments or offices within one company or between several different companies. Visual representation can be made via the keyboard and computer screens and any information which appears on screen can be printed out if necessary. Both computer conferencing and video conferencing save time, and therefore money, and give immediate contact. However, there is some loss in terms of personal contact.

(ix) Networks
A network is quite simply the linking together of several computer terminals and their peripherals (printers, data storage, telex and so on) and can consist of several terminals within one company or can incorporate several hundreds or thousands of terminals spread around the country (Viewdata—Teletex, Prestel, Ceefax, Oracle already have their own networks). The 'electronic office' seeks to combine as many facilities and services together to form a large network through which as many companies' computers as possible can 'talk' to each other, access information, process data and so on.

(x) Security
Use of equipment by more than one person inevitably holds risks in terms of security—access to computer files, photocopies, documents left behind, microfilm and fiche. Within a small company or a large network, concern for security is of paramount importance and has already been given some consideration in Chapter 1. Apart from the usual concern for keeping documents confidential, the secretary must

make sure she is aware of any special security measures to be taken within her company. If she is at all concerned with computerised records then she should familiarise herself with the important points of the Data Protection Act 1986. Several specially written booklets explain the Act and are available from the Data Protection Registrar in Wilmslow, Cheshire. An extract from the Introduction to the Act is given in Figure 1.1.

(xi) Electronic diary

Many of today's computers have automatic time and date recognition. This, in conjunction with a diary program, means that, again, what has been done on paper before can now be done electronically. Diary pages can be called up by an executive or his secretary, amended and checked while other programs are in use and on screen.

(xii) Datel

Datel is a service operated by British Telecom which enables computer data to travel over the present speech telephone network. In order to be transmitted the data must first be converted from its digital form to the 'analogue' form which telephone speech uses and then converted back again at the other end to the digital form used by computers. This is done by means of a **modem** (modulator-demodulator) at each end. Through Datel expensive computing facilities are now available to small and large companies alike throughout the country. Remote offices can be linked to a central computer, thereby saving overheads on payroll, personnel and other business functions. Specialists— engineers, scientists and so on—are able to have immediate access to valuable information which would otherwise take time to acquire.

(e) Audio equipment

Working from audio equipment, rather than taking shorthand, has become widely accepted in today's office. It is convenient for both the executive and the secretary in terms of time. There is no longer the need for the executive to give dictation at restricted times of day.

- He can prepare his correspondence at times to suit himself: at home, on the train, plane and so on although dictation while driving is not generally to be encouraged unless it can be done without a hand-held microphone.

- He can take his time to consider what he wants to say without wasting valuable secretarial time.
- He can amend what he wants to say, as much as he needs to, by redictation.
- His speed of dictation is not restricted to the capabilities of his secretary.
- With a portable machine he can instantly put ideas on to tape before they are forgotten.
- Dictation already done can be scanned easily to make corrections or amendments.
- Some units will record telephone conversations.
- With remote microphones, interviews, conversations and meetings can be recorded.
- Dictation units can be as small as hand size, and battery operated—particularly useful for travelling and conference reporting.
- Cassettes are small and convenient to carry.
- The newer recorders give a graphic display indicating:

  recording time remaining
  visual count of length of dictation
  total number of documents on tape.

  In addition:

  separate instructions for dictation can easily be located
  'conference button' enhances the power to pick up low level discussions.

Dictation can be transcribed using a desk-top transcriber with foot pedal and earpieces. For the secretary there are advantages also.

- Transcription can be done at her own pace—she is not restricted to the speed of her executive's dictation.
- Transcription can be done at times to suit her own schedule.
- Transcription equipment may indicate any or all of:

  priority correspondence
  amount of dictation on each cassette
  tape position
  beginning and end of documents (audible signals)
  areas of special instructions
  'fast play' enables quick checking of transcription.

(f) Office copiers

Most people are familiar with the standard copier, or 'photocopier' which produces exact copies from an original.

Public libraries, schools and colleges generally have copiers for student use. Unfortunately, all too frequently, these copiers give a false impression of the quality to be gained from these invaluable machines. In actual fact, copiers in common use in offices produce copies which are barely distinguishable in their quality from the original. They also offer a bewildering array of facilities from straightforward, minimum cost, desktop copiers to the all-singing, all-dancing copier which can enlarge, reduce, print in a selection of colours, sequentially copy, collate, staple and fold.

From the secretary's point of view the office copier offers a means of reproducing documents accurately, cleanly and quickly. Many companies have dispensed with carbon paper altogether believing that it is cheaper in terms of time, and hence money, to produce immediate, exact copies on a copier than to let typists and secretaries battle away with messy carbon paper which inevitably results in copies which are poorly corrected (if corrected at all). In addition, the psychological release for a typist who knows that there is no need to take one or more of the dreaded carbon copies can have a marked effect on her output.

When considering a copier there are a number of basic factors which have to be taken into account.

- Budget: probably out of the secretary's control.
- Average number of copies required: this will govern the size of copier needed.
- Location: several small copiers strategically placed around the company and/or one large, sophisticated copier centrally placed.
- Size: where is it to be placed—what will fit in?
- Speed: multiple copies need a fast copier, over 50 copies per minute is average, and increasing all the time.
- Reliability: a company cannot afford to lose time and money through avoidable breakdowns—also consider the follow-up and maintenance available.
- Type of copying to be done: single sheets, long reports, booklets, colour work.
- Quality of copy: external work needs good copy on good paper.
- Quality and size of paper—A4, A3, A5, card?

Once the initial factors have been considered it is time to look at the more sophisticated facilities.

An understanding of how the machine works is not altogether necessary although it is important to know how to cope with the more common occurrences. Depending on how sophisticated the machine is, some facilities will be automatic while others will require manual operation such as paper refill or change, colour change. Learn how to react to simple machine faults such as jammed paper and so on. If the machine is leased or loaned then maintenance will be arranged for you. If on the other hand your company has purchased the machine then it is likely that there will be a maintenance contract. Do not tamper with anything you are not authorised to touch; reference to a manual will tell you what you can do and what should be left. Clearing jammed paper is usually a simple task, as is chemical refill, but it cannot be stressed too often that if you are in doubt, leave well alone.

Intelligent or smart copiers
Smart copiers are linked to computer terminals and can reproduce documents direct from a digital (computerised) source. There is no need for original 'hard' copy since any data (text, charts, graphics, signatures, etc.) which is stored electronically can be reproduced at will. Smart copiers can also act as a link within the 'electronic office' and produce copies of material sent down the line from a computer terminal elsewhere.

(g) Calculators

Thought by some to be the secretary's next best friend after her keyboard, diary and notebook, calculators are, for many of us, a necessity in our everyday lives — we have grown up with them and it is second nature to use them. To this end it could be claimed that this paragraph is redundant, particularly since many calculators can cost as little as a good ball-point pen and in some cases are as disposable. Nevertheless there are several factors to consider when making a choice about purchasing a calculator:

- Do I need to run it on mains or batteries? (Consider if you need to take it out of the office.)
- Do I need a written record of calculations? (Some provide a print-out.)
- How complicated will my calculations be? (Don't pay extra for what you don't need.)

— Is it likely to be borrowed by my executive—what functions will he need?

— Is it likely to be 'borrowed permanently' by my executive or anyone else? (Battery operated calculators tend to 'walk' while mains calculators are more difficult to borrow!)

7.2 The Print Room

In a large company there will probably be a centralised reprography department, or print room. You, as secretary, will not be expected to concern yourself with the actual operation of available machinery, in fact you may be actively discouraged from doing so. However, it is sensible to know what can and can't be done, how quickly it can be done, how costly it will be and how easy or difficult the task is. A wise secretary will take care to co-operate with, and not antagonise, the print room staff, who in times of crisis can prove to be great allies (and vice versa!).

Print room equipment

All the equipment mentioned so far in this chapter is likely to be found in a print room as well as in individual offices. Depending on the size of the company and on its particular needs you may find that telex is a thing of the past and that fax has taken over. On the other hand your company may be involved in publicity, promotions or training, in which case it will equip itself with sophisticated machinery which will produce promotional leaflets, booklets, posters, and so on.

In addition to all or some of the above machinery a print room may have additional equipment.

(a) A collator   This is used for putting any number of pages of leaflets or booklets together in the correct order after they have been printed. A job which would take maybe 20 minutes by hand can be done in only a few minutes or even seconds. Bigger machines will collate, fold, staple, bind papers into booklets and finally trim them to give a professional and clean finish.

(b) Binding machines   After papers have been collated they can be bound to give a professional finish. The alternative to specialist binding is to use ready made card report bindings. These are available with clear and transparent plastic or coloured covers, with a variety of pre-prepared plastic binding strips or spirals, or securing clips inside the binder.

(c) Laminating machines   These cover papers with clear plastic, thus providing a permanent protection. This facility is particularly useful for documents which will be handled a great deal and which need to be long lasting. It is particularly suitable for notices, identity cards, route maps, price lists, report covers and so on.

Remember

For a professional finish don't forget the use of lettering machines or computer graphics which can easily and professionally do a job that takes much longer with Letraset.

(d) Offset lithography   Offset litho, as it is commonly known, is a printing process which gives excellent quality reproduction without the high costs involved in traditional 'block' printing.

Masters or **plates** can be made by means of a typewriter or printer with carbon ribbon, by hand with special pencils with high carbon content, or on electrostatic copiers. The plates come in three varieties: paper (for short runs or small numbers of copies), plastic coated paper (for medium runs) or metal for particularly large quantities (many thousands) which need to be kept long-term and used over again.

Printing is done by attaching the plate to a roller on the machine. A second roller wets the plate and a third inks it. The principle behind offset lithography is that 'oil and water do not mix':

 — As the plate is wet the carbon image rejects the water.
 — As the plate is inked the water rejects the oily ink and the carbon image accepts the ink.
 — The inked image is transferred to a 'blanket' as a reverse image.
 — The reverse image is printed on paper as the paper passes through the machine.

Some machines can take several colours of ink at the same time but a separate plate is needed for each colour.

Although a secretary is unlikely to have to operate an offset litho machine herself (although in a small company she can expect to do anything!) she does need to know what its uses and advantages are. It is particularly useful for producing the large quantities of internal stationery which a company will use, it can print high quality standard letters, leaflets, advertising literature and pictures. Once the master is made production of the documents is relatively cheap and costs, apart from overheads, are only for relatively inexpensive materials and operator time.

Remember to keep up with new developments

The world of office equipment and machinery is a fast changing one and you may find yourself moving overnight from a traditional office with a minimum amount of equipment to a sophisticated, well-equipped company which makes full use of the services of the electronic office.

Make it your own responsibility to keep up-to-date with developments— go to exhibitions, browse through office equipment journals when you have an odd minute. Your executive may expect you to keep him in the picture. And always remember that when you do need new equipment always support your request with well researched facts and recommendations. If your executive or office services manager sees that you have good reasons for needing a new typewriter, that the office would benefit from an improved or additional copier or that investment in Telecom Gold would improve communications, he is much more likely to consider your application positively.

It cannot be denied that improved equipment can lead to increased efficiency and it is up to you as secretary to weigh up the pros and cons of purchasing new equipment—taking into account factors like cost, output, quality, speed, needs and so on. Doubtless you will receive advertising literature and visits from sales people. You must use your judgement on how valuable the information you receive is. Balance your time carefully and don't always reject anything new or expensive. You should always keep up-to-date with developments, prices and so on so that when the time does come you have some facts and experience on which you can base your recommendations and decisions.

Do You Know?

1. What useful features can be found on new photocopiers?
2. How to produce colour work without using a professional printer?
3. What facilities may be offered by the 'electronic office'?
4. When the use of an offset litho machine would be most appropriate?
5. What equipment might be used in the preparation of a training booklet?
6. What are the most useful features to be found on dictation machines?
7. What are the most useful features to be found on transcription machines?
8. The usual features found on an electronic typewriter?
9. What is meant by hardware and software?

10. How to make a choice of ribbon for your electronic typewriter or daisy wheel printer?
11. What desktop publishing is?
12. How an electronic diary may be used?
13. What Datel is?

Do you know the difference between:

1. Daisy wheel   and dot matrix printers?
2. Prestel   and Ceefax?
3. Continuous stationery and cut sheet?
4. Database   and spreadsheet?
5. Electronic diary   and electronic mail?
6. Audio equipment   and answerphone?
7. Binding machines   and laminating machines?
8. Collator   and calculator?
9. Offset litho   and photocopier?

Secretarial Task Seven

Your old manual typewriter has finally given up the ghost and you have put in a request for a new electronic typewriter which has been approved. It has been suggested that you make some enquiries for yourself and look at the manufacturers' specifications before the purchase is made.

Among the facilities offered by the electronic typewriters you consider that the following features would be particularly useful:

variation of pitch
decimal tab
automatic underscore
bold print
automatic carrier return
automatic indent
page format
automatic centring.

Collect together as much literature as you can from office suppliers. Prepare a memo to your office manager supporting the case for the machine of your choice. Point out what the features do and why you would find them valuable in your work.

Examination Questions

1. Comlon International plc uses computers for a wide variety of applications in its offices, the major ones being:

   Ledger work
   Personnel records
   Payroll calculations
   Stock records.

   (a) Give three advantages and three disadvantages of using computerised systems in a company of this size.
   (b) Give three ways in which computers can be used for the maintenance of personnel records.
   (c) What information would be required by the computer to process payroll calculations?

   LCCI OO&SP

2. The company has decided to centralise the reprographics facilities at Head Office and offer a variety of machines, although any large amounts of printing will be carried out by the Printing division.

   (a) What are the advantages and disadvantages of such centralisation?
   (b) Describe how modern photocopiers could help the company.

   LCCI OO&SP

3. Distinguish between the terms 'hardware' and 'software' in connection with computers. Illustrate your answer with suitable examples.

   PEI SP INTER

Chapter 8

Visual Aids in the Office

How much do I need to know?

Your involvement as secretary with presentation of data and statistics in visual form will depend very much on:

the nature of your company's business
the department in which you work
the expectations of your executive.

8.1 What are 'Visual Aids'?

From your own experience in school or college you are no doubt aware of the existence of a wide variety of visual aids, from the traditional blackboard and chalk to videos and three-dimensional charts.

More specifically the visual aids with which most people are familiar consist of:

Blackboard	Statistical tables
Whiteboard	Diagrams
Posters	Flow charts
OHPs	Maps
Graphs, pie charts, bar charts	Pictograms
Films and slides	
Videos	

The same means of displaying data (facts and figures) applies in the office. Each topic, department, project, subject area will have its own favourites.

– The Sales Department may favour graphs and pie charts.

– Training and Public Relations make extensive use of films, slides and videos.

– Planning will find diagrams, maps and models of use.

166

8.2 Who Uses Visual Aids, When and What For?

There are few departments who cannot make effective use of good visual aids. Amongst an almost endless list of possible uses are:

sales statistics—current situation, changes and predictions
profits
numbers of customers
geographical distribution of customers
achievement against targets (sales, production)
progress charts (production)
holiday arrangements
forthcoming events   planners
location of staff   in and out of the office
office planning   three dimensional boards.

Effectiveness and image are the key

Old habits die hard and any changes need careful consideration. This is not to say that the adage 'but we've always done it like this' is to be taken as the only view. The possibilities of displaying information are immense and growing all the time as technology moves forwards at an increasingly fast pace. Any forward looking company will take every opportunity to provide clear and accurate information both for internal and external use and to promote an image which is efficient and up-to-date.

For any presentation to be effective it should:

- be appropriate to the situation
- be clearly set out
- be easy to read and understand
- make use of colours and symbols where appropriate
- be economical in use of words
- be easy to use
- should not be too time consuming to set up
- have immediate impact.

On the other hand, visual aids can be counterproductive if:

- they are time consuming to set up
- they are difficult to understand because they incorporate either too much information in one chart, etc., or too much coding and are therefore unclear
- no-one is given particular responsibility for their updating or maintenance which leads to out-of-date and untidy information.

Charts and display boards in particular need to be carefully maintained if they are to be used effectively. Employees will soon stop referring to them if they are cluttered, difficult to understand or contain old and therefore useless information.

What do visual aids do?

— Give clear, up-to-date information which is easily understood and assimilated.
— Make information accessible at a glance.
— Enable comparisons to be made between sets of figures.

8.3   Preparation, Presentation and Understanding

(a)   Graphs and charts

All material of this type should be:

    — clearly and adequately titled and labelled
    — suitable for the purpose for which it is chosen
    — drawn to a suitable scale.

Many people mistakenly think that 'graph' covers the whole range of visual representation of figures. This is not true. It is important that the secretary knows the difference. There are three common types of graph:

    line graph
    bar chart
    histogram

The basis for all three graphs is the same.

    — A vertical and a horizontal line which cross and are called the vertical or X axis and the horizontal or Y axis.
    — Each axis represents a different group of figures or classification.
    — A scale is used which is suitable for the amount of information to be portrayed and the available size of the display area, e.g. paper, slide, etc.
    — Different classifications are represented by colours, shading or broken lines which are explained in a key.

(i) Line graphs

These can show the changes in one or more different variables within the same graph and are useful for comparison or prediction purposes.

Fig. 8.1 *Line graph*

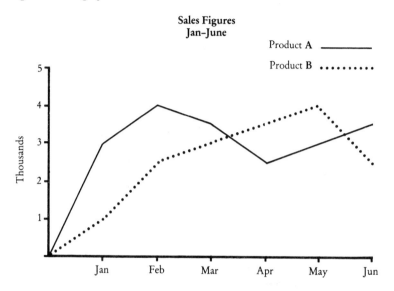

Line graphs can be used to display almost any type of information and are particularly useful for showing figures which change over time, such as sales, population, profits, births, deaths, and where increases and decreases are important.

(ii) Bar charts

The length or height of a series of bars are used to indicate amounts. Colours or shading can be used if more than one product or category appears on one chart. Individual bars or blocks in series are used to indicate figures within a given period, or field. For instance, one bar may indicate sales in January, the second bar sales in February and so on. Rapid comparisons can be made between bars. Comparisons of different commodities, sales etc., can also be made within a period by 'stacking' one bar on another.

Fig. 8.2 *Bar charts*

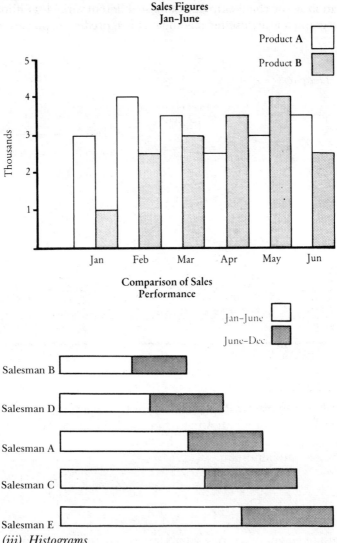

(iii) Histograms

These are a special form of bar chart used in statistics. One specific application is to represent a frequency distribution. Here the width of each rectangle represents a range of values in a population (such as an age range of pupils in a school), while the height is the associated frequency (for example the number of pupils in the school which fall into that age range). Unlike bar charts, the rectangles must be touching. Histograms are particularly suitable for indicating annual sales figures, population distribution and similar statistics. The word histogram is often mistakenly used to describe bar charts. Take care with this particular area of terminology.

Fig. 8.3 *Histogram*

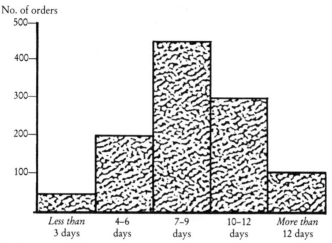

Shipments Received

(iv) Sector and pie charts

These show percentages as segments of a circle or rectangle (where the whole circle or rectangle adds up to 100 per cent). The circle or rectangle is divided up in proportion to the percentage each section is to represent.

Fig. 8.4 *Pie charts*

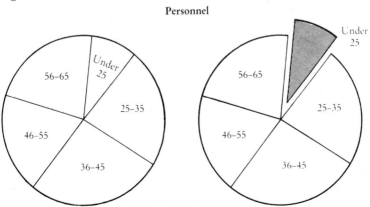

Personnel

Both forms are excellent ways of demonstrating statistics which relate to any specific situation, commodity, time period and so on. They give 'at a glance' information and can be enhanced by colours to indicate related products.

(v) Gantt charts

These are used to compare estimated or projected figures with actual ones. It is normal, for example, for companies to make predictions on their sales figures. In reality the predictions may not compare well with actual sales; or they may be better. Such comparisons are useful for analysing progress and making changes in sales programmes, staff, etc. In figure 8.5 the work scheduled is shown by heavy lines and the work completed by the end of the second week by light lines.

Fig. 8.5   *Gantt chart*

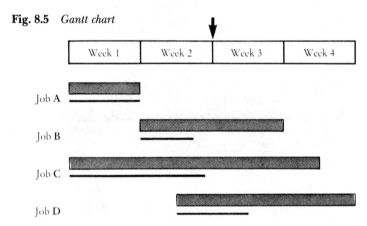

(vi) Flow charts

These have become a fashionable and important means of demonstrating information. Flow charts can replace a numbered set of instructions by boxes and arrows. Their use was originally confined to computer programs but they have now become a common way of describing movement of documents or processes within an organisation. Simple examples can be seen in figures 5.3 (p. 109) and 12.3 (p. 249).

Flow charts should be clear and accurate. Standard symbols are used which avoid an excessive use of words. A few of the more common ones are given below.

Fig. 8.6   *Flow chart symbols*

There is a much greater range which is used extensively in computer programming, but in general the secretary does not need to concern herself with such details providing she has a basic understanding of the concept and presentation.

(vii) Pictograms

These are a familiar means of demonstrating figures and are used to a great extent on TV and in the press. You will have seen the 'half man' or 'half car' in charts which demonstrate, for example, the number of cars or drivers on the roads in a given year. Other uses are many and varied. Pictograms are particularly easy to understand 'at a glance' since they use an appropriate pictorial symbol instead of lines or bars. Each symbol represents a quantity of the item being described.

Fig. 8.7 *Pictogram*

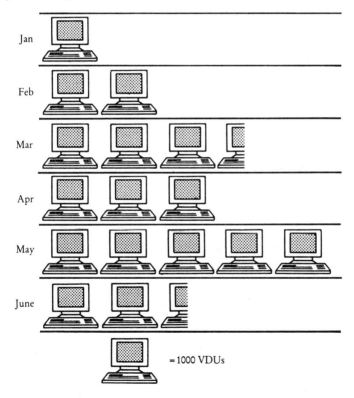

(b) Maps and diagrams

These are old, familiar and valuable visual aids. They can be used on an individual basis and large-scale in talks, demonstrations and so on. Always ensure that reproduction is of good quality and that information is up-to-date.

(c) Overhead projection transparencies (or OHPs)

For many these have replaced the use of the blackboard. The information is prepared on transparent film in one of several ways:

— Extracts of books, articles, photos, illustrations may be permanently copied on to a transparency using a photocopier which has this facility.

— Information may be directly typed on to the transparency using either an ordinary typewriter with carbon ribbon for better quality print, or a word processor with software and printer capable of producing larger print.

— Handwriting using coloured permanent or non-permanent pens. Non-permanent ink may be wiped off using a dry cloth at any time and is a valuable means of adding information to a permanent transparency while speaking to an audience or meeting. In this way it can replace the blackboard or whiteboard and has the added advantage in that different coloured pens may be used with ease.

Transparencies may be mounted in card which aids storage and use. Anyone involved in using such aids regularly, e.g. in training, will find a combination of all types valuable. Once again clarity is of paramount importance. An illegible or faded transparency is worse than none at all and can be counterproductive.

Once prepared the transparency is projected on a wall or screen by means of an overhead projector (OHP). The size and clarity of the projection are controlled simply by means of distance and focus.

(d) Electronic writing board

This reproduces, on paper, any material written on a white board. Reproduction is immediate and exact and allows material which has been written spontaneously during the course of a lecture or meeting to be distributed to participants as necessary.

(e) Slides, films and videos

Material presented using slides, films and videos should be clear and up-to-date. We have all, at one time or another, watched an old information film where there is great entertainment to be had from the out-of-date clothes and general appearance of the characters, with the result that little of the original message of the film is absorbed! By the same token a well-used video with plenty of 'crackle' and picture distortion can actually have the opposite effect to that intended since viewers will 'switch off' mentally when there is any unnecessary distraction.

As secretary it may be your task to book and prepare such equipment. Always check that it is in good working order before the meeting or talk begins. Slides and film projectors have become increasingly sophisticated and many companies will have specialist staff who not only prepare and operate equipment but make films and videos for in-house use. They are particularly appropriate to training. The more sophisticated slide projectors can be linked to sound tracks and have the facility to fade in and out from one slide to the next.

Videos are gaining popularity fast. They have the advantage that they are:

— easy to use
— cheap to run once the equipment has been purchased
— reliable
— allow for projection on to large screens (with appropriate equipment)—useful for meetings.

(f) Visual planning control boards

These boards offer a quick and easy way of updating information which changes either regularly—daily/weekly—or irregularly. A visual planning control board is a large board which can be used to suit individual requirements. Some are designed with flexibility in mind so that a company can arrange them according to their own needs while others are suited to specific purposes.

The most basic charts are little more than large sheets or boards which can be written on directly or which make use of coloured adhesive strips and symbols. Some are magnetic and reusable. Boards consisting of channels or racks into which cards are slotted can be used for stock cards, job cards or time cards. Peg boards are popular for demonstration purposes (coloured pegs can be used for coding) and magnetic boards are gaining popularity since, while they are expensive initially, they are quick and easy to use, and durable and flexible in application.

Visual planning control boards are commonly used for simple holiday rotas, sales figures, timetables and planning and progress through the year. A new development of the magnetic board is the 3D planning board which allows for geographical horizontal planning and is particularly useful for planning office layout both for future use and general reference. Small magnetic blocks representing any items required, such as office equipment and furniture, can be moved around the board to assist replanning of office space.

Visual control boards must be kept up-to-date—information should be cleared as soon as it is out of date. The position of the board is very important. It should be placed where it can be seen easily by whoever needs to refer to it, whenever they need to see it—in a meeting room or by a telephone, etc.

Checklist on use of visual planning control boards

Ask yourself:

Is it right for the purpose?

Does it say what you want it to say—in the way you want to say it?

Is it clear?

If necessary can it be seen and understood from a distance?

Is it to be studied in depth on an individual basis?

Is it necessary to compare information?

Would colour aid understanding?

Is colour available?

Is cost a limitation?

How up-to-date must the information be?

Who has responsibility for updating the information?

Fig. 8.8 *A white board—with clear messages*

8.4 Secretarial Involvement

As secretary your involvement with visual aids will depend to a certain extent on the nature of your company's business and which department you work in. Training is likely to keep you involved with preparation of teaching material—OHPs, slides, videos, booklets, handouts, and so on. If you work in Sales, however, it may be your responsibility to chase and collect monthly sales figures and present them to management in an acceptable form—graphs, charts, etc. Marketing on the other hand concerns itself with advertising and promotion material—posters, videos, exhibition stands and so on. In production you may be responsible for up-to-date progress charts or flow charts showing stages reached for particular items, production targets or up to the minute stock figures. The possibilities are endless. Often requirements will already be set out and you will be expected to carry out those requirements efficiently whether it be chasing sales figures, putting the figures together in a graph or interpreting graphs prepared by someone else. At a more senior level you may be left to your own devices or work closely with your executive to improve ways of collecting and presenting information. At a simple level, but equally valuable, you could be responsible for putting together and presenting the holiday rota.

Remember

One copy or several?
Don't be misled into thinking that visual aids stop at one copy. OHPs, for instance, need handouts to back them up. Copies of graphs are often circulated to interested management. Key points from lectures or films are valued as backup material. Chapter 7 will tell you more about ways and means of reproducing papers and articles.

Computer Graphics

Computers offer immense facilities in terms of visual presentation. Apart from large conference screens which display computerised information, facts, figures and pictures, any data can also be printed immediately for distribution to personnel in a meeting.

Secretarial Task Eight

Problem 1
You are secretary in the Marketing Department of a company selling crisps and snacks. The company has just launched a new range of crisps in three varieties. You are responsible for displaying sales information. How would you portray:

1. Last month's sales figures for the new crisps in each region of the country to an area meeting of sales staff?
2. Up-to-date sales figures of the new crisps over each region of the country to the whole work-force?
3. The organisation of the company to six new employees on an induction course?
4. The location of a promotion team on a promotion tour of the country (their location changes daily)?
5. Sales figures for three varieties of crisps over the last year for comparison purposes?
6. Promotion material for the new range of crisps and snacks for the promotion tour?

7. Up-to-date sales figures for the new crisps—figures come in daily?
8. The age distribution and numbers of people who like the new crisps, following a survey.

Problem 2
After receiving sales figures for the last year you have put together the following table which will form the basis for graphs and charts.

SALES OF 'CRUNCHY CRISPS'
('000 packets)

		Period				
Crisp Type	Area	Jan-Mar	April-May	June-Sept	Oct-Dec	Total
Hot Chilli	North	60	20	25	35	140
	South	50	40	40	50	180
	East	40	10	15	30	95
	West	20	10	10	20	60
	Midlands	70	60	50	70	250
	TOTAL	240	140	140	205	725
Ploughman's	North	60	50	40	50	200
	South	70	40	50	70	230
	East	40	20	20	30	110
	West	60	60	50	60	230
	Midlands	20	30	40	20	110
	TOTAL	250	200	200	230	880
Turkey & Mushroom	North	90	80	90	90	350
	South	90	60	50	30	230
	East	20	40	50	60	170
	West	60	50	40	60	210
	Midlands	90	90	80	90	350
	TOTAL	350	320	310	330	1310
TOTAL SALES (all crisps)		840	660	650	765	2915

In preparation for the monthly sales review meeting you have a number of displays to prepare in order that progress on the new range of crisps can be reviewed. It is your task to prepare draft outlines of the graphs and charts for submission to the Sales Director. Your drafts will then be produced in the form which you recommend.

1. Prepare a bar graph to show which has been the most popular of the three types of crisp (use total figures).

2. Prepare a line graph to show how total sales of each crisp have changed through the year. The Sales Director has asked you to indicate:

    (a) any significant differences
    (b) which is consistently the most popular crisp
    (c) if you have any suggestions as to the reasons for any differences.

3. Draw three pie charts—one for each type of crisp—indicating the breakdown of sales by area so that immediate comparisons can be made.

4. The Sales Director has also asked you to recommend ways of presenting the information you have prepared. There will be ten members of staff present at the meeting. Prepare a memo which you will attach to your draft graphs, etc., giving your recommendations.

Examination Questions

1. Your Office Manager has decided to man the switchboard and the reception of your office on Saturday mornings in future and it is suggested that this is done by the present staff on a rota basis. There are ten members of staff employed in the office and they are all experienced on the switchboard and in reception. The staff list is as follows:

    Julia Brown, Cynthia White, Amanda Green, Anne Black, Lynda Grey, Penny Hulbert, Caroline Godden, Janet Masters, Mary Holmes and Victoria Lang.

    (a) Make out a duty rota for the month of July, commencing Saturday the 3rd, which could be placed on the staff notice-board.
    (b) How would you set about allocating duty days?

(c) Give two ways in which staff could be compensated for such additional duties.

LCCI SSC

2.   Information is often displayed visually. What does this mean? Give two reasons why this method is thought to be better than other methods. Name three types of visual display and briefly describe one use for each.

PEI SP

Chapter 9

Finance and Figures

How much do I need to know?

As with so many other areas of responsibility the secretary's involvement with financial matters depends to a large extent on the size of her company and the department in which she is working. If you are working for a small manufacturing or service company you will need to have a broad knowledge of financial matters. However, it does not necessarily follow that if the company is large you can dismiss this chapter. If you are secretary to the Chief Accountant of a multi-national company you will find yourself very much concerned with all the financial aspects involved in running such a company. In other departments you may find that your involvement is somewhat less.

There are three main areas with which you can expect to be concerned:

Banks.
Petty Cash.
Wages and Salaries.

Stationery and control of stock makes up a fourth area which is more directly concerned with figures rather than finance. The topic 'Banking' is given much publicity, both in the media and in education. It creeps into many subject areas and there are few school or college students who have not studied the services of the banks in some depth. Handling petty cash, on the other hand, causes much heartache to many students and is a subject which is often put to one side when it comes to examination revision. However, a good secretary must know how to deal with petty cash—obtaining, issuing and handling it. A secretary concerned with petty cash is in a position of trust and no mistakes should be made. The topic of 'Wages and Salaries' causes yet more problems for many students. The emphasis and depth of knowledge has changed considerably in recent years due mainly to the fast increase in the use of computerised wage systems. If you work in a small company or in Personnel or Accounts your understanding and knowledge in this area must be greater than if you are based in some other departments. However, it is also essential that from a personal point of view you know what is happening to your own income—what the forms mean and how the figures are arrived at.

9.1 Banks and Their Services

You probably already have a reasonable idea of the services offered by banks—either you will have a bank account of your own or you will have spent some time in your other studies looking at banking services. A secretary must have a clear picture of how the banks are used:

- by her company
- by her department
- by her executive for his personal use
- by herself.

To help with this understanding the following is an outline of the services which are offered by the major banks. It is worth noting at this point that building societies and banks are moving closer together in terms of the services they offer and that there is now a considerable amount of overlap in their services.

Which account?

There are several types of account to choose from—most of which are standard and offered by the High Street Banks although they may appear under different titles. Barclays Bank, for instance, call their current account a Cheque Account. Amongst the many types of account on offer the main ones are:

Current account.
Instant credit account.
Loan account.
Deposit account.
Savings account.
Budget account.

In addition most banks also offer several other services, some of which can be found as part and parcel of an account service, while others are independently offered:

> credit and cash cards
> financial advice
> foreign currency
> storage of valuables
> mortgage facilities
> import/export advice
> loans and overdrafts
> acting as executors for wills
> financial advisors.

One of the first considerations for a secretary from both a personal and employment point of view is to understand the major differences between the types of accounts. Remember that while the services are broadly similar, there will be minor differences between the major high street banks—Barclays, Lloyds, Midland, National Westminster, and Royal Bank of Scotland—as well as between other banks such as the Co-operative and Trustee Savings banks.

In business you will probably find yourself most concerned with current, deposit and loan accounts; savings and budget accounts are commonly opened for personal use.

(a) Opening an account

In the majority of instances the accounts with which you will have dealings at work will have been opened for some time. If you are opening an account for yourself or on behalf of your company social club or similar society then you must be confident in the procedure, which is to:

— complete an application form

— give personal details—name, address, etc.

— give references

— provide specimen signature(s) of anyone authorised to sign cheques.

The bank will process your particulars and take up your references to check that you are credit-worthy. Once the bank is happy with your application details they will ask you to deposit a small amount of money in order to open the account.

(b) Current accounts—what they offer

Current accounts offer a facility for depositing money with the bank either directly by handing it over the counter (cheques, cash, postal orders, etc.) or by Bank Giro. The account holder is given a cheque book and cheque card. The bank pays no interest on a current account and may make charges for services, particularly when your account is overdrawn (you have taken out more money than you have in your account). Once you hold a current account there are several services available which as an individual you will probably make full use of. As secretary you will be concerned with some services more than others, but mostly in terms of collecting information and completing forms.

(i) Paying money into a current account
Bank Giro or credit transfer slips are used to pay money into your own or someone else's current account. Slips printed with the account holder's details (name, account number, branch and branch number) are available which are used to make payments into the account. Slips which are not personalised can be used to make payments into any account. Bank Giro is also used to pay wages and salaries to employees. One form is completed with all the employee's details. The total amount is deducted from the company's account and the individual amounts are paid directly into the employee's accounts. Similarly, you can pay several bills with one cheque—gas, electricity, telephone. With Bank Giro no cash changes hands and you can make the payments at any bank although if you do so at a bank other than your own you may have to pay a charge.

To make more than one payment it is also necessary to complete a credit transfer schedule (a list of all details of all payments).

When completing Bank Giro slips ensure that you get the following details correct:

– recipient's (Payee's) bank details:
  account name and number (if known)
  name of bank and branch (if not printed)

– amount being paid in:
  total
  breakdown (details of cheques and/or amounts and denominations of notes and of coins)

– date

– signature of person paying money in.

— complete counterfoil with:
    total amount
    name of account holder
    account.

(Note—credit transfer for payment of wages and salaries is gradually being replaced by BACS and Autopay.)

(ii) Cheque book
On opening the account you will be issued with a cheque book which will have printed on it three groups of numbers together with the name or names of people authorised to sign the cheques.
    The numbers indicate:

    account number
    branch code number
    cheque number.

Fig. 9.1   *A completed crossed cheque*

Cheques may be 'open' or 'crossed'. Open cheques may be exchanged for cash over the counter of a bank. However, open cheques are not very secure since they can easily be cashed by any dishonest person posing as the payee. The more usual and safer cheque is a 'crossed' cheque, which has two vertical parallel lines printed or written on it. A crossed cheque must be paid into an account—bank, building society or similar. Instructions to the bank may be written inside the crossing so further safeguarding the security of the cheque.

Examples of 'special crossings' are:

 - 'not exceeding £20' where the amount payable may be left open to be filled in by someone who is not the drawer

 - 'not negotiable' and 'a/c payee only' indicate that the cheque may not be passed to a third person.

Cash may normally only be obtained over the counter by presenting an open cheque, or a previously crossed cheque which has had the crossing cancelled, i.e. 'Pay Cash' and a signature written over the crossing. However, most High Street Banks will pay cash to customers presenting crossed cheques at the branch where their account is held. Otherwise a cheque card must be presented at the same time as the cheque.

(iii) Plastic cards—cheque cards, credit cards, debit cards, charge cards, store cards, cash cards

Cheque card—with cheque book. Cheque book holders will be issued with cheque cards which are used in conjunction with a cheque book. Cheque cards have two major purposes (a) they provide some protection against fraudulent use of cheques since the signature on the cheque and cheque card can be compared and (b) they guarantee to the payee (the person in receipt of the cheque) that the cheque will be honoured (paid) even if the account holder does not have sufficient funds in his account to support the payment. This is not to say that the bank will not notify such an account holder that he or she is overdrawn in such circumstances. However, a cheque supported by a cheque card will not 'bounce' (be returned unpaid).

Note that:

 - most businesses, retailers, etc. will only accept payment by cheque if supported with a cheque card

 - cheque cards only guarantee payment up to £50

 - a cheque supported by a cheque card cannot be 'stopped'—the drawer (account holder) cannot ask the bank to withhold payment if, for instance, he gets the goods home, sees that they are faulty and decides not to pay for them.

Credit card—buy now pay later. The most well-known credit cards are Barclaycard (Visa), offered by Barclays Bank, and Access (Mastercharge), offered by Lloyds, Midland, National Westminster and Royal

Bank of Scotland. By purchasing goods or services with a credit card, payment may be made without using cash or cheque. The card is handed to the assistant who completes a sales voucher in triplicate. With the use of a small machine, the retailer's and cardholder's details are transferred from the card to the voucher. The purchaser signs the voucher and takes a copy as a receipt. The retailer retains one copy and send the remaining copy to the credit card centre where the account holder's account is debited with the amount. A monthly statement is sent to the account holder who may pay the total amount by cheque or credit transfer within a given period with no interest charged. If payment is delayed longer than the stated time the credit card company charge interest, usually in the region of 2-3% for each month. The supplier is credited with the amount owing, regardless of when settlement is made by the credit card holder. Although the retailer is charged a small percentage fee by the credit card company to operate this service, most retailers find that the charge can be incorporated in their costs with no detriment to the customer. In fact, the public increasingly expect a retailer to accept credit cards and, if the service is not offered, may go elsewhere to shop.

Remember

Keep credit cards safely.
Make sure you are given your card back after making a purchase.
Destroy your old card immediately the new one is received—*cut it in two* before throwing away.

Fig. 9.2   *A credit card*

Debit card—immediate payment. The latest development in payment without cash is known as a **debit card**, launched in 1987. The 'Connect' card is offered by Barclays Bank and the 'Vector' card by the Midland Bank. The debit card is intended to take the place of the ordinary cheque with cheque card. It can be thought of as being half way between a credit card and a cheque card. It can be used to make payment over the counter. No credit is allowed and the purchaser's current bank account is debited with the appropriate amount straight away. The retailer fills in a debit slip, similar to a credit card slip, and the customer merely signs it—he does not have to write out a cheque. Unlike cheques there is no £50 upper limit on transactions because the retailer can get authorisation from the bank, 24 hours a day, telling them whether they can accept the debit. The retailer has to pay a fee to the bank for each transaction. Eventually debit cards will be used for EFTPOS—Electronic Funds Transfer at Point of Sale (see p. 152).

Remember

Charge card   In addition to the usual credit cards your executive may also use an American Express or Diners Card. These are charge cards and are run by private companies on similar lines to credit cards, independently of the banking system. Card holders pay an initial enrolment fee and an annual subscription. No interest is charged but full payment in settlement of the account must be made each month.

Store card   Store cards operate on similar lines to Access and Barclaycard and, like charge cards, are independent of the banks. They are becoming increasingly popular with major stores such as Marks and Spencer and House of Fraser and allow store card holders to purchase goods within the store on credit. A specified amount of initial credit is given and account holders receive a regular statement.

Cash card—immediate access to cash.   Provided the bank considers that you are a responsible person it will issue you with a **cash card** which enables you to get money from a cash machine outside banking hours. You are issued with a personal number which you should memorise (only write it down if you absolutely need to, and certainly don't keep the number anywhere near your cash card). If you work for a small company take great care that only staff authorised to do so know the cash card number and ensure that if you need to record it, it is locked away and unobtainable by anyone else.

Cash cards enable you not only to obtain cash but also to order a new cheque book or statement, or request an up-to-date display or print-out of the balance of your account. Some machines, particularly in building societies, enable you also to pay money into your account.

Fig. 9.3   *A cash card*

Fig. 9.4   *A cash dispenser*

(iv) Automatic payment—standing order, direct debit, Bank Giro, BACS and Autopay

Standing order.   A standing order is an instruction to the bank by an account holder to pay on his behalf and directly from his current account, a regular payment at a regular time, such as monthly or yearly. The amount of the payment must remain the same over a period of time and may only be changed with written notification from the account holder. The final date of the payment may be left open, in which case the account holder must inform the bank in writing that payment should cease. A standing order form must be completed by the account holder authorising payment. **Standing orders** are particularly useful for payment of regular accounts such as savings, insurance premiums and loan repayments.

Direct debit.   Direct debit is similar in principle to standing orders in that it gives the bank authorisation to make payment on the account holder's behalf without the use of cheque, cash or credit card, *but:*

- the amount may be different each time payment is made
- payment may be made at any time, at regular or irregular intervals.

The account holder signs a **direct debit** form, prepared by the company receiving payments, giving authority for that company to request irregular amounts from the bank whenever payment is due.

Some account holders may have reservations about signing a form giving such freedom in demands for payment. However, the direct debit system is carefully controlled and the company asking for payment must inform the account holder of the date and amount due *before* payment is made by the bank. Direct debit payments may be cancelled by writing to your bank. It is not necessary to inform the company.

Remember

Standing orders and direct debit save time and trouble.
Standing orders pay *regular* amounts at *regular* times.
Direct debit pays *any* amount at *any* time.
Direct debit is safe—banks keep careful control.

Bank Giro.   Money can be paid into your own account using a credit slip which may also be a Bank Giro slip. **Bank Giro** may also be used to pay money into someone else's account at a different bank or branch.

One cheque is written and a credit transfer or Giro slip is completed giving details of the account to be paid. Many householders use Bank Giro to pay bills such as gas and electricity, where the credit transfer slip forms a tear-off portion at the bottom of the bill. It is possible to pay several bills at once by completing a summary slip in addition to the slips and writing one cheque to cover the whole amount. Many companies use Bank Giro to pay wages to their employees. A summary sheet is completed giving all necessary details of employee's names, banks and account numbers and one cheque is made out to cover the entire amount. The individual amounts are transferred to the employee's accounts and the total is deducted from the company's account.

BACS (Banker Automated Clearing Services Limited) and Autopay. Using these systems banks and their customers can transfer money electronically between accounts. Since their introduction, growth has been outstanding and while Credit Transfer is still widely used, increasing numbers of companies are favouring **BACS** and **Autopay** for payment of wages and salaries. With both methods all necessary details are stored on computer and the data is transferred directly to the computer of whichever bank the company uses. Both systems save time and paperwork and mean that an employee's account can be credited almost immediately the company's account is debited.

The success of these systems is due mainly to the resulting savings in terms of efficiency and cost saving.

- Administrative costs are reduced since there is no need for handling of cash, cheques and paper bank giro credits.
- BACS charges are considered to be lower than traditional charges.
- Delays in making and receiving payments are reduced.

Remember BACS provides credit	
without cash	with accuracy
without cheques	with flexibility
without delay	with security
without paper	with economy

A company using BACS may submit information (data) on tape, diskette or cassette either direct to BACS at Edgware, London or through its City Reception Office. Delivery can be made by messenger, security transport, Datapost or normal mail. Data received at BACS by

9.00 pm on Day One can be processed on Day Two with funds avail-able in the Payee's account by 9.30 am on Day Three. Any company not having access to a computer compatible with BACS may use a computer bureaux who will submit data on behalf of their clients. There is also the facility to use BACSTEL, a direct telecommuni-cations link which connects directly with the BACS computer centre at Edgware. Using Bacstel, processing is almost instantaneous.

(v) Overdraft
By arrangement with the bank an account holder may withdraw cash or make payments for amounts in excess of the balance held in the current account. The amount of the overdraft may be repaid over a period of time which is usually also agreed with the manager of the branch. Interest is charged on the amount still owing at any given time.

(vi) Banker's draft
A banker's draft is a cheque drawn on the bank and can be used to make large payments when the payee is reluctant to accept one of the drawer's own cheques. For instance, you may be buying a car and the seller asks for payment before the car is driven away. You, as the purchaser, are naturally reluctant to carry large amounts of cash around and so choose to use a banker's draft. To do this you must present your branch with a cheque for the amount of the purchase price of the car. The bank will then debit your account and give you a cheque drawn by them, e.g. a Barclays Bank cheque, for the same amount as your own cheque. Such a cheque guarantees payment to the garage and will not 'bounce'. Companies trading with new customers for the first time may ask for payment by banker's draft if they have no guarantee of the customers' creditworthiness.

(vii) Statement
The bank issues **statements** at regular intervals agreed with the account holder (usually monthly) showing all transactions which have taken place and been processed over the period. Statements are usually self-explanatory and indicate the nature of the transaction such as DD (direct debit), SO (standing order), CD (cash dispenser) and similar. It is important to note that the statement dates transactions as they are processed, a date which may not necessarily be the same as the day the transaction occurred. For example, a cheque will usually be presented at the payee's account a few days after it was originally written. Processing can take three days and only then will the transaction appear on the drawer's statement.

Personal account holders should make a habit of checking their statements and keeping a careful record of all their transactions. Business account statements will be more detailed and complex and will normally be dealt with by the clerical staff in the Accounts Department.

(viii) 'Home banking'
It is important to note that there are moves towards '**home banking**' services whereby account holders can link into computerised records of their own accounts via a modem at home. With such services they can obtain immediate up-to-date records of all their banking transactions. Bank of Scotland were the first bank to introduce such a system.

(c) Accounts for borrowing

(i) Loan account
Loans are available for specific amounts and are usually taken out for particular purchases or projects. Private individuals may borrow money in this way to buy a car or extend a house while business organisations may use the loan facility to purchase machinery, or to build or expand their factories. A loan account is opened in which the account holder will be credited with a specific amount which must be repaid within a given period of time. Interest may be charged in one of two ways:

Personal Loan—normally a fixed rate of interest is decided at the outset and does not change throughout the period of repayment. Also the amount of interest payable is based on the original sum borrowed and does not reduce during the period of the loan. For example, if £1000 is borrowed to be repaid over a period of two years with interest at a rate of 20%, then the interest is calculated on the original amount borrowed, i.e. 20% of £1000 = £200, therefore the total amount to be repaid is £1000 + £200 = £1200 over the two year period.

Loan Account—interest is charged on the balance outstanding at any particular time during the period of the loan. Therefore as the balance reduces the amount of interest payable reduces accordingly. If say a loan was originally taken out for a period of two years and is repaid in less time, the amount of interest chargeable will be correspondingly lower, unlike a personal loan where the amount of interest payable is fixed at the start. This is referred to as a 'reducing balance'. Calculation is done as for an overdraft, the major difference being that a separate loan account is opened. The rate of interest on this account may be higher than with a personal loan even though the total amount of interest paid may be lower.

Depending on the size of the loan the bank may require either a guarantor (someone who guarantees to repay the loan if the account holder defaults) and/or collateral (items or valuable papers offered as security against the account holder being unable to repay the loan).

(ii) Instant credit account

Barclays Bank, amongst others, offer a service whereby a customer may open a special account which allows money to be borrowed when needed and which pays interest when the account is in credit. Barclays Bank run an account of this type called Cashplan. The account holder must make a minimum monthly payment into the account and is then given instant credit to an amount which is based on the monthly payment. For example, a monthly payment of £10 could allow credit up to £3000. Interest is payable on the amount borrowed and charged to the account quarterly.

(d) Accounts with interest

(i) Deposit account

Money may be left in a deposit account where it will receive interest for as long as required. The amount of interest can vary from bank to bank and, in addition to the current bank rate, may depend on the amount deposited in the account, with larger amounts receiving a higher rate of interest. It is customary for notice to be required if a withdrawal is to be made but many banks will allow money to be withdrawn on demand. Indeed there are deposit accounts which specifically allow for immediate withdrawal and require no notification.

(ii) Savings account

Savings accounts are intended for saving small amounts of money and are particularly useful for teenagers and children. Interest is given, together with other attractions such as saving club membership and a magazine.

(e) Budget accounts

Budget accounts are particularly suitable for householders who may transfer regular amounts to the budget account from which the bank will undertake to pay household bills, such as gas, electricity and so on. These accounts relieve the account holder of the problems incurred when large amounts have to be paid to settle bills at irregular times during the year.

(f) Other services

(i) *Travelling abroad*

Travellers cheques may be purchased from the bank and cashed at any time.

Eurocheque and Eurocard can be used abroad in exactly the same way as cheques and cheque cards are used in Britain. Apart from being more secure, one of the major advantages of Eurocheque and Eurocard is that unlike travellers cheques and foreign currency, no pre-payment is necessary. The money only comes out of the personal cheque account when the cheques are used and processed. Eurocheques are written in the local currency and can be used to pay bills in shops, hotels, restaurants and garages in most European countries guaranteed for up to £100. A set charge is made for each cheque used plus a percentage handling charge.

(ii) *Night safe*

Cash, cheques and valuables may be deposited in a night safe after banking hours. The company using the service will be issued with a key and identity.

(iii) *Financial help and advice*

In addition to the above services banks provide financial help and advice, and service in other ways, including:

mortgages
investment
pensions
tax, wills and trusts
insurance

Words to remember

Bank Giro Credit   This allows you to pay money into your own or someone else's account by filling in a form and paying the money in at the bank.

Clearing a cheque   A cheque is an instruction in writing from you to your bank, telling them pay the amount indicated to the person or company named on the cheque. That person will pay the cheque into his own bank who will collect payment from your bank. This collection process is called clearing. It is carried out by computer and usually takes three to four working days.

Drawer   The account holder who pays the money from his or her account.

Payee   The person who receives the money when you draw a cheque in his or her favour.

Bank Service	Secretarial Involvement
Cheque book	Collecting relevant figures and completing cheques ready for signature. Keeping an up-to-date balance of cheques issued.
Cash card Cheque card Credit card Access Visa American Express Diners Eurocheque	Ensuring they are up-to-date, signed and that old ones are destroyed. Keeping a note in your diary or follow-up system of renewal dates.
Standing order Direct debit	Completing S/O and D/D forms for loan repayments, insurance premiums, etc. Changing payment amounts and dates. Checking and following up final dates.
Overdraft Loan	Writing letters of application or completing forms. Completing transfer payment forms. Checking that repayment is going through.
Credit transfer	Collecting necessary details (e.g. employee work no, bank account no, etc.) and completing documentation.
Night safe facilities	Completing documentation.
Bank statements	Checking against documentation in the office and filing.

Bank or building society—keep up with developments

It is very important that you, as a good secretary, should know something about the services with which you are dealing. Keep abreast with developments and news and pick up leaflets whenever you can. This chapter has tried to cover much of the basics of what you need to know. Take care to keep up with current bank information since banks are striving all the time to provide new and improved services. Take note, too, of building society services. Many of the restrictions on what they *were* allowed to offer have been removed and therefore there is now much overlap betwen the services offered by these two major establishments. In addition to innovations there is also much competition between the individual banks and building societies.

Do You Know?

The difference between:
1. Standing order and direct debit?
2. Cash card and credit card?
3. Current account and deposit account?
4. Overdraft and loan?
5. Eurocheques and travellers cheques?
6. Credit transfer and BACS?

How to:
7. Make a large payment in this country without using cheque or cash?
8. Make small payments in this country that are guaranteed by the bank?
9. Make small payments abroad that are guaranteed by the bank?

9.2 Understanding Wages and Salaries

How much do I need to know?

If you have spent any time already considering the topic of 'wages and salaries', you may, at this point be saying 'no thank you—I've done this one before—so many forms, so many figures, I'll give it a miss!' However, you will very soon realise as you begin work (if you haven't already), that some of the figures which concern you most during your working life will be those connected with your salary. You will soon realise the importance, from a personal point of view, of taking some note of how the figures are arrived at, what they mean and why they change. In spite of the increased use of computers in the process of payment of wages and salaries there are, in addition, several forms which you will come across during your working life.

There are three levels on which you as an employee and secretary must take note.

(a) As an employee: you need to understand your own salary, pay-slip and other documents.

(b) As a secretary: you may have junior staff asking for advice and explanations of their own pay slips.

(c) At a specialist level: in a department which deals with wages and salaries (Personnel or Accounts): you will need more detailed knowledge of your own company systems.

(a) As an employee

If you understand how your own salary is arrived at you will be in a much stronger position to help other employees with any queries they may have about the figures and forms involved.

You may begin your first job having completed no forms at all. However, there are several you will come across during the course of your working life. To begin with you may not consider that they are important but as you move through your career—change jobs, increase your salary and your commitments—you will find that it becomes increasingly important that you know what the forms are all about.

(i) *When you start work: Form P15*

Your employer will give you a brief form to complete which he returns to the tax office. You will also receive a Coding Claim Form (P15) which you must complete. A P15 gives the tax office (Inland Revenue) the information they need on which they can calculate the amount of tax you must pay. If you are in a part-time job or on a government scheme you may not need to pay tax (this will depend on your total annual earnings from any other sources, which you should be honest about).

(ii) *Tax Return: Form P1*

If you have worked before you must every year (or every two years if your tax affairs are fairly simple) complete a Form P1, commonly known as a **Tax Return**. The purpose of the Tax Return is to enable the Inland Revenue to calculate how much tax you should pay. In the early stages of your career completing the Tax Return is a relatively simple task. But as you get older and your personal circumstances get more complex (children, savings, other income, expenses), completing of the P1 becomes a more difficult task and many families with complicated incomes entrust the job to an accountant.

(iii) *Notice of Coding: Form P2*

Either when you take your first job or when you inform the Inland

Revenue of any changed circumstances, you will receive a P2 (Notice of Coding) which tells you what your **code number** is. The code number is used to calculate the amount of tax you must pay and is based on your personal circumstances. Whenever your circumstances change you must inform the tax office. If you do not complete a P2 or are not allocated a tax code before you are paid for the first time you will be put on **emergency code** which may be higher than the correct figure and will result in your paying too much tax. If this happens tax will be refunded after the correct code has been issued and your employer knows how much to deduct.

(iv) Pay-slip

You may be paid weekly or monthly, and you may receive your pay in cash, or by cheque, or by direct transfer to your bank account such as Bank Giro, BACS or Autopay (see Section 9.1). When you are paid you will receive a '**pay-slip**' which details how the final figure has been arrived at and will show gross salary, overtime, backpay and deductions.

(v) Deductions

To understand what the figures mean you must know a little about the two types of deductions from your salary:

Statutory: (compulsory by law)	Pay As You Earn (PAYE)
	National Insurance
Voluntary:	Savings
	Social Fund
	Union Contributions
	Pension Scheme
	Health Schemes

Pay As You Earn.   Tax is deducted weekly or monthly from anyone who earns a regular income over a specified amount, known as the **tax threshold**. The tax threshold changes with each government's successive budgets. The advantage of PAYE is that employees can spread their tax payments over the year—a proportion is paid to the Inland Revenue each time the employee is paid. Tax allowances are made for various personal circumstances, and income up to a government specified figure is tax free. The conditions of the allowances are susceptible to change and you should make a habit of taking note of annual government budget changes.

National Insurance. National Insurance contributions are also deducted weekly or monthly and are paid by both the employer on the employee's behalf and by the employee. Contributions are calculated as a percentage of your earnings to cover such medical treatment as is provided by the state (hospital, optician, etc.) and also covers benefits such as unemployment, sickness, pension and other state allowances. Both amounts and benefits are liable to change and successive governments are likely to take out old and bring in new schemes at any time. When you begin work you will receive a National Insurance number which you will keep for your working life. Although it will probably appear on your pay-slip you should also keep a careful record of it elsewhere since you are likely to have to quote it at any time in the process of applying for jobs, health treatment and so on.

(vi) At the end of the tax year—Form P60
At the end of every tax year each employee receives a P60 which shows the total amount earned and tax deducted that year. (The tax year runs from 6 April to 5 April the following year.)

(vii) Changing jobs—Form P45
When you change jobs you will receive a P45 from your old employer which you should hand to your new employer. A P45 shows the amount of tax deducted up to the date of leaving and your code number. If you do not take a P45 with you to your new employment, tax will be deducted according to an emergency code. If you lose your P45 or do not work for some time you may need to complete a P15.

(b) As a secretary

When you are a secretary you must expect junior staff to come to you with their problems. A major concern of all employees is that of their income figure and how it has been arrived at. In addition to recognising the tax forms and their purposes it is also necessary to understand how employees' wages and salaries are arrived at. There is often confusion as to why some payments for work are referred to as **salary** and others as **wages**.

(i) Salaries
These are normally negotiated at interview and are fixed, regardless of the number of hours worked. Secretaries are normally on a salary, as are management and professions such as nurses and teachers. Staff on a salary may be on an **incremental** pay structure which means that the

increases are pre-arranged and progress yearly, until the employee reaches the top of the incremental scale. Other annual increases are discretionary and are decided by employers on an individual basis; often they will depend on how well the individual is seen to be doing their job, e.g. 'merit awards'. Many businesses today carry out STAFF APPRAISAL, whereby an assessment of an individual's progress is made by both management and the individual themselves. The appraisal may be in the form of a written or verbal statement or a combination of both.

(ii) Wages

These are generally paid weekly, although there is a move towards fortnightly and monthly payment. Contrary to popular opinion, the majority of wages are still paid by cash although many companies try to encourage their employees to open bank accounts so that direct payment or payment by cheque may be made. Companies prefer not to handle cash for security and administrative reasons. Some large companies have found it beneficial to allow one of the major banks to open a branch on their premises with part-time hours. This arrangement is particularly suitable where the company is situated a distance from any of the major banks.

Wages are calculated in a number of different ways, all of which centre around a **basic** figure.

Time or hourly rate   Rate set for each hour worked. Any extra time worked is paid for at a higher rate (overtime)—double time or time and a half. Encourages longer hours and quality is maintained.

Example—service industries where production can't be measured, e.g. canteen staff, draughtsmen, or production staff, such as foremen and supervisors.

Workers 'clock in'—i.e. take personal time card, insert it into machine, which automatically prints time of arrival and departure. This can be a computerised process entailing the use of 'keys'. The clocking in machine or computer provides record of attendance which is used to calculate wages.

Bonus Scheme   Paid flat-rate (basic) wage per week PLUS bonus for extra work done over and above basic. Encourages extra production but quality may suffer.

Example—packing boxes.

Piece work   Paid for each item produced or operations carried out. Encourages fast work, but quality may suffer.

Example—sewing buttons on shirts.

Commission Usually paid to salespeople who receive a small basic wage and extra payment for every sale made (commission). Encourages sales.

Example—area salespeople, door-to-door sales staff.

With an understanding of how wages and salaries are arrived at, together with some knowledge of forms, terminology and deductions, you should be able to clarify any basic problems a junior might have. However, where queries are centred around actual calculations and figures then you must refer the junior to the Accounts, Wages or Personnel Department.

(c) At a specialist level

If you work in a department which deals with payment of wages and salaries your knowledge needs to be much greater. Equally, if you work in a small company you will need to have a much more detailed knowledge of the process. This book cannot hope to give you all the detail you will need for three reasons:

1. The whole area of tax and insurance is constantly changing. Successive governments change the figures—allowances and thresholds (the amount you can earn annually before you must pay tax) and the form design. Also computerisation of tax offices is taking place which will lead to different forms and procedures.
2. Each company has its own procedures and it could be misleading to be too specific about the technicalities.
3. Many, many companies are moving towards computerised systems. Small businesses with only a few employees find it economical to use one of the many programs available, even though they may still pay their employees in cash. (Computer programs make the appropriate calculations, indicate how the wages should be made up in cash and will prepare and print wage slips for insertion into the wage packets.)

It cannot be stressed too much that computers are playing an increasingly major part in calculating wages and salaries. They can do in seconds what it takes even the quickest calculator operator hours to do. Many computer companies will take the burden of calculating wages from small companies and do the job for them—processing the figures, issuing the paperwork and storing the data. There is also an abundance of specialist computer programs for small businesses to choose from which can be run on desk top computers. Such facilities benefit everyone since the small business is relieved of a major headache at a relatively small cost while the computer company can offer an excellent personal service in which they are specialised.

(i) Tax Deduction Card—P11

In addition to the forms already mentioned you will come across the P11 or Tax Deduction Card. One card is held for each employee and gives a complete picture of their current wages and deductions. It is calculated cumulatively, beginning in the first week of the tax year and shows:

- Gross pay each week.
- Total amount earned in the current tax year.
- Total deductions (statutory and voluntary are shown separately).
- Total figure on which tax must be paid.
- Total tax payable to the current week.
- Tax deducted (or refunded) in the current week or month.

Payment direct from disc

It is also worth noting that the major banks prefer computerised services such as BACS and Autopay (see Section 9.1) rather than Bank Giro since it speeds up the process and cuts down on paper handling. It is now possible for large companies to take computer discs, tapes or cassettes to their bank and the bank is able to process the information direct from disc. (The disc contains all the information the bank needs to make the week's or month's wages payments.)

Remember—PAYE and Tax Tables

Every employee pays a proportion of his yearly income tax each time he is paid by his company. The exact amount is set out in the Tax Tables supplied by the Inland Revenue. Traditionally these lengthy tables (many thousands of numbers) have been referred to by hand.

The Tax Tables can now be stored on disc as part of a 'wages package'. Typically, a mainframe computer can now calculate the wages of many employees in only a few minutes.

(d) Types of pay

Basic pay   the amount you earn without overtime or deductions

Back pay   additional payment which amends any short pay which may be due to:
—miscalculations on the part of the employer
—wage increase due from a date already passed

Sick pay   paid by employer if employee is ill and completes appropriate certification (self-certification if absent for a limited number of days, a doctor's signature for a longer period)

Holiday pay   employees are allowed an agreed period of absence on holiday during which time they will be paid—the paid holiday entitlement usually increases in proportion to the employee's length of service with the company

Equal pay   the law stipulates that men and women doing the same job must be paid an equal amount.

Do You Know?

1. Which forms you may have to complete when you start work?
2. Which form you will receive every year around the end of April?
3. Which information you receive on the form around the end of April?
4. Which annual form asks for information?
5. Who fills in a Tax Return and why?
6. What a P60 is for?
7. What a P45 is for?
8. What the purpose of a Tax Return is?
9. What the figures on your payslip mean?
10. What deductions you can expect to be made from your salary?

9.3 Petty Cash

How much do I need to know?

During the normal routine of business life there are many times when small amounts of cash are needed for incidental expenses. The obvious items are tea and coffee, stamps and travel expenses but there are other occasions when you or your executive may need items which are not available from existing office services. Naturally you are not expected to finance such purchases from your own pocket and most offices keep a cash box for this purpose. This cash is referred to as petty cash and it must be carefully accounted for. Procedures for obtaining and issuing petty cash will vary but the basic principles are the same and the secretary must be familiar with these principals since she may find herself involved at any level:

- purchasing incidental items with petty cash
- issuing petty cash to other staff
- obtaining petty cash from Chief Cashier or bank.

(a) What is petty cash?

Petty cash is the cash used to pay for incidental items and bills. It is usually kept by the secretary or senior clerk in a lockable cash box and a careful record is kept of cash received and cash issued in a petty cash book. The petty cash book is usually kept on the 'Imprest' system.

- A sum of money estimated to be sufficient for a given period (e.g. a week or month) is 'disbursed' (issued) to the petty cashier (secretary or clerk).
- During the period this money is used to pay for small purchases or expenses.
- At the end of the period the petty cashier receives an amount to cover the expenditure of the period just gone, thus bringing the total cash up to the original amount.

For example:

Petty cashier starts week with	£20.00 in cash box and recorded in petty cash book
During the week she issues	£18.50 in expenses and purchases
At the end of the week	£1.50 is left in cash box and recorded in book
Petty cashier receives	£18.50 from cashier or bank
Total is restored to	£20.00 to start the next week or period

(b) Issuing petty cash

(i) Vouchers and receipts

Petty cash may be issued either in advance of any expenditure, particularly if larger amounts are involved, or after the purchase or payment has been made. In either case a **petty cash voucher** should be completed and signed by the claimant and usually also by a second person responsible for authorising the claim. This second signature may be an executive, if a junior is making a claim, or the petty cashier herself. If you make a purchase for which you intend to claim a refund out of petty cash you should endeavour always to obtain a **receipt.** Similarly you should encourage your executive and others to do the same. Some companies will not reimburse cash if no receipt is issued.

Fig. 9.5 *Petty cash voucher*

Petty Cash Voucher	Folio			
	Date			
Required for	VAT amount		Amount including VAT	
	£	p	£	p
Total				
Signature				
Authorised by				

(ii) The petty cash book
The petty cash book provides an important record of all receipts and expenditure and must be kept up-to-date. It is subject to the usual accounting checks and auditing and therefore must be accurate. Ensure that all items are entered in the correct columns, that the totals are correct and that all the figures balance. The procedure is as follows.

1. Enter all details of receipts on one side (usually the left)—date, amount, reference number (CB number).
2. Enter details of each expense claimed on the other side (usually the right)
    (a) date
    (b) voucher number
    (c) total details of expense (amount + VAT) in total column
    (d) breakdown of expense in appropriate column with VAT in VAT column

3. At end of period (week or month) prepare to restore imprest:
   (a) total each expense column
   (b) ensure that total figures agree—vertically and horizontally
   (c) subtract the total cash paid out from the imprest and enter it underneath as the balance
   (d) total the cash received column and cash paid out column and draw a double line underneath each total (these figures should now be the same)
   (e) transfer the balance (amount left) to the receipts column (balance b/f)
4. Obtain cash from the cashier equal to that which has been spent; details from the petty cash book are transferred to the ledger account by the cashier.

Do You Know?

1. Where to obtain petty cash?
2. What to use a petty cash voucher for?
3. Who signs a petty cash voucher?
4. How to balance a petty cash book?
5. What sort of items are paid for from petty cash?

9.4 Control of Stationery and Stock

How much do I need to know?

The degree to which you will be concerned with stationery and other stock will depend on the size and policy of your company. In a small company you must expect to take a major role in ordering stationery and organising its storage whereas in a large company the organis-ation of all stock will probably be controlled from a central point.

(a) What kind of stock?

A secretary's major concern will be stationery, although she may, and hopefully will, find herself being consulted about major changes in office furniture and other necessary equipment.

Types of stationery you will use

plain paper	bond, bank (flimsy) and card
printed paper	letterheads, memos, message pads, circu-lation and action slips, forms, compliment slips, business cards
envelopes	numerous qualities and sizes

notebooks	shorthand and general purpose
ribbons	typewriter and printer, carbon and fabric, corrector
forms	particular to your department
files and folders	various types for paper, microfilm, computer printout
essential 'sundries'	sellotape, paper clips, staples, etc.
carbon paper	different qualities available: one-time or film

(b) Stationery control

You may be responsible for ordering all the stationery in a small company. Most large companies order stationery centrally and each departmental secretary is responsible for maintaining her own supplies from a central store. The normal method is to complete a stationery requisition form and present it to the person who is responsible for issuing stock. The stock may be issued immediately or there may be a procedure for requesting stock during a given period before the issue time. Most central departments have restricted times for issuing stock so you must be organised and forward thinking in your requirements. It goes without saying that you must take care not to run out of paper, envelopes, or any other important stationery, but it is equally important to remember that stock costs money and that unnecessary stockpiling (keeping more than you need in your cupboard) is not only wasting valuable funds, it is also taking up valuable space which could be used for something more immediately necessary. Have a system for recording your own stock in your cupboard. Many people have a simple list on the cupboard door on which they make a record every time they remove a ream of paper or packet of envelopes.

If your department supplies stock to many office staff you may need to develop a more sophisticated system. If you have access to a computer system or have your own stand alone computer it may be advisable to investigate the several different stock control software programs available. Once you know how to set the data up and enter the figures you will find that keeping records of your stock is a very simple process.

(i) *For stock control to work efficiently*

 — Stationery should be available when it is needed (don't take the cupboard key home and lose it!)

- Stationery should be stored in cool, dry and dark conditions where it will not deteriorate in quality (a lockable cupboard away from a radiator is adequate for small quantities of stock).
- Stationery should be easily accessible—label shelves and stock clearly and keep the cupboard well organised (old stock at the front and new stock behind and little used stock at the top).
- Packets should only be opened as and when needed (not several at once).
- One person should be in charge overall to issue stock to other staff.

(ii) Stock records

To ensure that stock levels are always sufficient, anyone in control of stock should ensure that an adequate system for the maintenance of correct levels of stock is used. Whether this system is carried out on paper or computer the principles are the same.

- One record is kept for each item, and each variety of that item (colour, size, etc.).
- The record shows a description and a reference number.
- A maximum level over which stock should not go is set; this avoids overstocking and tying up too much capital in unnecessary stock.
- When setting the maximum figure consider:
  rate at which stock is used
  storage space available
  how quickly the item will deteriorate
  whether the item will become out-of-date (names, numbers, etc.)
  financial resources to purchase the stock.
- A re-order level or re-order interval should be set:
  re-order level: when stock level reaches this figure orders should be placed to replenish the stock
  re-order interval: stock is ordered at regular intervals regardless of quantity remaining.
- Both methods should take account of how long delivery of new stock takes and the level should be set to ensure that supplies are always available.

In addition to the above information a stock record card will show dates that stock was issued and received together with the balance remaining. It may also show a re-order level and name or names of suppliers of the item.

(iii) Things you should know

- Quantities of paper are measured in REAMS—1 ream=500 sheets.
- Paper size is measured in terms of a number prefixed by A—A0 is the largest (841× 1189 mm) A1 equals half A0, A2 equals half A1 and so on.
- Envelopes are measured in terms of a number prefixed by C to correspond with paper sizes.
- Quality of paper is measured in weight for a given area—the heavier the paper the better is its quality.
- Better quality paper is generally referred to as BOND.
- Flimsy paper is generally referred to as BANK.
- Envelopes can be made from:
    bond paper
    cartridge (strong brown) paper
    padded or bubbled paper
    polythene or fabric.

(c) Stocktaking

Normally a physical count is taken of all stock. Even when the procedure has been computerised, many companies still prefer to do a manual count of stock since computers do not take account of the human factor. Many companies find that security—theft and pilfering—is a major problem.

Large organisations use one of two methods for stocktaking—periodic and perpetual inventory.

Periodic stocktaking is done at regular intervals (often twice a year). Actual stock is compared with records held on stock cards or computer files. For some companies this is an immense task and involves the whole work force. In some cases production is stopped for the period of stocktaking or weekend overtime is worked by many of the staff.

Perpetual inventory is considered (a) to be a more reliable deterrent against theft and (b) to give a more accurate overall picture since it is done at random throughout the company. With this system there is no need for production to cease since professional staff will take any department at any time and usually without warning.

Computerised stock records
Computers are increasingly being used to maintain stock records even by the smallest companies. The process is very similar to the manual

process except that the information is input by keyboard, light pen, bar code reader, EPOS or some similar device (see Chapter 7). **Stock cards** are completed on screen and stored. Each time an item is issued or received the data is recorded and the program updates the figures immediately. Re-order levels are registered immediately they are reached and where a system is centrally linked to the supplier, goods too can be ordered 'down the line' without the need for any paper work changing hands.

Stock valuation (how much the stock is worth) can also be done automatically since prices are also stored within the program. In fact stock value is updated immediately there is a change in the quantity of stock held, in its price, or any other appropriate data.

Be organised and be thorough

Poor stocktaking and poor control of stock are caused by bad organisation and lead to wasted resources and wasted capital which could be put to other more profitable uses. They also may lead to a situation where there are insufficient materials for a company to continue to trade profitably. If you are in a small company it is imperative that you do your own stationery stocktaking at regular intervals.

Remember 'FIFO' and 'LIFO'

FIRST IN FIRST OUT—the oldest materials and stationery should be used up first.

LAST IN FIRST OUT—the newest materials and stationery should be used up first.

Do You Know?

1. How stationery should be stored?
2. What factors to consider when deciding how much to order?
3. When to use bond paper and when to use bank paper?
4. What FIFO means?
5. What information must be included on a stock card?
6. The difference between a re-order level and a re-order interval?
7. Why stocktaking is important?
8. How computers are used in stock control?

Secretarial Task Nine

Problem 1

You are secretary in a medium size company which imports electrical kitchen goods. In the company there are five senior management staff, two sales staff who spend two days each a week in the office and three clerical staff and a junior. You provide secretarial services for all the management staff. You have only recently joined the company and when you arrived you quickly became aware that each of the executives were in the habit of helping themselves to stationery and other office supplies as and when they felt like it. Stationery is stored in a small windowless office which is lockable but there is only one key which sometimes disappears. When you began work with the company the stationery room was quite chaotic and you have since spent some time attempting to organise it.

The final straw came, however, when the Managing Director asked you to send out an urgent letter to all your customers, (numbering approximately 500) informing them of an electrical fault on one model of kettle which had come to light that day. After preparing the letter and address file you find to your horror that there is insufficient headed paper left for you to send the letter that night. You then have an additional problem since it takes at least a week to have more stationery printed.

After this incident you decide that drastic action is needed and that an acceptable and reliable system needs to be introduced to avoid similar incidents. You decide to prepare a report for the Managing Director outlining the system which you would recommend.

Prepare a report which clearly explains your recommended system and reasons for its introduction.

Problem 2

The company runs an induction course every six months for all employees who have joined the company during that period. The Personnel Manager normally likes to back up the information he gives the new staff with handouts. He considers that the three areas which cause much confusion are:

wage slips
petty cash
stationery

In your previous job you had experience in similar areas and the

Personnel Manager has asked you to assist with the handout for the induction course.

He has asked you to prepare three handouts explaining:

(a) wage slips
(b) reimbursement for purchasing small items necessary for use at work which are not available from stores
(c) how to use the system for obtaining items of stationery.

The company pays all employees using BACS and since many new staff do not have bank accounts when they join the company the Personnel Manager would also like to spend a short time explaining to them:

all they need to know about current accounts
how the BACS system works.

In addition to the handouts the personnel manager would also like to illustrate his talk and has asked you to prepare OHP transparencies which he can use to support the points he is making.

Prepare clear handouts and transparencies which he would be able to use as part of his talk.

Examination Questions

1. Choose three of the following cards and explain how they are used. Suggest an occasion when John Brown could make use of each card.

    (a) charge card
    (b) cheque card
    (c) service card
    (d) business card
    (e) phone card

    LCCI PSC OO&SP

2. (a) What information would you expect to find on your pay advice slip?
   (b) Show how Comlon International plc could arrange for the net pay amount to be paid into the employee's bank account rather than paying him by cash or giving him a cheque.

    LCCI SSC OP

3. Your Office Supervisor is concerned about the lack of any system of stationery control in the office in which you work and has asked you to recommend a suitable system which would cover the following points.

    (a) There should always be an adequate stock of each item.

    (b) Issues of stationery should be supervised.

    (c) Stock levels could easily be determined without physically counting all the stock.

    (d) Due attention should be paid to safety and security.

Make your recommendations in the form of a memorandum.

LCCI SSC OP

Chapter 10

Meetings

How much do I need to know?

You may be involved in meetings at any level, from straightforward arrangements to taking minutes and follow up. You must be prepared at all levels since any oversights on your part can result in bad feelings and bad organisation.

10.1 What Constitutes a Meeting?

Meetings play a vital part in the running of any business, whether it is a large multinational organisation or a small family concern. Meetings, formal and informal, take place during most of the working day. Two partners in a small company may have an 'informal' meeting about a particular current problem or project over lunch or in the office. In this type of meeting is may be that nothing is written down formally, but that decisions are made which will lead to one of the partners taking further action, such as making enquiries about purchasing a wordprocessor or costing the employment of temporary staff during the summer. Other meetings may involve several people and major decisions on expenditure, staffing, planning and so on. Such meetings will require careful records to avoid misunderstandings and to ensure that all participants have a clear understanding of the discussions which took place and decisions which were made.

Meeting

A discussion between two or more people, with or without a written record of what was said or of any decisions which were made.

10.2 Why Have Meetings?

Some small businesses may appear to run without 'meetings'. Of course, in the case of a self-employed tradesman or anyone who works on his own, there would be little need for meetings within the firm, since only one person is there to make decisions. However, once running a business involves more than one person then there is an obvious need for consultation and discussion.

Some employers issue instructions to their employees without consultation and run businesses quite successfully; however, most companies are involved in negotiations and discussion at all levels. Open any daily newspaper and you will find instances of management/union negotiations—some more successful than others. The success of these negotiations, which contrary to popular opinion are *not always* concerned with pay, will vary according to the style of management in the organisation.

So why have meetings at all, why not leave all decisions to the Managing Director or owner of the company? The meetings which are going on in any company all the time may have one or more of several functions:

- to make formal reports, for example, to shareholders, and committees
- to provide an opportunity for face-to-face discussion
- to provide an opportunity for decision making
- to report on progress
- to inform the workforce of management functions
- to dispel rumours by giving accurate information
- to gauge the feeling of management or workforce
- to suggest ideas
- to plan for future activity.

10.3 Types of Meetings

Meetings held within a business may either be 'formal', 'informal' or 'semi-formal'. They may also be by pre-arrangement, or impromptu, but frequently involve only a small number of personnel. In addition they can consist of members from within a department or representatives from several departments; those in attendance may be on the same management level or meetings may be held by the management to inform or brief less senior staff within one, or more than one, department. Meetings can be held, for example, to follow up the sales progress of a new product, to discuss a change in policy, or perhaps to establish the viability of a new marketing and advertising campaign. Such meetings may not just involve the sales staff—representatives of other departments may need to be involved in order, for example, to provide any necessary technical information which may be required as part of the advertising material.

Formal meetings will be held less frequently and generally involve more people than informal or semi-formal ones. One formal meeting which is usually held in a large company is the **Annual General Meeting**, at which up to several thousands of the firm's shareholders may be present.

The procedures for such meetings follow a much stricter pattern and to a large extent are governed by the Companies Act in terms of the frequency with which they should be held and the procedures involved. All limited companies, both public and private, must give 21 days clear notice of Annual General Meetings and must file appropriate documentation with the Registrar of Companies.

The most common formal meetings held by large companies are:

- Annual General Meeting—required by law and which all shareholders are entitled to attend. The Directors are usually elected at this meeting.

- Extraordinary General Meeting—called by representatives of 10% of the total number of shareholders to discuss a company matter of some urgency.

- Statutory Meeting—required by law when a company begins trading.

- Board Meetings—normally chaired by the company chairman and which, while formal by nature, may be carried out in an informal manner.

10.4 The Secretary's Involvement

The secretary is primarily concerned with preparations and arrangements for meetings. It is normally her responsibility to ensure that:

- adequate notice is given to everyone concerned
- rooms and refreshments are booked well in advance
- paperwork is prepared and distributed to the right people at the right time
- minutes of the meeting are taken, typed, approved and distributed
- follow-up work is carried out by herself and others concerned.

The secretary may or may not have assistance, or may herself be assisting a more senior member of the meeting. In all cases the degree of her responsibilities will vary according to the size and type of meeting. For instance, a secretary to the managing director in a large company may have to arrange a meeting of marketing and sales staff to discuss the progress of a new product on the market. The standard procedure she would follow is:

(a) Before the meeting

The secretary should:

- make a note of the date of the meeting
- book or confirm availability of a suitably sized room
- issue **notice** of meeting to all concerned
- prepare and distribute the **agenda**
- collect together relevant documents and reproduce enough copies for all members if required
- prepare:
  (i) a file for the chairman with all important documents which will be needed during the meeting
  (ii) the chairman's agenda.
- consult the chairman about required refreshments and make appropriate arrangements
- prepare name tags and/or place markers if required and arrange for distribution, either at reception or in the meeting room.

(b) On the day

Check:

- availability of the room
- seating
- ventilation
- heating.

Ensure that each place has the following:

- notepaper
- pen
- agenda
- minutes of previous meeting

- copies of any necessary documentation
- water and glass.

Prepare the **attendance register**.

Arrange for clear notification of where the meeting is and inform reception.

Check availability of name tags.

(c) At the meeting

Ensure that everyone signs the attendance register.

Read minutes of the previous meeting, if required. (It is quite usual to distribute them before the meeting, in which case they are not normally read at the meeting.)

Have the minutes of the previous meeting available for the chairman to sign.

Have files and documents at hand for reference either by yourself, the chairman or other members of the meeting.

Take minutes if required (there may be a minutes secretary in attendance, or a member of the meeting may take the minutes).

(d) After the meeting

Collect all documentation and return to the office file anything which is not needed for further reference or which is confidential.

Prepare minutes:

- type or word process the draft minutes
- agree the draft with the chairman before distribution
- prepare the final copy
- arrange for enough copies to be produced for all members (including those who did not attend)
- distribute minutes to members, perhaps with reminders to those who are to take action following the meeting.

Then:

- send out any necessary correspondence arising from the meeting
- file any outstanding papers
- note the date of the next meeting in your own and your executive's diary.

(e) Checklist

It is a good idea for the secretary to prepare for her own use a check list which covers her duties in relation to meetings. It may be that the meeting will be less formal than that outlined above, in which case she may not be involved in such detailed preparation. However, whatever her degree of responsibility, she must remember that she is the kingpin on which the smooth running of the meeting rests—a room which is too small, a typing error on the date or time, a wrong file brought to the meeting—just one of these could cause major inconvenience and annoyance. *Remember* efficiency and accuracy are vital in meeting preparation.

10.5 In More Detail—the Documents

(a) Notice of meeting

If a meeting is a regular event, say monthly, then the date will have generally been agreed at a previous meeting. In other cases, the date will be arranged by the chairman. In either case the secretary should send to all members a **notice of meeting**. If you look at the example you will see that the important information contained in a notice is

Title of meeting
Place
Date
Time.

A NOTICE OF MEETING IS SHORT AND TO THE POINT

(b) The agenda

The agenda is a list of items to be discussed at a meeting. The items are arranged in the order in which they are to be raised. It is the responsibility of the chairman to ensure that the meeting follows the agenda and does not linger too long on one topic. This helps to avoid the possibility of time running out before other, perhaps more important, issues are reached. There is, however, an agreed order for certain items at the majority of meetings which is as shown in the example following:

Fig. 10.1   *Notice of meeting and agenda*

```
THE DESIGN COMPANY LTD

NOTICE OF MEETING

To:  All Sales Staff

The monthly meeting of all sales staff will be held on
4 March 19.. at 2.00 pm in the Conference Room.

AGENDA

1  Apologies for absence

2  Minutes of previous meeting

3  Matters arising from the minutes

4  Progress report on current sales promotions

5  Proposed promotions for next half year

6  Any other business

7  Date of next meeting
```

(i) **Apologies** for absence are read out.

(ii) The **minutes** of the previous meeting have to be approved by the members. This is to ensure that any inaccuracies and important omissions are rectified. Having an accurate record of the meeting is vital, particularly when important decisions are involved such as those regarding finance, personnel and policy. Once the meeting has agreed that the minutes are an accurate record then the chairman will sign them. Once he has signed them they may not be changed.

(iii) Following the previous meeting, it may have been necessary for further action to be taken on a particular matter. For example, it may have been decided that a sports hall should be built for the use of employees and that at the previous meeting it had been agreed that quotations for the project would be invited. At the following meeting, the quotations received would be made available for the members to study, further discussion would take place and the most competitive one (after taking into account price, suitability, completion date and reputation of company) would be selected and its bidder awarded the contract. Such points come under **matters arising**.

(iv) Other new items for discussion are then listed. This section may be confined to one only or there may be several. The chairman will have taken into account the time available and the complexity or likely length of discussions when arranging the agenda.

(v) The majority of meetings conclude with the following two items:

Any other business (AOB) at which point the members of a meeting may ask for discussion on any topics which are not on the agenda. At this stage the chairman may ask for these topics to be put on the next agenda if they are of major importance, alternatively the topic may be delayed until a later meeting, particularly if it requires detailed discussion and time is limited.

Date of next meeting. If the meeting is a regular occurrence then the date is usually decided at this point. Otherwise members are informed nearer the time in the notice of meeting.

(c) The minutes

The minutes are a written, accurate record of discussion and decisions which took place at a meeting. They should be concise and accurate— although it is important that they are not so brief as to omit important details. Traditionally minutes of meetings were handwritten in a bound **Minute Book** and read out at the next meeting. Only when those in attendance at the meeting had agreed that the minutes were an accurate record would they be signed by the chairman. Once signed they could not be changed.

Today it is more common to type or wordprocess minutes and to keep the signed copy in a looseleaf book or folder. This does mean that it is easier for them to go astray since single sheets can easily be removed and borrowed. Consequently it is wise to take certain precautions.

– Keep the folder carefully locked away in a fireproof cabinet.
– Ensure that only one or a maximum of two people have a key.
– The pages should be numbered and a separate record kept of the last number inserted.
– Every page should be signed by the chairman to ensure the validity of each page.

Normally the minutes will be taken in shorthand by the secretary, or perhaps in longhand by a member of the meeting. Sometimes a 'verbatim' record is required of a meeting. This means that an accurate record of *everything* which was said must be taken. For such records high shorthand speeds are essential—the secretary must be competent at 140 plus. Alternatively a recording machine may be

Fig. 10.2   *Minutes of a meeting*

```
THE   DESIGN   COMPANY   LTD

MINUTES OF THE MONTHLY MEETING OF ALL SALES STAFF HELD ON 4 MARCH
19.. AT 2.00 PM IN THE CONFERENCE ROOM

PRESENT:   Mr John Moore - Chairman
           Mrs Marion Lyon
           Mr Joseph Pearson
           Mr Steve Reeves
           Miss Mary Stevenson


1  APOLOGIES            Apologies were received from Mr Brian Clayton
                        who is attending a conference in Geneva.

2  MINUTES             The minutes of the previous meeting, having
                        been circulated, were taken as read and signed
                        as a correct record of the proceedings.

3  MATTERS ARISING      Mr Reeves reported that he had begun an inves-
                        tigation into the reasons for the unsuccessful
                        advertising campaign of last month and would
                        report on his findings at the next meeting.

4  PROGRESS REPORT      Mrs Lyon reported that this month's promotion
   ON CURRENT SALES     seemed to be very successful and had been
   PROMOTION            well received by most retailers.  A detailed
                        outline of retail outlets and quantities
                        distributed was studied and discussed. Fore-
                        casts suggest that sales will show an increase
                        on last month of at least 75 per cent.

5  PROPOSED            Mr Pearson suggested that in view of
   PROMOTIONS FOR      last month's failure, further promotions
   NEXT HALF YEAR      may prove to be uneconomical.  After lengthy
                        discussion Mr Pearson was asked to prepare a
                        report, in consultation with the Accounts and
                        Marketing Departments, showing full financial
                        details of previous promotions together with
                        suggested reasons for successes and failures.
                        The report should be circulated to all sales
                        staff before the next meeting when further
                        discussion would take place.  It was agreed
                        that no further promotions should be planned
                        before the report had been discussed.

6  ANY OTHER BUSINESS   There was no other business.

7  DATE OF NEXT         5 April 19..
   MEETING


........................ CHAIRMAN

........................ DATE
```

used, although such machines have several disadvantages: the sound may not be clear—there may be interference from other noises in the room such as coughing and traffic noise although newer machines have facilities for overcoming these problems; also a recording gives no indication of who is speaking and, in a large meeting where not every voice may be known to the secretary, identification would be difficult. Where a record of a lengthy speech is required, it is quite common for the speaker to provide a copy of the speech for reproduction if necessary.

When the meeting is over it is usual for the notes taken during the meeting to be produced as draft minutes which are normally shown to the chairman for his approval. The secretary must then prepare the final copy which will be inserted into the Minute Book and usually reproduced for circulation to all who attended the meeting so that they can read the approved minutes before the next meeting. In certain cases the secretary may add reminder notes to the minutes for anyone who has further action to take following any decisions made at the meeting. It is often the case that managers depend on the secretary to remind them of tasks and duties following a meeting and some are notorious for being absent-minded and forgetful. Some secretaries would claim that it is they who run the company rather than the managers.

Secretarial Task Ten

You work for the Company Secretary of a medium size company. He has expressed concern that some secretaries who arrange meetings are not always thorough in their approach to meeting preparation and follow-up and there have been a number of embarrassing moments when valuable customers have been misinformed and misled. He plans to talk to all of the secretaries involved about meeting procedure and would like to give them all two checklists in the hope that the situation will be improved. He wants you to prepare the drafts:

> *Checklist one* Preparation for the meetings and follow-up procedure.
> *Checklist two* At the meeting—points to remember (include some hints on taking minutes).

Examination Question

1. Arriving back at the office after lunch you find the following note from your employer:

    > Have been called out urgently—notice of Sales Managers' Meeting *must* go out, together with agenda. It's scheduled for a fortnight tomorrow at 10.30 in the morning in the Committee Room. Apart from the usual items can you please include 'Target figures for next financial year' and 'Report on Campaign Europa'.

    Draw up the notice of meeting and the agenda.
    PEI SP INTER

Chapter 11

Safety in the Office

11.1 Understanding the Law

Since the Health and Safety at Work Act 1974 came into force, both employers and employees have had responsibility for maintaining a safe working environment. Employers have a duty towards their employees, and employees have a duty towards themselves and each other to maintain a safe environment. Much theory is expounded about safety at work, but it is still too easy, once involved in the job you are doing, to forget the rules and regulations. Unfortunately there are many hundreds of accidents a year which are avoidable–they are caused either by neglect on the part of employer or by laziness and carelessness on the part of the employee. Not only could many of these accidents be avoided completely but the degree of severity of deaths and injuries could be significantly lessened if both employers and employees followed the rules and guidelines laid down by two major Acts of Parliament, and used a great deal more common sense.

The two Acts which the secretary needs to concern herself with are *HASAWA (Health and Safety at Work Act) 1974* and the *Office, Shops and Railway Premises Act 1963*. The whole area of safety–research, education and training, publicity, staffing–is the responsibility of the Commission for Health and Safety at Work. The Commission is headed by an Executive which has the power to ensure that the safety regulations and requirements are carried out in the working environment. They are also empowered to prosecute anyone (employer and employee) in breach of the regulations.

11.2 What does the Law Say?

(a) The Offices, Shops and Railway Premises Act 1963

The Office, Shops and Railway Premises Act 1963 sets down minimum standards for acceptable working conditions. It gives guidance regarding basic requirements such as:

- standards of cleanliness—floors swept at least once a week
- amount of available space per person—minimum 400 cu ft per person
- amount of lighting necessary—windows must be kept clean
- permitted levels of noise
- minimum working temperature—16° C
- amount of ventilation necessary
- provision of drinking water
- provision of separate toilets for men and women
- provision of first-aid facilities—first-aid box available and if more than 150 people are employed then one person must be trained in first-aid
- provision of eating facilities
- precautions against fire—in accordance with the Factories Act and Local Authority fire regulations.

In addition, the Offices, Shops and Railway Premises Act stipulates that it is the responsibility of the employer to ensure that employees are protected from injury or health hazards arising from:

- excessive noise or vibration from machinery on the premises
- stairways and floors which are unsafe
- dangerous machinery which does not have adequate guards or other safety devices
- untrained staff or staff who are unsupervised working on dangerous machinery
- unsafe power points
- trailing cables or wires
- lifting of heavy weights.

(b) Health and Safety at Work Act 1974

Until HASAWA became law, safety of workers and staff was in the hands of the management, although many of the requirements of the Act were not specific enough to satisfy many employees and employers. Remember that HASAWA does not replace the Offices, Shops and Railway Premises Act of 1963 which still applies. HASAWA sought to expand and broaden the area of safety in the working environment so that safety is now no longer just the responsibility of the employer. As an employee, safety is just as much your responsibility as that of your employer and your fellow workers. The joint responsibility of all parties forms one of the major features of the Act. Both management and employees have a legal responsibility to be actively involved in the maintenance of health and safety in factories, offices, building sites and so on. This is fine in theory, you may say, but what does it mean in real terms? What can I do about safety if my employer refuses to co-operate? Equally your employer may ask where his responsibility ends if his employees refuse to wear safety masks which he has supplied them with? Both are fair questions so let us look at the issues in more detail. What, in fact, does HASAWA have to do with today's secretary?

(c) HASAWA and the secretary

First and foremost it is important to understand some of the common causes of accidents in any business. When reading through the list you may say 'but that's obvious, no sensible person would do that'. But reconsider. How often do you act without thinking—reach across a boiling kettle because you can't wait, switch a light off without drying your hands properly, leave a trailing wire across a room because it is difficult or inconvenient to move your equipment nearer the socket? The list of your own short cuts may go no further but spend some time thinking through this list of common causes of accidents:

— emergency exit routes blocked by chairs or boxes

— emergency exit routes kept locked because the key is mislaid or no-one has responsibility for unlocking them in the morning

— boiling kettles left on the floor or edge of a desk because either there are no kitchen/canteen facilities or staff are too lazy to walk

— staff climb on unsuitable chairs to reach high shelves; steps are not provided, they may be broken or inconveniently located

— staff carry too many books, files, etc at once and do not look where they are going; perhaps trollies are not provided or are inconveniently placed

— the layout of the office means that electric machinery can only be used in certain places which results in trailing flexes across the office

- smoking is allowed in offices and smokers do not take sufficient care (a danger to smokers' and non-smokers' health and to safety)
- staff rush along corridors and through doors—maybe they are overworked and therefore need to rush to meet deadlines, or they may just be careless and not think of the consequences of rushing.

The list goes on and on and it doesn't take much imagination to visualise further dangerous situations and their consequences. Unfortunately, the thought 'It won't happen to me' is all too common and without due care on everyone's part you may find yourself numbered among the statistics which show that over 700 000 people suffer accidents at work each year.

11.3 Whose Responsibility?

How can accidents be avoided? What can everyone do to help? Looking at the above list it is easy to see that many accidents are caused because of neglect on the part of the employer. The table on page 230 shows the responsibilities that are borne by employer and employee.

Cause and effect of accidents could form a never-ending list. Common sense normally will tell you and your fellow-employees what is safe and what isn't. Unfortunately common sense does not always prevail and far too many accidents are caused by:

- neglect
- carelessness
- rushing
- lack of concentration
- inadequate training
- poor equipment
- an unhealthy life (insufficient sleep, insufficient exercise, too much alcohol, smoking, drugs)
- inadequate working environment (lighting, poor floors, etc.)
- silly, inappropriate behaviour, i.e. fooling around.

In a perfect world this long list would be much shorter but the world is not perfect and there will always be accidents. All the law can do is give guidance and protection.

Fig. 11.1 *Responsibility for a safe working environment*

Situation	Employer	Employee
Exits blocked by boxes	To ensure that there is a correct place to store the boxes	Not to leave boxes in the way
Exits locked	To ensure that the door is unlocked during working hours	To report to management that the door is locked
Boiling kettles in dangerous positions	To provide adequate facilities for refreshments—kitchen, canteen, drinks machine	Not to boil a kettle in a place that may cause an accident to their fellow employees
No step ladder available	To provide correct equipment	To request adequate equipment, to use equipment provided, and to report broken or missing equipment
Employee carrying too much	To provide the equipment needed to perform a task adequately and safely	To carry only what they can manage comfortably and safely
Trailing flexes	To provide safe office equipment and the facilities which enable work to be carried out without danger	To use machinery only when it is safe, and not to leave either equipment or flexes in a dangerous position
Smoking	To non-smokers to provide smoking areas away from the general work-place, or to ban smoking altogether, particularly in open plan offices	To themselves to maintain a healthy body. To fellow workers not to inflict on them a polluted atmosphere
Staff rushing	To ensure that staff are not overworked, so that they will not need to rush, and to ensure that the environment is such that working at a fast pace (not the same as rushing) does not lead to accidents	Not to put themselves under stress by rushing when it is not necessary. To fellow workers not to cause injury to others by rushing around carelessly

This is not an exhaustive list of the many hazardous situations which can exist in the office environment.

11.4 Safety Committees and Safety Officers

Two important areas in which the law helps is to insist that every organisation:

- provides a written statement with regard to health and safety and its implementation within the company, i.e. a safety policy
- makes provisions for the appointment of a safety officer from amongst the employees.

Most large companies will have a safety committee as a matter of course. However, if one does not exist and two safety officers within a company make a written request to the company then the law states that such a committee must be set up.

A safety representative may be a union representative and is responsible for ensuring that all safety procedures are carried out. She will consult with management over safety matters, investigate unsafe situations and make regular inspections of the work place. Although not obligatory, most safety representatives will undergo some training in safety and maybe first aid. Any company may have more than one representative.

11.5 How can Employees be Made Aware of Their Own and Their Employer's Responsibilities?

Large companies will provide an induction course for all new employees. An important feature of the induction course should be an illustrated talk, video or demonstration of safety policy and practice within the company. In addition to the general safety requirements every company, factory and office will have circumstances and risks which are special to its business.

Dangers in a solicitor's office are not normally of the kind found in a bottling factory. Most accidents in offices probably occur through such things as careless maintenance of furniture, carpets, and so on, scalding from a carelessly placed boiling kettle or electrical faults. Office staff today must be particularly careful not to overload electrical sockets. With so much electric and electronic equipment in use it is all too easy to add yet one more plug to a well used socket. This is a highly dangerous practice and one which should be avoided at all costs. If you find that your office will not accommodate all the equipment you need to use then you must not cut corners—report the situation and ask for additional sockets. Factory employees, on the other hand, face different dangers—badly maintained machinery, broken safety devices. Equally many factory workers have horrific accidents through their own negligence—long hair or a tie caught in machinery, failure to report broken equipment, or failure to wear protective clothing provided by the management. The results of such negligence do not bear thinking about but unfortunately are all too common.

A safety officer has an enormous part to play in educating the employees with regard to their own safety. Employees should also be made aware of their rights and what they can expect from their employers. All too often accidents occur because of ignorance on one side or another. Many staff will continue to work in an unsatisfactory environment because they are not aware of the procedures which can be followed to put things right.

11.6　A Duty to your Fellow Workers

An employee's duty to his fellow workers falls into three distinct areas:

- — maintain a safe and healthy environment—do nothing which will put your fellow workers at risk
- — report any unsafe situations to a safety officer and to the management immediately
- — report any accidents immediately they happen, enter it into the accident book and complete an accident report form.

Remember:

- — Clear doorways and corridors of books, papers, wires etc.
- — Report dangerous office furniture, carpets, electrical points, etc.
- — Ensure that electrical equipment is safe to use.
- — Beware of loose plugs, trailing wires, overloaded sockets.
- — Arrange furniture to give clear access.
- — Tuck chairs under desks when not in use.
- — Use steps to reach high shelves.
- — Place files and papers within easy reach where possible.
- — Store dangerous liquids and substances under lock and key in metal cabinets.
- — Unlock emergency exits and do not obstruct them.
- — Display safety notices prominently.

— Display clear fire procedure notices in every office.

— Warn with a notice of any unusual and temporary hazards.

— Don't overload filing cabinets.

— Have a first-aid box easily available in every office and well-

11.7 Health is as Important as Safety

Health is becoming a major issue in the latter part of the twentieth century. Few people can escape the publicity given to improving our bodies and our minds through good exercise and good diet. From a personal point of view it is a good thing to exercise regularly, eat well, and get sufficient sleep. Smoking is becoming increasingly unpopular socially and at work and it has been proven over and over again that we stand a much greater chance of dying young if we smoke. Many large companies now offer facilities for exercise during or after a day's work and if you are in this situation you should take every advantage. Find a form of exercise you enjoy—squash, jogging, swimming, aerobics—and stick with it. Try to persuade one or more work colleagues to join you and you will enjoy it all the more. If you can combine your exercise with healthier eating and drinking all the better. It isn't always necessary to go on a strict diet—you can improve your eating habits just by thinking carefully about what you eat and concentrating on healthier foods.

If you are fit and healthy you will find you can improve your efficiency and effectiveness which will benefit both you, your executive and your company.

Do You Know?

1. What to do in case of an accident in your office?
2. What to do in the case of a fire in your office?
3. What the Offices, Shops and Railway Premises Act set out?
4. What HASAWA stands for?
5. What meaning HASAWA has for the office worker?
6. What meaning HASAWA has for the factory worker?
7. What meaning HASAWA has for the management?
8. How to avoid accidents from electrical equipment?

9. How to ensure employees are aware of safety procedures?
10. What the major causes of accidents are in any office?
11. What improved fitness and diet means for an employee?

Secretarial Task Eleven

You have recently been on a health and safety course. Your executive, Mrs Jennings, would like you to take an active part in the forthcoming YTS Induction course by giving a short talk to the new employees on health and safety in the company. She considers that the new employees will take more notice of what you have to say since you are of a similar age group and she is anxious to avoid a number of the minor accidents which have been happening in the company in recent months.

Every morning Mrs Jennings leaves you a tape on which she has prepared messages the evening before. On today's tape she leaves you the following message:

> 'Jane, about next month's YTS Induction course—can you let me have an outline of the content of your talk please? Say a little about the relevant Acts which the employees should be aware of. Can you give them some idea of why they should take note of the law—most of them seem to think it has nothing to do with them! Also stress the personal aspect—their own responsibilities to themselves and to each other as well as our responsibilities as their employer.
>
> 'I think in particular you should also cover:
>
> > protective clothing
> > accident procedure
> > accident prevention
> > defective machinery
> > inadequate equipment.
>
> 'I suggest you take advantage of our excellent resources and include some visual aids to give some weight to what you want to say. If you can give me some ideas of what you need I will try to arrange it with our Resources Department—I am sure they will be able to provide you with whatever you need (within reason!)
>
> 'If you can let me have a clear outline of your talk, together with a memo outlining your visual aids, I'll see what I can arrange for you.'

Examination Questions

1. A recent fire in the Classical Music section of the company was apparently started by an electrical fault in a lead setting light to some waste paper in a basket underneath the photocopier. Although not causing extensive damage the fire resulted in the loss of some files kept in a box file containing names and addresses of club members. Also destroyed were some valuable manuscripts which were kept in a wooden cupboard. What advice would you give to Miss Prior to improve security and safety in the office?
LCCI SSC OP

2. You have been appointed Safety Representative for your office which is situated on the fifth floor of a modern office block. You are concerned that there has not been a fire drill during the past year and that there are no instructions to employees in the event of a fire.
    (a) Give reasons why regular fire drills are necessary
    (b) Draft a notice which can be placed on the office notice-board outlining the action to be taken when:
      (i) a fire is discovered by an employee and
      (ii) the fire alarm is heard.
LCCI SSC OP

3. You have been asked to prepare a list of ten important hints on safety in the office which can be placed on the office notice-board. There are ten people working in the office which is equipped with an electrostatic copier, electric typewriters, two 4-drawer filing cabinets and a small spirit duplicator.
Select ten hints which you feel are important and explain what could happen if each hint is ignored.
LCCI SSC OP

4. There are two matters Mr Blackstone, the General Manager, wishes to resolve before he retires, on which he has asked you to draft a memo:
    (i) Health hazard—what steps should be taken to prevent a further outbreak of skin infection which has recently affected office staff handling sample goods packed in straw and coloured tissue? To which Act of Parliament will you refer Mr Blackstone in this connection?
    (ii) Electrostatic copier—what advantages has this copier over the present company policy of carbon copies of all correpondence and copy-typing of documents?
RSA

Chapter 12
Travel and Absence from the Office

Arranging a business trip for your executive is a task which you must be able to do efficiently and without fuss. You may know several months in advance of a forthcoming trip, on the other hand he may announce that he has to make an urgent trip abroad tomorrow or even that day. Whichever is the case you must be prepared and have a routine which allows for no mistakes, oversights or delays. You need to be aware of time schedules, possible means of transport, documentation, time and cost limitations, and the comfort of your executive.

It may be entirely your own responsibility to make arrangements. In a large organisation, however, there will probably be specialist staff who will do this for you, all you will then have to do is to pass on the details of a trip to the relevant person who will make the arrangements. Always make sure you get the initial details correct and that you follow up your requests to ensure that nothing is forgotten.

What kind of trips does the business person take?

They may be:

- conferences at home and abroad
- sales tours
- meetings
- exhibitions and trade fairs
- fact finding tours.

The arrangements for each trip will be particular to the occasion. For instance, at a conference, hotel arrangements will probably already be made as part of the conference booking. On other occasions it will be up to you to find an appropriate hotel, bearing in mind such factors as price, location, service and comfort. You may also find yourself making hotel arrangements for overseas visitors to your company. Most companies have favourite hotels which they use whenever they have visitors.

A checklist is a valuable aid when making travel arrangements, firstly to indicate what has to be done for any specific trip and secondly to check off when each task has been completed.

Think about your own holiday arrangements, your checklist might look something like this:

Decide **date** of holiday.
Collect **holiday brochures**.
Make **choice of holiday**.
Book **flight/ferry/package**.

Check **passport**.
Arrange **currency/travellers cheques**.
Check/arrange **insurance**.
Receive and check **tickets** and details.

A checklist for a business trip would not be very different, except that you, as secretary, would not have the services of a holiday travel company to help you. On the other hand it is wise to make regular use of a favourite travel agent who will give you advice and make any travel or hotel bookings you require.

It is necessary for you to find times of planes and trains, book cars, taxis and find suitable hotels and restaurants.

Arrangements for passports and currency will not be dissimilar to your own arrangements except they may be in large amounts and in someone else's name. In addition, you may need to arrange meetings with other business people and travel between meetings.

12.1 Making the Arrangements

If you do not have the luxury and convenience of a travel department you must establish for yourself a routine to ensure that nothing is missed or forgotten. Prepare several copies of a blank checklist which you can use for all trips—firstly ticking off what needs to be done for any one particular trip and secondly ticking off when the task or arrangements are complete.

Your checklist might look something like Figure 12.1. The first column should cover the maximum number and type of arrangements that may need to be made for any trip. The second column provides space to tick the arrangements necessary for the particular trip you are concerned with at the outset. For instance, a visit to the USA would require a visa in addition to the normal documentation

Fig. 12.1   *Travel checklist*

		NEEDED FOR TRIP	IN PROGRESS	COMPLETE
VISIT OF				
TO				
DATE				
CHECK	— passport	....	....	....
	— visa	....	....	....
	— inoculations	....	....	....
	— health insurance	....	....	....
MAKE APPOINTMENT	— provisional	....	....	....
INVESTIGATE ACCOMMODATION provisional bookings		....	....	....
		....	....	....
BOOK TRAVEL	— plane	....	....	....
	— boat	....	....	....
	— train	....	....	....
	— car	....	....	....
	— taxi	....	....	....
ACCOMMODATION		*amend*	*book*	*confirm*
ARRANGE CURRENCY	— English	....	....	....
	— Foreign	....	....	....
	— Travellers cheques	....	....	....
CHECK CREDIT CARDS are up to date — Access				
	Barclaycard/Visa			
	American Express			
	Other			
IN THE OFFICE — Enter arrangements into both diaries				
Make alterations to diary entries as necessary				
Prepare Itinerary (at least 3 copies)				
Prepare Files		....	....	....
	Documents	....	....	....
	Speeches	....	....	....
	Sales Literature	....	....	....
	Samples	....	....	....
	Phrase Books	....	....	....
	Maps	....	....	....
	Addresses	....	....	....
	Telephone lists	....	....	....
	Visiting cards	....	....	....
	Company stationery	....	....	....
Prepare file for papers which arrive in the office during his absence.				

On the other hand, extra inoculations are unlikely to be necessary. However, a visit to any African state *would* require inoculations. Hotel bookings, too, are not always necessary since they may be part and parcel of a conference booking and be made automatically for you by the conference organisers.

As each task has been completed and followed through, the final column would be ticked. Marker and highlighter pens would give 'at a glance' information and any additional arrangements not covered by the form may be inserted at the end.

12.2 In More Detail

(a) Passport

Anyone who travels abroad on a regular basis will most likely be more aware than you of the expiry date of the passport. It is wise to keep a careful eye on the date and to mark in your diary or follow-up system a suitable date (well in advance of the renewal date) for arranging the passport's renewal at the nearest passport office, in person, or by post. If the passport is out of date it is possible to obtain a one year British visitor's passport on demand from a main post office, although this passport is not valid in all countries. It is not unusual for a well-travelled executive to have two passports for the following reasons:

— he may split his time between two or more locations and need to travel at short notice from either

— to allow for overlap while one passport is being renewed, or if its renewal gets forgotten

— to allow him to travel freely between countries which have restrictions (you are not allowed into some countries with a stamp on your passport from other specified countries)—he could then use one passport for travel across the border in one direction and the second passport for his return journey

— he has a passport to fall back on if the first gets mislaid.

(b) Visa

If in doubt whether a visa is necessary, contact the relevant embassy immediately. There can be considerable delays in obtaining visas and, although visas for some countries are available from travel agents, some countries insist on personal attendance at their embassies.

(c) Health certificates/inoculations

In most cases travel out of the UK does not involve inoculations and certificates, particularly within the EEC. However, it may be that your company has dealings with countries such as those in Africa and Asia, in which case a variety of inoculations against diseases such as smallpox, cholera, etc. may be necessary and, from a personal point of view, desirable.

Once again it is important to check well in advance on any health requirements and regulations. Some countries ask for health certificates and many inoculations are given well before travelling, as a course of two or three. Time should be allowed for the complete course and also for possible after-effects or reactions.

(d) Insurance

Check insurance already available. Some companies have their own arrangements with insurance companies. In the case of specialised travel or equipment special arrangements may have to be made.

(e) Business appointments

All other arrangements rest on the timing and location of appointments. Make provisional appointments (entered into both diaries, yours and your executive's, in pencil) either by telephone, letter, fax or telex and confirm later in writing after all other arrangements are finalised. When making appointments bear in mind distances from hotel and previous/subsequent appointments allowing breathing space and time for unexpected delays such as traffic hold-ups. If your executive is attending a conference ensure that you prepare one or more labelled folders containing the programme and all other relevant papers, and remember to keep an identical copy of everything in the office. It may be that he will extend the time of his visit and make further appointments while there.

(f) Travel arrangements

Your executive may have a preference for one type of travel over another. Inland he may prefer to drive or to take advantage of first-class rail in order to work while travelling. Always respect his likes and dislikes even though you may have your own ideas. Where he expresses no such preference it is up to you to arrange travel most suited to his needs. You must consider:

— distance

— time available

— cost: many managers operate on a tight budget in which case a cheaper but slower means may be chosen (e.g. train rather than an internal air flight)

— convenience: air may be quicker, but if the airport is not near his destination then train or road may be more convenient; also city centre to city centre can be quicker by train than by air where airports are a distance from the centre

— comfort and service: relaxation is an important preparation for business meetings; a tense journey can lead to tense and unsuccessful discussions or negotiations

— numbers of calls and their geographical spread: travel by road enables more visits to be made in a given time, i.e. more calls in a day

— time of travel: need to sleep, relax, eat, etc.

— frequency of public transport: if times available do not coincide with required times then alternative means of travel may be necessary and preferable.

Take note of preferences:
If you are starting out on a secretarial career your travel experience will probably be confined to local and holiday travel. You are able to make your own decisions based on your own likes and dislikes. When making arrangements for someone else, in addition to considering the requirements of the trip, it is important that you take into account your executive's preferences. If he reads and writes many reports he may be glad of a longer first-class train journey, when he can work away from a telephone; he will probably prefer a non-smoking compartment (unless he is in the minority and smokes) and he may have a preference as to whether he faces forward or backwards on the train. If time but not cost is of greater importance and if he can easily reach an airport at each end, then a shuttle flight would be an obvious choice. Contrary to popular opinion travel overseas is not always by air—sales or marketing staff in a company concerned with exhibiting new equipment abroad may wish to travel with their equipment by sea and road. Here safety, cost and ease of conveyance will be your prime consideration.

Fig. 12.2   *Means of travel—internal and international*

Mode of travel	Advantages	Disadvantages
Train	Intercity—fast comfortable leisurely	Service can be poor except on Pullman or equivalent
	Facility to work	Punctuality, can be unreliable
	No stress	Can get crowded
	Less expensive than air	Lacking in personal attention
	Refreshments usually available	Refreshments not always available
	Available in bad weather	Need to fetch own refreshments—awkward on moving train, no security for personal belongings
	Safe	May be necessary to change trains
Car	Door to door convenience	Less safe
	Good for carrying samples and small items of equipment	Tiring
	Useful if transport needed once arrived at destination	No opportunity to work
	Inexpensive, especially carrying colleagues	Need to stop for refreshments relaxation, etc.
	Inexpensive if using company car	
Taxi	Can work	
	Relax	
	Available at short notice	Expensive for long journeys
Air	Speed	Waiting time
	Comfort	Journey time to and from airports
	Services	No work time
	Personal attention	Expensive
	On board refreshments	Can be affected by adverse weather
	Essential for medium to long distances	
	Dubious for less than 200 miles	

Mode of travel	Advantages	Disadvantages
Air (contd.)	Intercity shuttle available walk on/walk off No booking necessary Seat always guaranteed	
Sea	Safe Can take car Leisurely Inexpensive Refreshments Can take heavy or bulky equipment	Rough crossing can be uncomfortable Lacks personal attention
Hovercraft	Quicker for cross channel Can take car	

Hire car combined with air travel is convenient if there are many calls to be made.

Once you have selected the mode of transport it is important to make appropriate bookings, where necessary co-ordinating taxis, trains, planes and so on. Take care to consider check-in time, distance to travel by road with potential delays (rush hour, road works) and any other factors which will affect times of arrival and departure.

Set it out clearly
Make sure you set out on paper very clearly all relevant details such as:

```
Time to leave office
By air:   Departure: airport
                     check-in time
                     airline
                     gate number
                     time of departure
          Arrival:   airport
                     gate number
                     time
          PLUS details of transport from airport

By train: Departure: station
                     platform (if known)
                     time of departure
                     number of seat if booked
          Arrival:   station
          PLUS details of transport from station
```

```
By sea:   Departure: reporting time
                     dock details
          Arrival:   time
                     dock details
          PLUS details of route from dock
By road:  Details of route
          Route map
          Recommended places to stop: Hotels (meals and overnight)
                                       Pubs (lunch and light
                                         refreshment)
                                       Restaurants
Useful books—Egon Ronay
             RAC Hotel Guide
             AA Hotel Guide
             Michelin Guide
```

Remember also to include details of hotels, people to be visited, companies, and so on.

(g) Selecting the accommodation

For regular trips inland and overseas your company may have favourite hotels. If this is the case your only concern will be whether your chosen hotel has vacant rooms at the time you need them. If not there will often be a hotel in the same town or area which you use regularly or which is recommended to you by the hotel staff. If you are starting from scratch, ascertain from your executive any preferences he may have such as location, size, facilities (he may have a healthy attitude to fitness and like a work-out followed by a sauna after a day of meetings).

When selecting hotels either follow reliable recommendations from colleagues or business associates or use one of the many hotel guides available (RAC, AA, Michelin). Make a provisional booking by telephone, fax, telex or letter to be followed by a firm booking once arrangements are finalised. Remember to enter provisional bookings in both diaries in pencil and only in ink after you have received written confirmation from the hotel.

(h) Arranging currency

Firstly investigate restrictions—some countries allow only a limited amount of local currency to be brought in. In consultation with your executive and in accordance with his wishes arrange for the correct amount of currency in the correct form (cash, travellers cheques) to be available at least a week before departure. You will probably need to arrange this with your cashier. If travel involves more than one country ensure that he has sufficient funds in each denomination so that he does not find himself without the right currency as he crosses the borders. It is also helpful to check banking hours in each country if he is moving around a great deal. In a large company arrangements will be made for you but if you work on your own you will need to inform the bank of your requirements in currency and travellers cheques preferably well in advance of the trip. Your executive will need to sign the travellers cheques either at the bank itself or on company premises in front of someone authorised to act on the bank's behalf.

Remember—Eurocheque and Eurocard

Avoid the need to pay for currency before leaving. Eurocheques are obtainable from banks and are written in the same way as ordinary cheques (supported by a Eurocard) as and when they are needed.

In addition check that credit cards—Access, Barclay/Visa, American Express, etc.—are up to date and signed and that they are valid in the countries to be visited.

(i) In the office

After making provisional arrangements for visits, meetings and accommodation, and having made sure that everything is co-ordinated (remembering to allow 'breathing space' and adequate time for discussion, travel and relaxation), it is important that confirmation is sent in writing, well in advance, setting out dates, times and venues.

Ensure that you enter all arrangements in both your own and your executive's diary and use your follow-up system to remind you to carry out any further necessary tasks such as collecting together literature and files needed for the trip.

Prepare an **itinerary** (two or more copies) setting out clearly all details of the trip. The itinerary may be postcard size if the visits are few in number or, for a longer trip, as many as two or three sheets of A4 paper may be necessary. A good itinerary should be clearly set out and easy to follow. It should include the following details:

AIR   Airport, gate no, flight no, check in time, arrival and departure times.

TRAIN   Station, platform, departure and arrival times.

CAR   Route—major towns, road numbers, motorways, motor-
way exits.
Map.
Suggested stop-off points.
SEA   Port, dock, departure and arrival times.

When you are preparing the itinerary:

— take account of travel time between meetings and to destination
— allow breathing space for consolidation of information, report
and note writing after meetings, relaxation and recovery time
— allow for weather conditions which may affect travel, particularly in winter
— allow time for meetings to overrun
— use 24 hour clock to avoid confusion and misunderstandings.
Allow for time changes
— include an agreed time to contact you in the office or vice versa,
particularly on longer trips. Suggested times to contact his
home may also be appreciated.

Fig. 12.3   *Travel itinerary*

```
MR NICHOLAS BRAITHWAITE


ITINERARY FOR PARIS VISIT - 4 July to 6 July 19..


4 July   1000    Leave office for HEATHROW Airport (company car)
         1100    Check in
         1200    Flight BA 1202 (London/Paris)
         1310    Arrive Paris - Claude Arrieu from Paris Office will
                         meet you with car
         1530    Jules Ravel - briefing (Folder 1)
         1700    Company car to Hotel Internationale
         1930    Meet Claude Arrieu in Hotel Reception for dinner at
                 his home

5 July   0900    International Textile Conference
                 (all conference details in Folder 2)
         1930    Dinner with Michelle Lefevres - Paris promotions
                 (Folder 3)

6 July   0900    Taxi from hotel to airport
         1000    Check in
         1100    Flight BA 5623 (Paris/London)
         1210    Arrive Heathrow (company car to meet you)
```

(j) Preparation of necessary documentation

Apart from the usual vital documentation and papers (passport/visa, currency, tickets) you must ensure that all other necessary papers and literature are prepared well in advance of the departure dates. A sales promotion tour, for instance, may require leaflets and samples, while a meeting to negotiate a new contract may call for reports and specifications which may have involved several months of preparation. Again, consult with your executive—hopefully he will be efficient and well prepared. On the other hand organisation may not be one of his strongest points in which case he will rely heavily on you to give him a 'nudge' and to make the preparations for him.

These may include:

— Files Documents	Prepare photocopies of relevant documents (try not to part with the originals). These may include background information on the company, details of personnel, correspondence, draft contracts and so on. Prepare a clearly labelled and divided file or files—plastic, transparent files are lightweight and different colours can make quick access easy.
— Speeches Discussion points Lecture notes	Forgetting notes in business can be disastrous and have major repercussions on the company's business. Equally, arriving at a conference without lecture notes could prove to be a humiliating experience, but one which could be overcome by the use of a fax machine.
— Sales literature Specimens Samples	Advertising literature, 'give-aways' and so on are part and parcel of promotions at exhibitions. A secretary in Sales and Marketing will be very much concerned with this aspect and it may fall to her to arrange exhibition stands and promotions. Planning, preparation and printing must be done well in advance to ensure that material is available in time. Remember to allow time to get the material to the promotion site in the cheapest, fastest, safest and most convenient way.
— Phrase book	Aids to an easier life. If your executive is fluent in the language of the country he is visiting don't

insult him with a phrase book! On the other hand he may only *think* that he is fluent and be grateful for a discreetly placed phrase book amongst his papers! Use your initiative.

— Local maps

Local maps of home towns and towns abroad are desirable and are often overlooked. Conference literature often includes local maps indicating access from stations, airports and major roads and motorways. If he is travelling entirely by road then a good road map together with street maps of any towns he is visiting are essential.

— Addresses Telephone lists

Either within a short itinerary or in addition to a longer one, names, addresses and telephone numbers of companies to be visited are essential. Sales tours, in particular, involve many visits; details of additional potential customers, over and above those already on the itinerary, are useful for sales personnel. Often one visit will lead to another and for this the executive needs to be well prepared.

— Visiting cards

Check well in advance that your executive has sufficient cards to last him through his trip. These cards are a quick, easy and valuable way of making business contacts. They should include his name, his position and the name, address, telephone, telex and fax number of his company. They may include other information but should not be too cluttered to make reading difficult.

(k) Preparation of personal items

Some busy executives who travel a great deal at short notice keep an overnight case easily available. Your executive may have personal requirements which he has asked you to include as part of your check list: regular medication, spare glasses or contact lenses (anyone experiencing loss of a lens or broken glasses knows how debilitating this can be and also how difficult normal conversations, let alone negotiations, become).

12.3 A Quiet Time for the Secretary?

It is a fallacy that the secretary can take a holiday or have a restful time while her executive is away on business. Many secretaries will say that it is the only chance they have to catch up on the backlog of routine work. It is a good idea to draw up a list of jobs in order of priority with some sort of time scale which allows for daily tasks and non-routine tasks.

In addition there will be mail, telephone calls, visitors, meetings to arrange and so on.

It is important to know which tasks you are able to deal with. They will normally fall into one of three categories:

- those with which you can deal—routine or by prearrangement
- those which are to be passed to someone else (his deputy, superior or colleague in another department—by prearrangement)
- those which need to be left until his return.

How will you decide which category the matter falls into? Experience or company policy will often give you an idea but in the early stages of your career these points may act as a guideline. Very briefly, the pattern to follow is outlined in Fig. 12.4.

Fig. 12.4   *Questions to ask yourself*

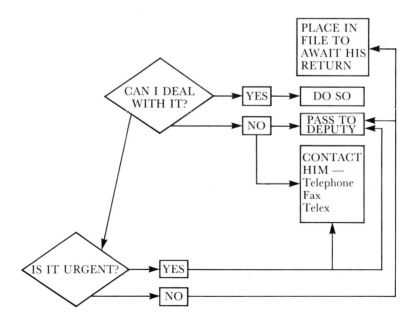

Remember not to open private and confidential mail unless you have been instructed to do so. Some executives ask you to either open and deal with it in an appropriate manner or to forward it unopened if they are away for any length of time.

Urgent matters may have come to your attention by letter, fax, telex or telephone, or via a visitor to the office. Once you have considered who is to deal with the matter you must also decide if you need to inform your executive. Generally it will depend on how you view the urgency of the situation and only your experience, initiative and knowledge of company affairs will enable you to make such a judgement. A genuinely urgent family matter will naturally require you to make some contact. If you are unable to speak direct you must leave an appropriate message which indicates the urgency. An urgent company matter which cannot be dealt with by anyone else and will not wait until the executive's return also needs you to make direct contact. If your executive is not immediately available by telephone and you are unable to leave a message—perhaps there is a time difference or a language problem—always remember alternative means of communication. Fax and telex can get round the problems of such time and language barriers and are as quick as the telephone. Whatever the means of communicating never forget to ask him to confirm receipt of your message by fax, telephone or telex—only in this way will you be sure he has received the message.

12.4 Dealing with Unexpected Visitors while your Executive is Away

You may find yourself battling with unexpected, unwanted visitors in your executive's absence. The nature of these callers will vary depending on the department you work in. In Personnel you may find yourself confronted by an employee who has urgent problems and needs to see the Personnel Manager; in Purchasing you will receive plenty of calls from sales people from other companies; in Public Relations it may be unhappy or dissatisfied customers or clients you have to cope with. Such examples can only give a small idea of the range of problems you may be confronted with. However, whatever the situation the usual rules of calmness, politeness and clarity apply.

- Try to take the heat out of the situation—offer a seat, coffee or tea and apologise.
- Be calm—do not get heated—it gets you nowhere.
- Get to the root of the matter by calm, careful questioning.
- Try to find another executive to deal with the problem if appropriate (your client may object to this but be positive).

— If an alternative executive is not available or not acceptable to the client do what you can to solve the problem and make an appointment with whoever they would like to see.

— Offer assurance that the matter will be dealt with as soon as possible on your executive's return.

— *Don't* make promises on your executive's behalf which he may not be able to keep.

— *Do* keep an accurate record of the procedures you followed and action you have taken and place the record in the file you have prepared for his return.

Helpful hints

1. Keep passport renewal date in your diary/follow-up system.
2. Keep a record of passport numbers safely in case of loss or theft.
3. Think ahead—visas, health requirements, currency regulations.
4. Cultivate the services of a helpful travel agent.
5. Keep a record of travellers cheque and credit card numbers.
6. As soon as you know about the trip open three files:
   — ONE for all preparations labelled with date and destination(s) or name of conference, with checklist on or at front.
   — ONE for documents and paper for your executive to take with him, together with list of contents.
   — ONE for you to keep during his absence—it will contain a record of all correspondence, telephone calls, fax papers, telex messages and action taken by you and his deputy during his absence for reference and action on his return.
7. Prepare at least three copies of the itinerary which should include hotels and telephone numbers:
   — ONE for him to take (maybe two)
   — ONE for you to keep (two would be better)
   — ONE for his wife or partner at home.
8. Check on alcohol rules in country he is visiting to avoid embarrassment. Certain Middle Eastern countries allow no alcohol.
9. Ensure he has sufficient company stationery and file paper to make notes and write letters.

Do You Know?

1. Where to obtain a passport?
2. What information to include in an itinerary?

3. Which books to refer to for hotel and travel arrangements?
4. Which essential documents to prepare for a business trip?
5. What extra items may be necessary for a trip?
6. What to do with urgent mail while your executive is away?
7. What to do with Private and Confidential mail while he is away?
8. How, when and where to contact him in an emergency?

What books will be useful?

Hotels and Restaurants in Great Britain (British Tourist Authority) indicates standard facilities (including conference), tourist information, plus additional notes.

AA and *RAC Handbooks*   maps, distances, hotels and other useful information.

Michelin Guides   published for specific countries (similar to *AA* and *RAC Handbooks*).

The Travel Trade Directory (Morgan-Grampian)   useful up-to-date information including travel operators, passport and visa offices.

Hints To Businessmen (Dept of Trade and Industry)   free booklets giving advice and information on hotels, customs, entry regulations, etc.

ABC Rail Guide   timetables and fares from London stations and other major stations (published monthly).

ABC Coach and Bus Guide
National Express Service Guide } routes and services in the UK.

ABC Shipping Guide   timetables, fares and services on major routes.

Whitaker's Almanac or *Pears Cyclopaedia* will also give useful general information.

A good atlas is invaluable.

Secretarial Task Twelve

Problem 1

Your executive, Mrs Bradbury, has been away on a business trip and unfortunately, you have been ill at the same time.

The company has recently taken on a junior secretary, Alison, who took over your duties while you were away. When you return to the office after your illness you find Alison very upset and asking for your advice. Mrs Bradbury, who had returned before you, has been annoyed because Alison has been unable to give her any record of what has happened in the office during Mrs Bradbury's absence.

Mrs Bradbury tells you that it had been hoped that Alison would act as relief secretary whenever any of the other secretaries are away but that unless Alison shows more promise this would be out of the question.

You decide to help Alison by preparing a set of guidelines which will help her to cope with office routines and procedures while any executives are away.

Problem 2
Mrs Bradbury has to fly to Washington on 2 December of this year. She is to visit the US Textile Federation, 1742 Constitution Ave, Washington DC, Tel 626 7328461 at 1000 on the morning after her arrival and Mr Chuck Armstrong at US Bank, also in Constitution Ave, Tel 626 34876 at 1400 (local time).

She would like some time for sightseeing, particularly the Capitol, and will travel back on 4 December.

   (a) Prepare a checklist for your own use to cover all the arrange-
        ments you need to make, in the correct order.
   (b) Using all the resources at your disposal, find out times of
        travel, details of hotels and any other necessary information
        and prepare a typed or wordprocessed itinerary in a form
        which would be suitable for her use.

Examination Questions

1. You are employed as secretary to Mr Paul Adams, one of the
    partners in a firm of estate agents in Swindon. The Manager of the
    Chippenham Branch will be attending a three-day conference in
    Leeds in April with Mr Adams. As the manager's secretary has only
    been with the company for a short time, Mr Adams has asked you
    to make some notes for her on her role and responsibilities while
    the Manager is away. She will have to deal with existing clients and
    new clients requiring appointments, advice, etc.

    Write a memo to Linda (secretary at the Chippenham Branch)
    including notes on matters to be checked with the Manager before
    he leaves, and during his absence.

    RSA SD

2. The Annual Electronic Games Exhibition is being held in Vienna
    from 18 to 21 February 19--. Mr Andrews will be visiting the
    Exhibition to promote the company's goods. You are to make his
    travel arrangements.

What arrangements should you make and where will you find the information you need?

Draw up an itinerary.

LCCI SSC OP

3. Your employer has decided to hold a one-day conference for all branch managers on the second Thursday of next month to introduce them to wordprocessing. As the managers will be travelling from various distant towns, he has asked you to arrange accommodation, at an appropriate central point, for all delegates for one night in a hotel with a conference room. You also have to arrange travel facilities to take your employer and yourself to the Conference Centre.

List the actions you would take, in chronological order, to carry out this task satisfactorily.

PEI SP INTER

Chapter 13
Information Sources—Where to Find Out What

How much do I need to know?

You will never be expected to have all the information you need at your fingertips. What is necessary, however, is that a good secretary knows where to look for it. There *will* be occasions when you have plenty of advance warning but it is not unusual for notice to be short and because of this you need a good selection of sources of information immediately available to you.

It is important to remember that information sources are not confined to text books. An increasing amount of data, statistics and general information can be accessed via a computer terminal. Viewdata, Prestel and Oracle provide valuable up-to-date computerised information on a wide variety of topics from weather conditions and forecasts to current stock-market prices.

13.1 What Books do I Need?

The minimum you need is:

- A good dictionary.
- Directories: telephone, and if you have the facilities, telex and fax.
- Recent hotel guide (if your executive travels).
- Recent maps, AA/RAC handbooks.

This is indeed a very short list and you may well question why many books for secretarial guidance have lengthy chapters covering a much greater range. The answer is, of course, that a competent secretary will need to find out many pieces of information during the course of her working day—from details about a visiting VIP to the times of trains to get her executive from town A to town B.

Know what's available and where

The title of most information books will give you an indication of their content. Your job is to know what is available to you. If it is not on your own bookshelf a secretary in a different department may have it, or there may be a central library within the company run by specialist staff. If all else fails remember that a large public library will have a comprehensive selection of books with trained librarians to help. If your local library does not have the book you need the librarians there are nearly always able to get it for you from another library.

Every company will have its own policy regarding the purchase of information books, and central libraries are common in large companies. Always ensure that you have easy access to at least the minimum you need and that your information sources are up-to-date. There is nothing less useful than last season's train timetable, or a 1970 road map where a recent motorway may have transformed the local road system, or last year's tax-tables!

It cannot be stressed too much that the nature of your specific job will to some extent govern the types of books you need. A glance down the following list may invoke the response 'but I'm sure I'll never need all those'. Indeed, it is not likely that you will ever find yourself referring to all of them. However, it is likely that you will find yourself in more than one type of company during the course of your career and that you will work in more than one department. To this end you must know the availability of books and other sources of information in order to make the correct selection and to acquire relevant up-to-date information.

13.2 Books in More Detail

Generally books fall into six major categories (although there is a certain amount of overlap):

- Correct use of English and presentation of copy
- Directories–Telecom and Trade
- Travel, accommodation and eating out
- Official and government
- People
- Desk books and manuals

(a) Correct use of English and presentation of copy

Dictionaries	There are several good dictionaries available, such as *Chambers 20th Century Dictionary*. Remember to use a dictionary not only for meaning and spelling, but also pronunciation, plurals and derivatives.
Thesaurus	*Roget's Thesaurus of English Words and Phrases* gives alternative words with the same or similar meanings. Look the word up in the index, refer to the given page and find the synonym (similar meaning) or antonym (opposite) you need.
Dictionary of Acronyms and Abbreviations	Full explanations of commonly abbreviated names, titles and other words.
English Usage	*Fowler's Modern English Usage* gives guidance in correct English (grammar, punctuation and style). Chamber's *Pocket Guide to Good English* is a concise and easy-to-use reference book of modern English usage.
Clear Expression	*The Complete Plain Words* gives help in using language simply, using straightforward English and avoiding unnecessarily complicated sentences (published by HMSO).

(b) Directories

Telephone, Fax and Telex

Trade—
useful for contacts, sales promotions, etc.

Yellow Pages Directory	Free up-to-date local area classified trade directory, issued by British Telecom.
Thomson Local Directory	Free up-to-date local area classified directory giving details of local business/trade/services.
UK Kompass	Register of British Industry and Commerce; Volume I —products and services Volume II—company information, geographical and alphabetical.
Kelly's Manufacturers and Merchants Directory	Each directory is specific to a trade or manufacturing industry and gives lists of all companies connected with the particular trade: manufacturers, wholesalers and retailers together with exporting connections and information.
Trade Journals	Many trades have their own journals which are published regularly and which give important information specific to the trade.

Specialist
for example:

Willings Press Guide

Directory of Directors

(c) Travel, accommodation and eating out

See page 252.

(d) Official and government publications

Hansard	A daily verbatim account of happenings in parliament; useful to companies and professions such as town planners needing to keep up-to-date with possible and actual changes in the law. (Note Hansard is *not* a list of MPs—a common mistake.)
Times Guide to the House of Commons	Details and photographs of current Members of Parliament, party manifestos and election statistics.
Statesman's Year Book	Details of governments throughout the world and international organisations such as NATO and UNESCO.
Municipal Year Book	Details of local government authorities.
Keesing's Contemporary Archives	Weekly newsheets with items of international news taken from world press and information sources.

(e) People

Who's Who and special editions such as: *Who's Who in Theatre*	Biographies and other details of important living people.
Who Was Who	Biographies of once important people who are no longer living.
Burke's Peerage *Debrett's Peerage and Baronetage*	Details of peers and their families with correct form of address.
Black's Titles and Forms of Address	It is important to address people correctly. Black's tells you how to address titled and qualified people such as doctors, the Mayor, Justice of the Peace.

Plus books in other categories which refer to people, titles, forms of address and so on.

(f) Other essential desk books and manuals

Secretary's Desk Book   All you need to know to do your job well!
Office Oracle (Chambers)

The Post Office Guide   Complete guide to all Post Office services.

Typewriter Manual   With the sophisticated typewriters of today you need to hang on to this—don't let it walk!

Word processing Manual   Keep them at your side and ensure that they are not
Database Manual   'borrowed' for too long and that you know where
Spreadsheet Manual   they are!
and others

13.3 Newspapers, Trade Journals and Periodicals

It is not unusual for it to be part of a secretary's job to scour trade journals and newspapers for current articles which have some relevance to the business which her company is in. In some companies it is the job of the librarian to do this but if you have no library then you should be methodical about extracting or photocopying relevant articles. Articles of interest may be about a new product, either of your own company or of a competitor, trade news or figures, and results of surveys (market or political). Keep all the extracts systematically in clearly labelled files and if necessary photocopy them for circulation to interested staff. Don't be afraid to use your initiative here—a busy executive will appreciate your doing the donkey work for him and providing him with information he may not otherwise have time to find.

The choice of newspapers and journals received by your company may be out of your hands but if you are aware of a publication to which you feel your company should be subscribing do not hesitate to bring it to the attention of either your executive, company secretary, or whoever makes such decisions.

For every industry or service there is an endless number of specialist publications geared specifically towards their needs. Your Sales, Public Relations and Marketing Departments will be aware of a whole range of magazines, newspapers and journals in some of which they may advertise and the company may be supplied with many of these. Often the company may obtain more than one copy for distribution to several departments such as Reception, Library, Marketing and Production. The Managing Director may receive a copy of all incoming publications as a matter of course. Some publications are free (usually those containing high advertising content) while others are very expensive per copy; cost will govern how many copies your company receives.

(a) Newspapers

Most companies receive at least one daily newspaper which will normally be one of the 'quality' newspapers such as the *Financial Times, Guardian, Independent, Daily Telegraph* and *Times*. Apart from news items these newspapers have business and financial information and all have a 'business section' in some form or another. Try, whenever possible, to read at least a little from one of these papers, if you are not already in the habit of doing so. If you have so far found them to be too heavy going, take it step by step. You will find that the more you are able to read, the more you will understand and the more you will find the 'tabloids' less satisfying.

For businessmen it is important that they keep up-to-date with current trends and movements in their own and other industries or services. There are always news items about possible mergers, export drives, export restrictions or bankruptcies which may affect their own businesses.

Once important articles have been located and, if necessary, brought to the attention of your executive, extracting articles from them for long term reference is a suitable task to be carried out in 'quiet' moments, although it should never be left so long that the task becomes overwhelming and the articles severely out of date.

(b) Trade journals and periodicals

There are several journals which are of interest to all businesses, regardless of their specific product or service. Those listed below are only a representative few.

General

> *Business Systems and Equipment*
> *The Economist*
> *Management Today*
> *Mind Your Own Business*
> *New Scientist*
> *Time*

There are numerous other specialist publications which will be of interest to specific departments or people. The following are just a few of the hundreds available. Some classify themselves as magazines, others as journals; some are costly and some are free.

Specific

> *Accountancy Age*
> *Drapers Record*
> *PC User* (IBM PC and compatible computer magazine)
> *Management Accounting*
> *New Scientist*
> *Textile Outlook International*
> *Training*
> *Which Word Processor?*

Remember—use your library

If you need to find out more about a particular publication or what is generally available, your company or local library will be able to help. Certain organisations such as Universities and Research Centres have their own specialist libraries where you may find information you need.

To consider ordering a publication you need to find out:

> the title
> the publisher
> typical content
> some idea of price

all of which your library will be able to give you.

If possible borrow or send off for a sample copy (you may have already received one by post, from an exhibition stand or from a salesman).

13.4 Information via Viewdata and the Television Screen

Obtaining information via the computer and the television screen is an obvious development and is growing in popularity, both in the home and in business. There are three major sources:

> Prestel   run by British Telecom
> Ceefax   run by the BBC
> Oracle   run by ITV

All three services operate on the principle that a large amount of information stored on computer is accessed by a keypad (in the case of Ceefax and Oracle) or by telephone (in the case of Prestel). The major difference is that Prestel is a two-way service whereby the receiver can feed information back—for example with Prestel you can find out if theatre tickets are available and if so book them—while Ceefax and Oracle are one-way information services.

More information about Viewdata can be found in Chapter 7.

Remember

Use your books!
Don't let the books lie unused on the shelf. It is one thing knowing which books to purchase and quite another to use them. Don't be lazy about referring to books and other sources of information. A commonly underused book is the dictionary—far too many typists and secretaries 'can't be bothered' to use a dictionary and rely on asking colleagues for the spelling of a word, or simply guess, with the inevitable result that work has to be re-done. What a waste of time!

Use your telephone!
Don't forget also that apart from Prestel there is a wealth of information at the other end of a telephone line. A combination of the telephone and Yellow Pages can save you many wasted hours 'asking around'. Libraries, Citizens Advice Bureaux, local councils, colleges and many other institutions are very pleased to help with information or to point you in the right direction.

Checklist

Basic books to have in your office:

- A good dictionary.
- Good national map.
- Local street map.
- Roget's Thesaurus.
- Post Office Guide.
- Directories (Local, Yellow Pages, Telex, Fax).
- Industry trade journals.
- Industry Year Book or similar.
- Black's Titles and Forms of Address.
- Secretary's Desk Book.
- Equipment manuals.

Remember—browse in your library

There is no substitute for browsing through the books for yourself—this is the best way to find out what is in them *and* you are more likely to remember.

Spend half an hour or so in your college, school, company or public library and find as many of them as you can.

Keep your eyes open for *free* magazine subscriptions and send for them for yourself or suggest that your college, school or employer sends for them.

Do You Know?

what information you will find in:

1. *The Post Office Guide?*
2. *Who's Who?*
3. *Whitaker's Almanac?*
4. *Hansard?*
5. *Statesman's Year Book?*
6. *Yellow Pages?*
7. *Michelin Guide?*
8. *Fax Directory?*

Also remember

In your office and in your examination the requirements are the same.

Not only are you expected to be aware of a wide variety of sources of information and the information they contain, you will also be required to extract information from given information— timetables, advertising leaflets and so on.

Your task as secretary is to obtain the correct information quickly and efficiently and to present it in a clear and concise manner for your executive to use or refer to—report, memo, list, note, whichever is most appropriate or requested by him.

Secretarial Task Thirteen

You have just started work with ELNEWS Publishing Company as secretary to Mrs Paula Hammond, the Publicity Manager. Your work is very much concerned with arranging promotional tours, contacts with authors in a wide range of industrial areas, trade conferences and other publicity events. You have in the office only three reference books: a dictionary, an AA book which is three years old, and a manual for your new electronic typewriter. You are finding that you waste a great deal of time searching for information you need in the public library and consequently you have written yourself the following reminder to be dealt with today:

'Prepare a list to give to Mrs Hammond asking for more reference material.'

You know that Mrs Hammond is reluctant to authorise unnecessary expenditure and realise that you need to make out a good case for each item otherwise she won't see the need to have it in the office.

Examination Questions

1. For an Anniversary dinner Mr Thomas wishes to know more about the guests and the correct form of address for introducing them and he has asked you to obtain the necessary reference books for him. The guests include a Member of Parliament, the Mayor and Mayoress and a titled Chairman of the local Sports Council.

    List the books you will obtain and the information your selected books will provide.

    RSA SD

2. Your company is considering expanding its range of products and is about to undertake a survey to assess the demand for new products.

    Describe the ways in which the necessary information might be obtained for:

    (a) Likely competitors—who they are, size, up-to-date product information, products manufactured, etc.
    (b) Statistical information on sales trends in the industry.

    LCCI OO&SP

Chapter 14

A Secretarial Career

The way ahead

By now you will hopefully have made a decision regarding your career and are on the initial rungs of the secretarial ladder. This last chapter is intended to help you in two ways. Firstly, from a personal point of view, you will find information to guide you along the next most appropriate route at whatever stage you are at the moment in your training and your career. Secondly, in your capacity as secretary, you may be called upon to give advice on careers, arrange interviews, advise on selection of clerical staff and generally contribute in a positive way to training and selection, particularly to school and college leavers. It is in the second area that the examination boards expect you to be aware and competent.

If you are keen to reach the heights in secretarial work it is important that you take the right step early on in your career.
You have two important routes open to you:

- take a secretarial college course which gives you good qualifications—a recognised diploma or group certificate together with individual subject examinations
- start at a lower level, clerk or typist, and take further training at the same time as working—evening classes and/or day release.

By either route you can reach the same goal. You should never feel pressurised to go further than you can cope with but equally you should strive to make the most of your career. Even if you interrupt your career for a short time—a few months or a few years—you must always remember that for many executives, experience counts for a lot. You will find in many places where you work that there are highly valued secretaries who have only basic qualifications. You may find this surprising but remember that experience and willingness to learn are major factors in a successful secretarial career.

14.1 'No Experience—No Job' and 'No Job—No Experience'

Doubtless at this point you are saying 'but how can I get experience before I have a job'? This is a recognised problem to which successive governments have given some attention with a variety of training and work experience schemes. Although some view government schemes with scepticism you must consider all avenues open to you and remember that the skills you offer are highly valued in the business world. There are major companies today who restrict all their new employees to those on government schemes and new employees are given excellent training and valuable initial all round experience. Such schemes offer a way out of the 'if I can't get a job I can't get any experience and if I can't get any experience I can't get a job' syndrome. What you must do is to make the most of all opportunities open to you now and be determined to improve both your qualifications and your experience at every turn of your career.

The first step is to consider your initial training. There are many options. The first one is what to do and where to do it. Having decided that you want to be a secretary the next stage is to decide where you are going to study.

14.2 Where Should I Study?

Skills at school?

When making decisions about courses at school ask yourself which subjects you will get the most value from and listen to the advice of parents and teachers. It can be very frustrating to be told that you should not take a wordprocessing course at school and that you should concentrate on more 'academic' subjects such as French or Physics. This is sound advice and you must remember that you can always follow on with secretarial subjects at college. For most people it is wise to concentrate on a basic education while still at school. For the higher secretarial/personal assistant jobs you will stand a much greater chance of success if you can show success in several GCSE subjects and maybe one or more 'A' levels, in addition to specialist training. If you are considering moving towards administration or management then it is vital that you build up a good groundwork of basic subjects while at school.

Skills at 14?

On the other hand if you are very keen to start work then it is wise to begin learning the skills as soon as you can. Hopefully your school will be well equipped with computers which will run word processing, database, spreadsheets and other programs. If so you will probably have the option of studying 'Information Technology' in the widest sense in addition to specific keyboarding, typing and word processing skills. If you are particularly lucky your school will also be equipped with at least a few electronic typewriters.

Secretarial courses in the sixth form?

Specialist courses in secretarial studies are a common feature of sixth forms in schools and sixth form colleges. The majority of such courses are identical to those offered in colleges of further education and it is usually merely a matter of personal choice based on your own preferences as to where you go. You may consider such factors as distance, facilities, friendships, staffing and how old the building is, although there are local authorities who have strict rules about which colleges you are allowed to attend.

Secretarial courses at a college of further education or college of technology?

In further education you will be able to choose from a wider variety of courses (depending on the size of the college) and many students value the independence of college life and a change from the school environment. You will have the benefit of greater specialist facilities, specialist staff and specialist courses such as medical, secretarial, foreign languages, tourism and information technology.

14.3 What Should I Study?

If you have worked hard at any secretarial subjects at school it is probable that you already have a good grounding in the skills, particularly typewriting or keyboarding, and word processing. If on the other hand you have 'played' at it or found it particularly difficult to get to grips with the fundamentals then you may do best to think about making a fresh start in a new environment, with new friends and new teachers. Think carefully about the course that will suit your qualifications and personality—there are several to choose from:

At school: GCSE, the groundwork

Several examining bodies offer certificates which include course work. What you do will depend on the choice of your school. It is worth noting that while not all boards offer the full range of grades, those that do offer a Grade 1 expect a very high level of achievement (the Southern Examining Group, for instance, requires candidates to pass at a level equivalent to RSA Stage II in order to gain a Grade 1 in keyboarding applications). If you have worked to this level at school you can feel justifiably proud since you have achieved an excellent groundwork on which you can build other skills.

You are not restricted to keyboarding and there are other examinations you can take which incorporate experience in word processing, database, spreadsheet and other office systems in addition to shorthand.

There are other GCSE examinations which are centred around a study of office precedures although they appear under different names.

At college: Secretarial courses

There are three major examination boards you may come across:

> The London Chamber of Commerce and Industry (LCCI)
> Pitman Examinations Institute (PEI)
> Royal Society of Arts (RSA)

On many secretarial courses you work towards a 'group certificate'. This means that although you will take examinations in several individual subjects at the end of your course, provided you reach the required standard in a prescribed number of subjects you will be awarded a certificate which states the overall level you have reached. Each board offers a different group certificate, each with its own emphasis. You can obtain syllabuses from all the examination boards and before embarking on a college course you may like to study them carefully to establish what the options are.

Remember that some local authorities insist that you attend the local college unless that college does not offer the course you want to study. Where you do have a choice of both college and courses, ensure that you do your homework and check which is the one which offers you what you need. The following is only a brief guide and do remember that all courses are prone to change. Increasingly examining boards are looking towards an integrated approach and are placing more emphasis on course work. You will probably be accustomed to this approach from school but again, when making your choice, bear in mind which type of approach suits you best.

The London Chamber of Commerce and Industry currently offers three levels of secretarial group examinations each of which prepares the would-be secretary for employment as:

 —shorthand or audio typist/secretary to junior or middle management
 —private secretary and assistant to middle and senior management
 —private secretary or personal assistant to higher management.

It is worth noting that it is not obligatory to pass a shorthand examination for the LCCI examinations and that audio typewriting is an acceptable alternative. In addition, at the two higher levels candidates are expected to be confident in oral communication and an interview plays a major part in the examination.

For those who prefer to concentrate on the clerical and administrative aspects, particularly in terms of communication, information and data processing, LCCI offer two levels of the Certificate in Office Technology.

Pitman Examinations Institute also offer Group Certificate examinations at two stages both of which recognise all-round secretarial ability. To pass the higher certificate candidates are expected to demonstrate that they have supervisory potential.

The Pitman group certificates are gained by passing a number of related single-subject examinations during the course of one year. Secretarial Practice (single-subject) examinations are set at two levels—Intermediate and Advanced, both of which can be taken separately from the Group Certificate.

The Royal Society of Arts offer a single subject in Secretarial Duties which also forms part of a group certificate. This examination sets out to assess a candidate's potential to become a secretary.

Remember

Most examination boards offer single-subjects examinations in some or all of the following skills:
 shorthand/typewriting/keyboarding/audio-typing/shorthand/word and data processing
plus related subjects such as:
 communications / secretarial duties / procedures / background to business/business arithmetic
There are also several courses and examinations you can take if you want to work within a specialist profession: medical, legal, travel.

Take note

Examinations have been through considerable change over recent years. Many examination boards have been rethinking their syllabuses, creating new subjects and giving new emphasis to new areas. For this reason it is wise to make your own enquiries from the major examination boards as and when you are thinking of further study.

14.4 Applying for a Job

There are two accepted ways of applying for jobs. One is to write a letter including all your details, perhaps in a 'CV', and the other is to complete an application form. Look carefully at jobs advertised in local and national newspapers. Most will ask you to apply in writing to a given address and some will state that further details are available and give a telephone number or an address.

Try to create a good impression, even on your first contact with the company. When you ask for particulars on the telephone you will give your name and address. If you make a mess of it at this stage you may be remembered! On the other hand a confident approach will immediately give you a good start.

Applying by letter

It helps to work from a standard letter which you can then reword to fit in with the job you are applying for.

You will doubtless have such standard letters that you used in earlier studies at school or college. However, when you are writing, include the following points and be clear and concise. No-one wants to read a lengthy essay which says very little about you; on the other hand they need to know enough in order to make a decision about who to select for interview:

- indicate where you first learned about the job—newspaper, Job Centre, careers office
- refer to the date, if an advertisement
- state clearly which job you are interested in (there may have been several advertised together and you don't want to find yourself being interviewed for the job of head cook if you applied for junior secretary!)
- give good reasons as to why you are attracted to the job
- support your application with some good reason as to why you think you will be able to do the job well
- say that you are including a Curriculum Vitae giving details of your qualifications and experience.

Fig. 14.1   *A curriculum vitae (CV)*

```
CURRICULUM VITAE


NAME

ADDRESS



TELEPHONE

DATE OF BIRTH


SCHOOL

ADDRESS                          TELEPHONE


COLLEGE

ADDRESS                          TELEPHONE



EXAMINATIONS TO BE TAKEN
Subject                          Date


EXAMINATIONS PASSED
Subject                          Grade      Date



EXPERIENCE

INTERESTS


REFERENCES (at least two)

NAME                     NAME

POSITION                 POSITION

ADDRESS                  ADDRESS


TELEPHONE
```

Curriculum Vitae (commonly referred to as a 'CV')

A sample CV is given on page 271. You will see that its purpose is to set out clearly all the important facts which have a bearing on your suitability for a job. A word processor is an ideal tool for preparing a CV—you can store the current version, or a blank form, and amend it whenever you need to, without the need to retype the whole thing. If you don't have access to a word processor it is wise to make a number of photocopies accurately dated, if you are applying for several jobs.

Applying by application form

Many companies prefer you to fill in a standard application form. This makes it easier for them to refer to the different aspects of your qualifications and make comparisons with other candidates.

When filling in a form:

- start by photocopying the blank one so that you can have a trial run in pencil

- plan carefully what you are going to put and where

- keep items in date order where appropriate

- write or type the form, whichever you can do most neatly (some companies stipulate handwriting or black ink for photo-copying)

- be concise and if you need more space use a separate sheet and refer to the sheet on the form

- be accurate about your information (some interviewers go through a form with a fine tooth comb and may ask you about any of the information you have supplied—if you have been inaccurate or 'bent the truth' you may find yourself in great difficulties either in the interview or afterwards if you get the job)

- give as many referees as required after checking with them first; it is usually expected that one will be someone in authority at your present place of employment, your college head of department or principal, or your headteacher. If you don't give any of these it may look suspicious and your prospective employer may think the worst about you!

Many forms have a space for you to give further details about yourself. Remember that this is where you have the chance to show that you have something special to offer. If you are stuck at this point talk to someone who knows you well. Identify your strong points—perhaps you are a good organiser, a determined worker, strong on initiative. This awesome blank space is the place to sell yourself to the company but remember in your eagerness not to go over the top.

Interests
One of the problem areas for many applicants is the 'Interests' section and far too many glibly write 'reading, walking, clothes' and have absolutely nothing to back this up with in an interview. There is nothing wrong with writing these interests down if they are truly your interests but remember that an interviewer is experienced in his job and can see through you very easily. During the course of the interview he will probably use this information to get you to talk about yourself. If you write down 'reading' because you think it looks good but haven't read a book for a year or more you are going to look pretty silly when the interviewer asks you what you thought of the last book you read. He is likely to be much more impressed if you say 'I do enjoy reading but have been so busy with my college course that I haven't had time to read much lately; or you might say 'I did a lot of reading last year but this year I seem to have spent most of my free time making clothes which I enjoy and it saves me some money'. The point to remember is that whatever you write down make sure that you can speak with authority about it since the interviewer is more concerned to know that you are an interesting person than he is to know the details of English literature in the twentieth century.

14.5 The Interview
Preparations
If you are called for interview there are several preparations you must make.
Getting there:
> —Find out exactly where the place of interview is (don't just assume it is where you think it might be).
> — Find out how you are going to get there—bus, train, car, etc.
> — Find out how long it takes by that method (do a dummy run).
> — Find out and write down the times of transport you will use.

Whatever happens *don't be late.*

The organisation:
> — Try to obtain leaflets and information about the company (try your library, careers department or if you've time, send for some from the company itself).

- Find out about the company's products or services.
- Find out about its structure and organisation.

This information will be useful for discussion or questions in interview.

Prepare yourself:
- Look clean.
- Look tidy.
- Dress appropriately for the job—smart, simple and businesslike.
- Dress comfortably—don't rush out and buy a new outfit, you are much better in something you feel good in and which gives you confidence.
- Avoid extremes of any kind—even the most adventurous employers will be suspicious if you don't conform to their expectations at interview.
- Carry a simple handbag or brief case and ask if you may leave anything else you have brought, such as an umbrella, at reception.

Get yourself organised the night before
First impressions are very important and your appearance can make or break your chances of success however unfair this may seem. Give it careful thought before the day of the interview, and then spend some time preparing yourself the night before—don't leave it until the last minute.

Before the interview:
- Arrive early.
- Check your appearance well before your interview time.
- Be calm and don't panic.

During the interview

- Shake hands firmly (hold out a firm, not limp, hand).
- Sit upright but be relaxed.
- Put your handbag on the floor or neatly on your knee (it is a good idea to have something to hold, it stops you fiddling with your hands).

- Speak positively—no 'ums' and 'ahs'.

- Answer questions firmly (not aggressively)—it is important to give an impression of confidence and competence, but remember that no employer wants a secretary who is 'too big for her boots'; an employer is also looking for someone who can work well with others, particularly her executive, and someone who can delegate, take and follow instructions.

- Have at least one question ready yourself; the type of question you ask and the way you ask it gives the interviewer an indication of your interest in the job; unfortunately many a time your carefully planned questions will have been answered during the course of the interview! If this happens then you must either think quickly or be honest and say 'Before the interview I was wondering . . . but you have explained that very clearly thank you'. Again you must hope that your honesty will be appreciated.

Good questions to ask:

- Could you explain how promotion is carried out in the company?

- I understand that the company has offices in several local towns. Are staff moved from one office to another at any time?

- Do you have sports facilities for staff?

- What communications systems will I be using—do you have Telex/Fax?

- Could you tell me what equipment I will be using?

- I would like to continue improving my skills—are employees allowed to take day-release courses?

You must take care to word your questions carefully—don't sound presumptious or banal and take care not to ask trivial questions.

If you have a genuine concern, query or reservation about the job this is the time to ask about it. Once you get home the opportunity will be lost. Very often a prospective employee will have already booked holidays and is concerned that her holiday entitlement at the new company may not allow her to take the time. A reasonable employer will honour holidays so do not be afraid to ask. If you have been shown round the offices and/or factory there may be questions that occur to you as you go round—if you think you may forget them make a note of them in a quiet moment.

Before your interview scan through this book and see where the likely new developments are, or keep your eyes open in newspapers and magazines where you will often find information about large or local companies and new technological developments. You can use any of this information as a basis for finding out more about the company.

The interviewer/s
For top jobs you may find yourself in front of an interviewing panel, which may include the Personnel Manager, and Departmental Head, each of whom will ask different questions. Whatever kind of interview, the interviewer will probably make notes while you are talking. Even though this may be offputting try to ignore it and carry on confidently. Remember that the interviewing panel will be interested in you as a person and will be encouraging you to make the most of yourself.

The test
You may be asked to carry out a small typewriting, audio or shorthand test as part of the interview. Depending on the company this can be a harrowing or relaxed experience. However difficult the task may be you must relax. Keep calm if dictation is involved and don't let an unfamiliar typewriter put you off.

Provided you have been sensible about being adaptable to different machines at college you will be able to cope with any strange typewriter. Remember that in general an employer is concerned primarily with the presentation of your work. It is more important to him that you can produce tidy, accurate and clean mailable copy. He will be concerned with the time you take to do it but if your copy is good he is more likely to overlook the fact that you may be slower than someone who zipped through it with disastrous results.

At the end of the interview

The interviewer will probably stand up, thank you for coming and say that they will let you know in a few days. Say 'goodbye' and 'thank you' clearly and remember to close the door after you leave! He or she may ask you to show the next person in, although there is usually a gap between interviews to allow for discussion and notes. You may be told the results of the interview immediately but, if not, all you can do is go home, cross your fingers and wait!

14.6 Successful?

When the letter arrives offering you the job it should also be accompanied by a Contract of Employment which will set out details and terms of your employment. You will be given details of starting date, starting salary and salary scale, hours of work, details of notice to be given by employer and employee, details of holiday allowance and any additional points referred to or agreed to in interview. Before replying and accepting the position read your contract thoroughly. It is important that you take note of what it says since you are required to sign it and return it. You should also receive a Job Description which sets out clearly what you are expected to do and this too will have been discussed in interview.

Remember the key points:

Find the job—Job Centre, Newspaper, Careers Office

Letter or form?—draft it first, then write neatly or type

Interview?—prepare yourself well—
> find out about the company—find out where it is—try getting there once before the interview—get yourself organised—be comfortable and smart—show that you are confident—organise your thoughts—speak slowly and clearly—answer sensibly—have more than one question ready—give a confident 'Goodbye'

You've got the job?
> read your letter and contract carefully—check dates, salary, job description—write your acceptance

---

14.7 Starting Work with Mixed Feelings

During your first few weeks at work you will probably have mixed feelings. There will be days when your college or school life is a foggy memory and you wonder what you did with all that spare time; then there will be others when you long for typewriting routines and communication lectures you probably grumbled about while you were there! Don't be downhearted. Office life has its good moments and its mundane routines as does any job, and while you are at the bottom of the ladder it is inevitable that you will get a fair share of the routine jobs that other people have been putting off! But very soon you will find that you are established in new routines, you will make new friends, take on more responsibilities, face new challenges and generally begin to feel confidence in your own capabilities.

Whenever you are in doubt don't be afraid to ask. Providing you do not pester and that you take care not to ask when someone is in the middle of a harrowing task, you will find that most staff are willing to be helpful. There is always the traditional 'office dragon' but she, invariably, has a heart of gold!

14.8 Where do I go from Here?

Induction courses

Large companies usually have a programme of induction for all new employees, whatever department they work in. An *induction course* will vary from a short talk by the person in authority (such as the Managing Director), followed by a tour of the premises and a brief instruction by a departmental head, to a much fuller course which may last a full week or more. However long or short the course is, its basic features remain the same:

  – introduction to the company–its structure and business
  – introduction to staff–management and departmental
  – tour of the premises which may be on more than one site
  – talk on health and safety in the company
  – talk about staff facilities–canteen, sports, social
  – introduction to any trade unions and their representatives
  – introduction to departmental staff
  – talk on company policy regarding promotion, training, sickness and welfare
  – time spent in one or several departments learning about different aspects of the company or job
  – distribution of staff handbook or information sheet

It is important to remember that staff from all departments will be on an induction course and a company may only hold such courses at certain times of the year so that they can accommodate several new staff at once. Induction courses also give new staff from different departments an opportunity to get to know each other, and senior staff a chance to introduce themselves to staff who they otherwise may never meet.

Application and training for all kinds of jobs

When you are established as a secretary, particularly if you work in Personnel or Training, you may find yourself organising all or part of a Training or Induction Programme.

Many of the points covered in this chapter relate to jobs which are not just secretarial and the procedures can be recommended to any new job applicant.

Further training

Having been successful in obtaining your first position you must now get to grips with the real world of work. While you are gaining valuable experience in your new job you may also feel that you want to continue to improve on your skills and qualifications. It may also be that your company encourages all young, new staff to follow a day-release course at the local college or they may leave it to your discretion. If you opt for day-release you must give all your energy to the course since you will probably pack quite a lot of study into one day with the result that at the end of the year you will have the opportunity to pass any of the higher examinations mentioned earlier. Some companies insist that staff must pass stipulated examinations before they are awarded a further pay increment while others insist on further qualifications for promotion.

Fulfilling your ambitions

If all goes well you will strike lucky in your first job—it will be the job of your dreams and you will go from strength to strength in the same company. However, there may be those amongst you who prefer to move around—'up, up and away' may be your motto and you will gain a wealth of experience from working in several different companies. There will be, in addition, those for whom a career as a secretary proves to be a disappointment and who will move across into administration or change lanes altogether. Of the successful secretaries talked to in preparation for this book most were happy to remain in their secretarial jobs for the remainder of their working lives. Others were looking for a change: one, a secretary from a computer marketing company, was keen to move across to training users of their systems. A personal secretary in a large chemical manufacturing company who had worked for 30 years had only one further ambition—to retire! Another secretary, with a market research company, was keen to 'expand' into other fields such as 'putting up billboard ads, being a lorry driver and car mechanic'!

So there you have it. A career as a secretary can be a satisfying and enjoyable way to spend your working life. As they say 'it takes all sorts' and hopefully you too will find your own niche where your 'sort' fits in, and you will be happy and successful.

Good luck in your new career!

Secretarial Task Fourteen

You work for Mr Johnson, the Manager of the Chapeltown branch of the Northern Estate Agency. Later today Mr Johnson is meeting the Area Manager. They have several points to discuss, one of which is the advertisement for a new secretary for the branch. They hope to appoint someone in her early twenties who must be capable of running the office during the times when Mr Johnson is out. The person appointed will also do some travelling to take details of properties and to show potential buyers around.

Mr Johnson has asked you to prepare some notes for him on the technical skills, abilities and personal qualities that the person appointed should possess. He will refer to the notes during discussions so they need to be clearly set out and he would like to take two copies so that the Area Manager can also refer to them.

Examination Question

1. As secretary to the Personnel Manager you are in the process of preparing a résumé of the work carried out in your department for inclusion in a company recruitment pamphlet. Your junior has just finished typing the following and has asked you to explain to her the words she has underlined.

   'The Personnel Department is not only concerned with firing and hiring—it fulfils many other functions. When applications are received it is often necessary to provide a short list of candidates. New employees are provided with an Induction Course and further education and training is company policy. We are also concerned with the welfare of our employees, and encourage the use of our sports and social activities.'

   List the underlined items and give a brief description of each which would answer your junior's questions.

   PEI SP ADV

Chapter 15
Secretarial Examinations— A Few Hints to Help You

Revision

- Check that you have covered all the syllabus—each examination board is different and will place emphasis on different areas of secretarial work.

- Read your notes carefully and clarify with your teacher or lecturer or from a text book any points you do not understand.

- Highlight the topics for revision.

- Prepare an outline pattern of revision for yourself which is realistic and which you know you can keep to.

- Take one topic at a time but also try to notice where they overlap, as many secretarial tasks do.

- Make a note of the *key points* and prepare brief notes on each.

- Use the key points and brief notes as self-test material.

- Read around the subject and keep up-to-date—office resources and hence secretarial tasks are developing and changing all the time and additional *relevant* knowledge demonstrates to the examiner that you have an all-round awareness and interest in the subject.

In the examination

Initial information

Most secretarial examinations, particularly RSA and LCCI, begin the examination by giving a 'scenario', i.e. an outline of the company around which the topics on the examination paper are set. Most of the tasks or questions will be based on this initial information, so it is *very important* that you take time to read it carefully and try to gain an overall picture of the company you are 'working for' during the course of the examination.

Read the initial company information carefully and take note of the key points.

- The *size* and *type* of company (partnership, plc, etc.); you will be expected to take this into account in your answers.
- The *type of business* the company is concerned with: manufacturing goods, providing a service (banking, insurance, etc.).
- The *department* you work in.
- *Other staff* in the department.
- The *name of your executive* and his or her *title*.
- Other departments you may have connections with, any other information you are given about the *company*, the *department* and *personnel*.

Relate your answers to the company on which the examination is based.

- Take all the information into account and use the relevant facts in your answers. Credit is normally given by the examining boards for this. For instance, if the initial information tells you that you work in the Sales Department of a textile company and one task if concerned with your secretarial duties, amongst your ordinary secretarial routines you would be wise to make some mention of tasks specific to the department, in addition to any which are specific to the textile business: contacting sales staff, collecting sales figures for fabrics, clothes, etc., preparing sales figures in a visual form and arranging sales or progress meetings.
- Think around the topic, don't confine yourself to 'textbook' tasks and duties, you will always be given credit for a more thoughtful answer.
- Make sure your answer has some substance; 'answer' the question or task put to you.
- Include all the facts you are asked for.
- Don't include information you are **not** asked for unless it is relevant. The examiners will get very fed up with reading answers which have no bearing on the question. They are not fooled by waffle.

Take careful note of the wording of the question:

- List—an itemised list with brief points.
- Outline—a brief description (a list is often acceptable).

- State what action you will take—relate the action to the problem.
- What qualities you will require—explain the qualities and give a brief example if it helps to make your explanation clearer.
- Prepare the information Mrs X requires—refer to the information you are given in the question and task, and ensure that your answer relates to it.

Remember that one task or question may be testing several areas of the syllabus. In one question you may be asked to do several things.

- You may be asked to prepare a memo, report or letter (to ensure that you can set them out correctly and that you can word them adequately).
- You may be required to extract information from a given source and use it in a particular way or to reword it.
- You may be required to use information from several parts of the syllabus and relate the points to each other.
- For example, in relation to a forthcoming business trip, a task might ask you to:
  (a) extract times of travel from a printed timetable
  (b) prepare a check list of travel preparations
  (c) prepare an itinerary
  (d) prepare some visual aids or suggest a means of presentation
  (e) write confirmation letters
  (f) make diary entries.

Remember

Prepare yourself well
Cover all sections of the syllabus
Read the whole paper through and read the wording of each question carefully
Answer clearly and concisely
Spell and punctuate correctly

Index